A Glimpse
of Fame

ALSO BY DENNIS SNELLING

Johnny Evers: A Baseball Life (McFarland, 2014)

The Greatest Minor League: A History of the Pacific Coast League, 1903–1957 (McFarland, 2012)

The Pacific Coast League: A Statistical History, 1903–1957 (McFarland, 1995)

A Glimpse
of Fame

Brilliant but Fleeting
Major League Careers

DENNIS SNELLING

McFarland & Company, Inc., Publishers
Jefferson, North Carolina

The present work is a reprint of the softcover edition of A Glimpse of Fame: Brilliant but Fleeting Major League Careers, *first published in 1993 by McFarland.*

All tables compiled by William J. Weiss

LIBRARY OF CONGRESS CATALOGUING-IN-PUBLICATION DATA

Snelling, Dennis, 1958–
    A glimpse of fame : brilliant but fleeting major league
careers / by Dennis Snelling.
        p.   cm.
    Includes bibliographical references (p.   ) and index.

    ISBN 978-0-7864-7749-4
    softcover : acid free paper ∞

    1. Baseball players—United States—Biography.   I. Title.
GV865.A1S6 2014
796.357092'273   92-44295
[B]

BRITISH LIBRARY CATALOGUING DATA ARE AVAILABLE

Cover graphics (Fuse/Thinkstock)

Manufactured in the United States of America

McFarland & Company, Inc., Publishers
    Box 611, Jefferson, North Carolina 28640
    www.mcfarlandpub.com

For Linda, Tyler and Garrett—
who made this possible.

THE LINEUP CARD

Acknowledgments   ix

Introduction   1

BILL KOSKI • Pitcher, 1951 Pittsburgh Pirates   5
The role of luck, fate, and circumstance in a player's career

ED SANICKI • Outfielder, 1949, 1951 Philadelphia Phillies   19
*Four straight 100 RBI seasons in the minors, his first three
big league hits are homers*

JOE STANKA • Pitcher, 1959 Chicago White Sox   35
An American wins the Most Valuable Player award in Japan

BILL ROHR • Pitcher, 1967 Boston Red Sox;
1968 Cleveland Indians   53
One pitch away from a no-hitter in his big league debut

AL AUTRY • Pitcher, 1976 Atlanta Braves   75
*The only major league pitcher in the last 57 years to win
in his only appearance*

JOE BROVIA • Outfielder, 1955 Cincinnati Reds   89
*One of the Pacific Coast League's most feared hitters gets
his chance at the age of 33*

JOHN LEOVICH • Catcher, 1941 Philadelphia Athletics   103
The best part of baseball is friendship

BERT SHEPARD • Pitcher, 1945 Washington Senators　　115
*An ex-fighter pilot becomes the only one-legged player
in the history of major league baseball*

RON NECCIAI • Pitcher, 1952 Pittsburgh Pirates　　135
The kid who struck out 27 in one game

DOUG CLAREY • Second Baseman, 1976 St. Louis Cardinals　　151
*His only major league hit is an extra-inning game-winning
home run*

MARSHALL MAULDIN • Third Baseman, 1934
　　Chicago White Sox　　167
Leaving behind a legacy for future generations

FLOYD GIEBELL • Pitcher, 1939-41 Detroit Tigers　　183
*The man who out-pitched Bob Feller to clinch the 1940
American League pennant*

BERNIE WILLIAMS • Outfielder, 1970-72 San Francisco
　　Giants; 1974 San Diego Padres　　201
*Touted as Willie Mays' successor, eventually traded
with Willie McCovey*

JOHN PACIOREK • Outfielder, 1963 Houston Colt .45s　　217
Three for three in his only major league game

FRANK LEJA • First Baseman, 1954-55 New York
　　Yankees; 1962 Los Angeles Angels　　229
The life and struggles of a "bonus baby"

Bibliography　　247

Index　　251

ACKNOWLEDGMENTS

If I had known what I was getting into when I began this book, it very likely would never have been undertaken. I now have a much greater respect for all authors who can complete a project and a little better understanding as to why they may sound strange once in awhile — it's a combination of living with one subject too long and many hours of banging one's head against the word-processor (not an easy thing to do, I assure you).

Of course, I did undertake this venture, and I was helped immeasurably by a number of friends and new acquaintances who are largely responsible for making this book possible. Don Frascinella assisted in the formative stages of this project, in gathering information on various players and helping me bounce ideas around. Lark Downs, Dan Langhoff, Jerry Frye, Gary Baker, and Steve Ensley each read most or all of the manuscript, providing encouragement and making a number of suggestions, many of which I actually incorporated. Their help was greatly appreciated.

The staff at the Research Library of the National Baseball Hall of Fame at Cooperstown was most helpful, and always quick to provide information requested of them. Special thanks go to William J. Weiss, one of baseball's foremost statisticians, who provided the year-by-year playing records of each player in this book. Also, special thanks to Jim Norby, who read all of the material for this book and was a constant source of advice and great encouragement.

Frank Jeans was a contact source for my first two subjects, which enabled me to get the ball rolling. Lucille Yancey Primm, companion and long-time friend of Marshall Mauldin, went out of her way to provide me materials pertaining to Marshall's career after his death in September 1990. I could not have completed his profile without her.

Anita Bologna of the *Waterbury Republican-American* provided articles and local sources regarding Bert Shepard on short notice.

I also want to especially thank all the ball players who allowed me a glimpse into their lives, and in some cases their homes. I appreciate the time, and the insights they gave me. This is their story, and I thank them for letting me be a part of it.

Finally, I want to thank the most important people of all, my wife Linda and my sons, Tyler and Garrett. Without their love and support I never would have made it through this book.

And a big thank you to baseball, a game that has provided me countless hours of fascination and enjoyment. I hope in some small way, this book gives something back as a way of saying thanks.

—D.S.

Not a day passes over the earth, but men...of no note do great deeds, speak great words and suffer noble sorrows.

—from Charles Reade, The Cloister and the Hearth

INTRODUCTION

You've seen him—the old guy sitting on a bench in the park observing a group of neighborhood kids play baseball and occasionally nosing his way into the contest with some kernel of unsolicited wisdom. Probably every town in America has such a character. He seems irritating and the youngsters generally ignore him—until they learn of his pitching a dozen or so games for the St. Louis Browns way back before World War I and hear his stories of having faced the great Ty Cobb.

I never pursued the opportunity to meet Jack Gilligan, the man on the park bench in my hometown, but I wish I had. I would have loved hearing the stories he could have related to me about an era beyond my perspective, an era I can never see except through the eyes of those who lived through it.

I think the public has always been fascinated by those who touched stardom, even for only a moment. I have always been fascinated by the stories of "everyday" people. It never ceases to amaze me that many of the most riveting personal experiences come from sources you would deem least likely. These two ideas were combined in bringing about this book.

This project is quite different than I imagined it to be at its inception in May 1989 and I now know what authors mean when they talk about a book taking on a life of its own. Originally, I envisioned short capsule biographies of perhaps 100 of the more interesting characters to have played only briefly in the major leagues. Four months of research went into cataloging and seeking out information on hundreds of these players and then placing them in one of roughly two dozen categories.

I was always curious, however, about the possibility of conducting extended interviews with the subjects of this book and pondered the possibility that these interviews might yield something more interesting than what began as a volume of trivia. On the day Pete Rose accepted his lifetime ban from baseball, I conducted my first interview and the book's focus changed immediately. I realized that instead of a collection of fascinating, yet obscure facts about men who played the game, I wanted to provide a subjective view of baseball from the vantage point of those who battled to the top of their profession only to, for one reason or another, remain there for only a moment. Men who, like Moses, were allowed only to the edge of the promised land.

Earlier research had revealed that of the more than 13,000 men to have worn a major league uniform, between one-third and one-half lasted the equivalent of a full season or less. I thought it intriguing that these men were not mere curiosities, but were in reality the most typical of those who played major league baseball.

Over the next year and a half, I conducted interviews and researched the careers of the men you find in this book. They were chosen to represent a cross-section of experiences. Their baseball careers span five decades. None are now in professional baseball. Some played on good teams, even pennant winners. Some played for really rotten ballclubs. Some were stars in the minor leagues, one setting a record that still stands some forty years later. Two had extensive careers in Japan. At the time of their interviews, the men ranged in age from their mid-thirties to their eighties. Some were bitter, many were not, although in fairness I would imagine that those especially bitter were among the group who did not reply to my inquiries. This collection is not meant to be a definitive study of professional baseball, but rather is intended to serve as a meandering through portions of the history of our national pastime, through the eyes of 15 men who had the type of career most common among those who reached the major leagues. It is also the story of 15 men who share a common type of career experienced at a common season of their lives.

Throughout the course of my writing, it became apparent certain themes kept repeating themselves—for instance the fact that these men faced entirely different dilemmas than the person we would normally think of as the "typical" major leaguer. For instance, Stan Musial never had to decide whether to continue pursuing his dream because his children were reaching school age and needed a more stable home life. Willie Mays never had to ask himself at the age of 26 whether he really had the ability to make it. Ted Williams never faced a career-ending injury at the age of 23 that stripped him of the only thing he knew how to do. These Hall of Fame athletes never faced the possibility of giving up their dreams short of the goal; of having had a taste of that success but not the opportunity to prove their abilities to others or to themselves.

The men portrayed here were obviously talented athletes, or they could never have reached that level of competition. Often, we treat these men as failures, or make flippant judgments about their abilities without knowledge of facts and circumstances. I was curious as to what happened to these men, and why? And how these experiences influenced their view of the game, or for that matter, the rest of their lives. We tend to lump these men into one category, taking for granted that they lacked talent and are now bitter, if we scrutinize them at all. I was convinced that each would have a unique perspective of the game.

I've always admired the premise of Orson Welles' *Citizen Kane*, with its plot mechanism of profiling an individual through offering the obviously subjective viewpoints of those in orbit around the central character, leaving the viewer his own interpretation of that individual. I decided on attempting that same approach to this book, with baseball serving as the central character and the players' diverse views of the game intended to shed light on the life of the "average" ball player.

Each profile represents a different side of athletic life: filling a role in a great pennant race, sitting on the bench for an entire year because of a logjam of talent, making the most of adversity, giving something back to the game, the frustration of a promising career ended by injury, the perils of front-office politics, the impetuousness of youth, dealing with the reality that one's playing days are over, the quality or lack thereof in professional instruction. The everyday hurdles facing the everyday ball player. And finally how the success and failures in negotiating those hurdles affected the lives of these men.

Every effort has been made to accurately present the personality of those profiled here. In some cases, for the purpose of shortening the telling of a story or for clarity's sake, I have interpreted the player's feelings within the author's narrative, outside of quotes. However, in all instances the players have seen and verified the accuracy of statements attributed to them and indicated any misquotes or misstatements of fact.

This book is essentially a series of *character studies*. I tried hard not to bring along any preconceived notions to the interviews, and waited to choose a theme until after transcribing the various conversations. In some cases, the theme would become apparent with the writing of the piece. The hoped for result is that each story is different as each person is different. Some are more articulate than others and take a more direct part in the telling of their story. Others are more hesitant about revealing themselves. You are encouraged to read between the lines and provide your own interpretations of the player's remarks. I have my own opinions but have tried to keep them to myself, concentrating instead on telling their stories from their perspectives. I want the reader to make his or her own judgments.

My rule of thumb as far as the accuracy of certain events was that, if possible, I would confirm that a certain event took place. When that was impractical, or impossible, I made sure that it could have happened (for instance that the people involved were present at the time in question), and always attributed the event to the player's recollection. I do admit to leaving one story in this volume where the incident happened, but a minor component of the story was incorrect. Since I was sure that the event in question *did* occur (and the story was so good), I left it in.

Once again, this volume of recollections is not meant to be a definitive history of the game. It's simply a look at baseball from a point of view many have before taken for granted. Generally it is assumed that these are men embittered by the failure of attaining their dream. In truth, there are more themes in their lives than that one. Indeed few seemed very bitter at all. They are justifiably proud of their accomplishments and most retain a great fondness for the game and the life-long friends they made. It was an experience all of them would repeat. It's an experience all of us wish we could have.

BILL KOSKI

Pitcher, 1951 Pittsburgh Pirates

Bill Posedel was our pitching coach and I said, "Porthole, I'm having trouble with my curveball." Now this is the pitching coach of the Pittsburgh Pirates. Now you'd think he'd say, "Okay son, let's go down to the bullpen and work on it," right?

We were playing the Philadelphia Phillies. Robin Roberts is standing there right behind the cage taking batting practice. So, instead of taking me down to the bullpen and getting a catcher and saying, "Let's work on that curveball," Posedel says, "Come with me." He takes me over and he introduces me to Robin Roberts, the opposing pitcher. He says, "Robin, I'd like you to meet Bill Koski. He's one of our young pitchers and he's having trouble with the curveball. Could you give him some pointers?"

Then he walks off and leaves me standing there with Robin Roberts.

Now, what's Robin Roberts gonna say to me — "Let's go down to the bullpen and work on your curveball"? Here's a Pirate in the Philadelphia Phillies bullpen throwing and Robin Roberts giving him lessons? You know it wouldn't work. I was embarrassed for Roberts, and it ticked me off — but that's the way Posedel was. He could not teach you.

When I left high school, I said, "I'm going professional, I'm gonna learn stuff." Well, what I found out the longer I was in the game was, the coaches didn't know. The managers would say, "You pitched a couple of years, be my pitching coach." Now, he may not know anything about pitching. All he could do was say, "Okay, you're in the next inning," or he'd come to the mound and take you out of the game. But he couldn't show you anything.

—Bill Koski

5

A teacher affects eternity; no one can tell where his influence stops.
                                    —Henry Adams

Although now a draftsman by trade, Bill Koski's greatest enjoyment comes from attempts to solve baseball "problems" in his spare time; how to teach someone to throw a better curveball, or throw harder, or hit to right field.

After retiring from playing professionally, Koski coached Babe Ruth Baseball for a number of years and assumed that 13- and 14-year-olds knew how to play the game. His teams lost and he slowly came to the realization that just because these teenagers had grown up with baseball, it didn't necessarily follow that they knew what they were supposed to do on the field.

"I went back to kindergarten level and started asking them questions and explaining *why* you do something," says Koski. "And they'd do it. I didn't have to yell at them to keep their gloves down on the ground to field a ground ball because when I told them *why*, it made sense."

When Koski signed a contract with the Pittsburgh Pirates in 1950, major league baseball was, for all intents and purposes, a closed society. It was not *what* you knew, or how well you could present what you knew that landed you a job with an organization. It was *who* you knew and how well you knew them. This applied not only to coaches and front office personnel, but to ball players as well. Farm systems at that time were vast: Most were three to four times larger than today's. The prevalent theory of player development went that if one player didn't succeed, another would always be available to take his place. Players were interchangeable parts. It was nearly as important for a young athlete to have someone at the front office level rooting for him as it was to succeed on the field of play. Of course, it never hurt a player if his team had made a significant monetary investment in his future.

The role of the coach at the professional level in the 1950s was essentially as it had always been: evaluator of talent and drinking buddy. Quite often not in that order. While Johnny Sain and Harry "The Hat" Walker gained reputations as "super coaches" in the 1960s, only recently has the importance of instruction been truly emphasized, enabling men such as Roger Craig, Walt Hriniak, and the late

Charley Lau to gain notoriety for their theories and ability to develop talent.

When the time came to negotiate a professional contract, Koski sought advice from his high school coach, Dick Windemuth, and his father, a star high school pitcher himself in his younger days. Koski had attracted a lot of attention; of the 16 teams in the major leagues at the time, only the Senators and Athletics did not make contract offers. The final decision to sign with Pittsburgh was made in part because the Pirates *weren't* a good team at the time. To put it politely, the organization was "rebuilding."

In baseball, bad teams are always rebuilding and a pennant is only one or two players away. It's part of the giddy incoherence that melds spring and spring training, where optimism is the watchword and reality is suspended — until about the end of April. The reality for Pirates' fans was that, outside of outfielders Ralph Kiner, Gus Bell, and pitcher Murry Dickson, there was little to be optimistic about. Pittsburgh had not won a pennant in 23 years, nor made a serious run since 1938 (a year the Chicago Cubs broke the hearts of others for a change). New ownership had more than tripled the size of the farm system and would bring in the inventor of that system, the legendary Branch Rickey, as general manager. But for then and some time after, the Pirates would be dreadful.

All of these factors actually worked to Pittsburgh's advantage in Koski's eyes. He felt that the Pirates' commitment to youth would translate into the opportunity to move through the system quickly. Of course, it didn't hurt that part-owner Bing Crosby telephoned his mother and assured her that he'd "take care of her boy."

So at the age of 18, Bill Koski was two thousand miles away from his central California home, playing baseball in Kentucky for the Mayfield Clothiers in the Class "D" Kitty League. He wasn't homesick, however, he was excited.

"I thought I was going to learn something about baseball. What I found out was my high school coach had taught me well. Because of his teaching of the fundamentals, it made me seem like a smart ball player. But I wasn't doing anything different than what I was supposed to do."

The painfully shy, gangly right-hander (he was listed at six-four and 185 pounds, but was closer to six-foot-six) had an impressive half-season for Mayfield in 1950. He tossed four shutouts en route to winning eight of ten decisions as the Clothiers captured their first pennant since 1939. Koski's success earned him a ticket to New Orleans, the Pirates' Double-A affiliate in the Southern Association, and an invitation to the major league camp for spring training in 1951.

Koski continued to impress at San Bernardino the next spring. He made headlines, much to his surprise, striking out Ralph Kiner with the bases loaded during an intrasquad game. As opening day approached, the Pittsburgh papers began speculating on the fate of the hard throwing 19-year-old pitcher. The Pirates broke camp and began the long swing back east from California, barnstorming their way across country, along with the Chicago Cubs, travelling through minor league towns of all shapes and sizes, each club unloading players along the way like so much cargo; players who would stock the teams in the small towns that made up the Pirate and Cub farm systems. Although he was still on the train and with the team, the young pitcher fully expected to be unloaded in New Orleans, the final stop before Pittsburgh. He began to notice one of the unspoken routines that signal one's status with a team.

"I got to where I understood if they gave you a big bundle of sanitary socks, you were gonna be around for awhile. The guy they didn't give any to, the next day or two, was gone. So I see the clubhouse man handing out sanitary socks and I get this big bundle. Fine, I'm gonna be here for awhile. As we'd go back, we stopped in New Orleans and played the Cubs. The clubhouse man is throwing these sanitaries out and I'm really sweating it. I'm getting down near the end because the next stop is Pennsylvania. And here comes Byron, the clubhouse man, running around with these bundles of sanitary socks and I'm watching him go around and it seemed like he bypassed me a couple of times and right at the end he throws me this big bundle of socks and it means, hey, I'm going all the way to Pittsburgh!"

Despite his mere half-season of professional experience, the teenager was not in awe of his surroundings as he stood atop the mound at Forbes Field, wearing number 26 for the Pirates and pitching to Ted Kluszewski of the Cincinnati Reds. It was not a matter of ego; it was a lack of comprehending what he'd accomplished in such a short time. Growing up on the West Coast, Koski and his friends followed the Pacific Coast League instead of the majors. The

National and American Leagues were foreign to them. At that time, no team was headquartered west of St. Louis and there seemed little likelihood of change; the major league map hadn't been altered in 50 years. Only during the World Series was there any interest in what the "big leaguers" were doing.

"I'm just now realizing what I've done. Like I met Honus Wagner. Honus sat in the dugout every once in awhile. He's a real old sucker and we got a Pittsburgh Pirate blanket around his shoulders and Honus is sitting right there in the dugout. I really didn't know who he was...I mean in California we didn't have big league baseball. Honus is just an old guy sitting there...I knew he was an old-time ballplayer and that he played shortstop, but that was it. He would sit there and watch and I'd be in the game pitching relief and I'd come in, and you'd think he couldn't see from here to the table there, and he'd say, 'Son, you got to get a little more aggressive out there,' or something. He'd talk to you. He could see all kinds of things going on that field out there. But he used to manage, which I didn't know.

"George Sisler. Hall of Famer. Great hitter. I'm just now reading about Hall of Famers...and George Sisler? *George?* Well, I used to call him George...'*Hey, George!*' you know. He was just walking around. I'm realizing these guys were real great big time and now I see them on TV. We didn't have that back then. So, I got to meet a lot of those people. Now I'm glad I got to meet Honus. Jeez—how many guys get to meet Honus Wagner?"

* * *

After tossing three hitless innings in his major league debut, Koski made his first and only major league start a week later at the Polo Grounds against the New York Giants. The Pirates, including Manager Billy Meyer, had been hit hard by a flu epidemic, and Coach/Acting Manager Milt Stock pressed the 19-year-old into service. Once again, Koski hurled three hitless innings before Monte Irvin's double in the fourth brought the Giants two runs. After walking two in the fifth, the rookie was lifted by Stock in favor of reliever Bill Werle, who subsequently surrendered a grand slam to Giants shortstop Alvin Dark. Koski was charged with the defeat—the only decision of his major league career. The Giants went on to greater conquests that season, thanks to some heroics from outfielder Bobby Thomson.

Although underage, limiting his access to big city nightlife, Koski was enjoying himself. He'd already earned the moniker "T-Bone," bestowed in honor of his trencherman feat of ingesting three complete steak dinners ("each topped off with a parfait"), at the encouragement of roommate Vern Law. He remembers team star Ralph Kiner as somewhat of a prankster, once teaming up with outfielder George "Catfish" Metkovich in a scheme that involved affixing a label marked "acid" on a bottle of harmless eye drops and tricking the team's aged trainer into putting the "acid" into Kiner's eyes. When Kiner screamed in "agony," his teammates thought the trainer was about to have a fatal heart attack, thinking he'd blinded the team's star.

When in Pittsburgh, Koski lived with several other Pirates in a rooming house run by "Mom" Daniels. She quickly adopted the gangly youngster as her favorite, often bringing him in to eat with the family in a separate dining room. Unknown to the other residents, the teenager would dine on steak while his buddies outside ate hamburger. It seems that "Mom" had an eligible daughter.

He also has fond memories of Branch Rickey, who became the Pirates' general manager the year Koski came to the big leagues. On occasion, Rickey would summon the younger players on the team to his hotel suite to find out how they were doing…if they were homesick or had anything bothering them, and to hold audience—to recount inspirational tales of baseball legends past.

After his lack of success in obtaining instruction from Bill Posedel, it was Rickey whom Koski called on for pitching advice.

"I was having trouble throwing a change-up so Rickey said, 'Well, let's go and work on it.' I was throwing on the sideline. I had no trouble throwing it when I was in the bullpen. I could throw a change-up anytime I wanted, and that's what I told him. He was watching me and he said, 'There's nothing wrong with your change-up. It's fine.' I says, 'Yeah, I can throw it all day here, but I can't throw it in a game.'

"He just came unglued.

"'You don't say you can't.' That's what he told me. 'When you say you can't, you're having intercourse with the devil!'"

By early May, it became obvious that the devil himself couldn't salvage 1951 for the Pittsburgh Pirates. At one point, they were swept in a doubleheader by the Philadelphia Phillies 17-0 and 12-4. True, pitcher Cliff Chambers had no-hit the Boston Braves and Kiner was always around to slug home runs, but the season was already beyond recovery. The team had too many green youngsters and over-the-hill veterans to compete. Typical of the veteran ballplayers was "Pistol" Pete Reiser, winding down his career with Pittsburgh after having lost too many battles to outfield walls over the years.

Koski remembers that Reiser would literally "come apart at night. His shoulder would separate, his hip would come out of joint. When his muscles relaxed at night, the bones would pop out of place."

In mid-June, Pittsburgh traded Chambers and outfielder Wally Westlake to the St. Louis Cardinals for five players, including veteran reliever Ted Wilks, two-time 20-game winner Howie Pollet, and a veteran catcher by the name of Joe Garagiola. It didn't help. By 1952, this team would lose 112 games.

Lack of control was Koski's weakness and it confined him largely to mop-up roles. His best performance came May 12 against the Chicago Cubs. Vern Law had started the game despite a sore arm and was knocked out of the box in the first inning. Koski came on to record seven innings of three-hit ball in a game the Pirates eventually lost by a score of 8-4.

By the time of trade with the Cardinals, Koski was scarcely pitching at all. With the arrival of Wilks and Pollet, he was optioned to New Orleans, returning to the parent club for two games in September. After that, he was then never again to appear in a major league box score. However, at the time of his demotion, Koski's future seemed bright. He'd shown some talent, was only 19, and had a live arm. The Pirates placed him on 24-hour recall, leaving Pittsburgh the option of bringing him back literally at a moment's notice. In fact, it took peculiar circumstances to prevent Koski's return to the big leagues.

In 1952, he was assigned to Burlington, the Pirates' affiliate in the Carolina League. The ballclub had a talented pitching staff. Several, including Ron Kline, Bill Bell, and Ron Necciai, went on to pitch in the majors, but by the end of the season Burlington finished nearly forty games out of first place.

With all the pitching talent on that team, it is ironic that the player who went on to possibly the most effective big league pitching career was the team's six-foot six-inch *shortstop*, Dick Hall. First switched to the outfield before moving to the pitcher's mound, Hall eventually established a long career with the Philadelphia Phillies and the Baltimore Orioles. Koski remembers Hall gaining a reputation as a sort of "intellectual" because he liked to study clouds and do crossword puzzles in Sanskrit.

Koski enjoyed what he felt was the best season of his career at Burlington, despite his 8-16 record. He pitched on the league's all-star team, striking out three in his stint during a 1-0 victory. He also tossed a one-hitter, completed 16 games and finished fifth in the league in strikeouts, while being victimized by 39 *unearned* runs.

While at Burlington, Koski was confronted with the first twist of fate that would ultimately end his chances of returning to the majors. In mid-August, Branch Rickey sent a telegram informing him that he was being recalled by Pittsburgh. As he packed to leave Burlington, another telegram arrived for the 20-year-old...from Uncle Sam. He had been drafted by the Army and was to report within the week. Koski flew to Pittsburgh to inform the team of his status, and then headed to California.

After serving 19 months in Special Services (among those in his unit were actors David Janssen and Martin Milner), upon his discharge in 1954 Koski immediately noticed a change in attitude toward him. It seemed that, for some reason, he was no longer considered a prospect. People in the organization seemed cool toward him; the keen interest in his welfare he had noticed before was missing.

He *had* lost something from his fastball (some years later he discovered the reason: he had unknowingly changed his pitching grip after spraining his thumb), but what Koski later discovered was that a former teammate had spread a rumor that he had hurt his arm while in the Army. That had not happened, but no one came to him and asked if the story was true and in the closed, country club atmosphere of that time, a rumor like that was often ruinous to a player's career.

One hope remained for Koski's return to Pittsburgh. Harold Roettger, the Pirates' travelling secretary (and a close friend of Branch Rickey), had always been a fan of the young pitcher. During the 1955 season, Roettger arrived to observe the Pirates' farm team in Brunswick, Georgia, where Koski was pitching. He had finally developed the change-up he'd worked on with Rickey and it was paying dividends. After starting the season in the bullpen Koski had moved into the rotation, completing six of nine starts and sporting an earned run average well below three. It seemed perfect timing for a visit from the Pirate front office.

"Roettger came down to Georgia when I was pitching this game, and I had struck out two or three guys on change-ups. When the game was over he comes up to me and says, 'Bill, wait till Mr. Rickey hears about this!' He said, 'Man, oh man, this is great.' He was all excited about this change-up I was starting to throw then. He says, 'I gotta go down to Florida, but boy, when I get back I'm gonna tell Rickey all about this.' He was just all excited, and I felt pretty good. I got a guy who's gonna go up there and get me some points.

"He goes down to Florida. They said he was sitting by the pool...typing...has a diabetic attack, falls off, rolls in the pool and drowns. Never got back to Pittsburgh."

* * *

Before entering the Army, Bill Koski had been a quiet, unassuming young man: the kind of guy who got along with everybody and always did as he was told. While playing for Burlington in 1952, he met and married Nancy Frazier in what has been described as a genuine whirlwind romance by those present at the time. Nancy was the first girl Bill had ever dated seriously (much to the disappointment of "Mom" Daniels), and she remembers that, in those days, her husband was the type who never displayed anger toward anyone, even when justified. Once, an outfielder named Joe Duhem made an error that cost staff ace Ron Necciai a victory, earning the outfielder a tongue-lashing from the pitcher after the game.

According to Nancy, Duhem later related what had happened and added sheepishly, "I must've lost a *dozen* games for Bill like that this year, and he never jumped on me once."

After his stint in the military, Koski had become older and perhaps less tolerant of what he viewed as incompetence. In 1956, he was back in the Carolina League, playing for Kinston and a manager named Jack Paepke.

"Worst manager I ever run across in my life. This guy was a joke. An absolute joke. I see this guy doing these antics, like when he went out to argue a pitch at home plate. He was our catcher, he has his catching gear on, right? He would run out there and do a hook slide on his shin guards into home plate, grabbing two hands full of dirt as he's sliding. He'd do a stand up slide, throw the dirt in the air, and he'd start arguing with the ump. He went through these antics and it just drove me nuts.

"We were playing Durham and their manager was Johnny Pesky...and [their center fielder], he comes up and bam...hits one out. The *next* batter...bam...hits one out. I'm in the bullpen warming up and Paepke's gonna put me in relief. So, two home runs in a row and I go in. Back in those days when guys hit two home runs in a row, the next guy's going down. Everybody knew that, even the hitter. He knew he was gonna be brushed back. So I wind up and I brush him back. Not to knock him down, just *tight*.

"Pesky gets on me from the third base coaching box. 'You don't throw at my ballplayers!' he starts yelling at me. When I was nineteen, twenty, I'd have never said a word, but I really ripped him good. I called him a 'half-man,' because he wasn't a big guy anyway. I ripped him good.

"I didn't know Pesky and Paepke were good Navy buddies. We were in Durham and Paepke was staying with Pesky at his house. They're drinking beer, and I could just hear 'em, Paepke saying, 'That Koski! Nobody's gonna get on my Navy buddy.'

"Two days later, Paepke calls me in the office and wants to send me to Waco, Texas. I said, 'No way. The kind of people they're sending to manage these ballclubs, I don't want anything to do with this organization. I want out.'"

Koski gained his release. In truth, he was prepared to call it a career; he now had a family and his son was about to start kindergarten.

Returning home to Modesto, California, Koski enrolled at the local junior college to study drafting and begin shaping a life outside of baseball. He took a summer job as a pitcher-first baseman for Las Vegas in the Arizona-Mexico League, one of those colorful little minor leagues that proliferated the baseball landscape too many years ago. His most vivid memories of that circuit concern a team owned by a copper mining company in Mexico. To get to the small town, the Las Vegas team drove its players via station wagons into the middle of the desert...and turned left. It was truly in the middle of nowhere.

As Koski recalls, the fans in the town hated baseball because each citizen was required to purchase season tickets out of their own pockets. Everyone was an employee of the mine, and wages were not always in line with the latest cost of living index. The atmosphere was imposing; the fans were separated from the all-dirt baseball field by a huge barbed wire fence. The only entrance or exit in the stadium was through a gigantic fortress-style gate. As one might infer, the visiting team was wise to beat a hasty retreat should they win.

After surviving the Arizona-Mexico League and completing junior college, Koski was hired for a position with the County Planning Department in Modesto. Bill and Nancy's original plan was to scrape together enough money to return to Burlington, where he already had an offer of employment. The position with the county, however, brought with it the promise of raises and promotions, and they realized that he couldn't walk away from the opportunities being offered.

Playing baseball with the local entry in the California League and Sunday ball kept Koski occupied and only once did he nearly succumb to the temptation of attempting a comeback. In 1958, the Pirates made their first trip to the West Coast to play the San Francisco Giants, and Pittsburgh General Manager Joe L. Brown invited the ex-Pirate hurler to throw batting practice. Nancy remembers vividly that it took two weeks for her husband to come down from the clouds. Pirate shortstop Dick Groat raved to Koski about his arm, and he really thought seriously about giving baseball one more try. But in the end he couldn't put his family through the rigors of minor league life anymore.

Even though it had been his own decision and he had more or less left the game on his own terms, Koski found going from the life of a player to that of an ex-player a difficult transition. He was working as a draftsman for the county in a new government complex, far from any ballfield both in distance and surroundings, and discovered that withdrawal from athletic life brought with it some rather eerie side effects.

"I was out at Center Three [the building in which he was working] when I got this job with the county, and we had one of those rooms out there with no walls in it. We had one whole big room. This *was* the Planning Department. We had only one partition and the secretaries were out front at the counter, and the drafting room was bigger than this whole house. There was just two drafting tables sitting in this big room and this whole bank of windows on the side.

"Every spring I'd be sitting there and all of a sudden I'd be working away and I'd hear bats and balls...balls hitting bats and

BILL KOSKI

Born February 6, 1932, Madera, California

Ht. 6'4" Wt. 190 BR TR

MAJOR AND MINOR LEAGUE CAREER

Year	Team, League	W-L	Pct	G	GS	CG	SHO	IP	H	R	ER	BB	SO	ERA
1950	Mayfield, Kitty	8-2	.800	10	—	8	4	78	59	25	21	37	51	2.42
1951	PITTSBURGH, National	0-1	.000	13	1	0	0	27	26	23	20	28	6	6.67
	New Orleans, Southern Assn	4-9	.308	15	15	7	0	91	99	63	53	70	31	5.24
1952	Burlington, Carolina	8-16	.333	30	—	16	0	187	181	112	73	78	117	3.51
1953				MILITARY SERVICE										
1954	Burlington, Carolina	2-2	.500	4	3	1	0	19	27	18	15	8	10	7.11
	St. Jean, Provincial	3-2	.600	9	6	3	0	50.1	46	29	26	39	18	4.65
1955	Burlington, Carolina	0-1	.000	12	2	0	0	13	20	19	16	13	4	11.08
	Brunswick, Georgia-Florida	8-6	.571	18	9	6	1	102.1	89	40	28	42	54	2.46
1956	Kinston, Carolina	2-2	.500	10	2	1	0	42	51	28	22	15	18	4.71
	Modesto, California	0-2	.000	2	2	0	0	8	16	15	13	3	5	14.63
1957	Las Vegas, Arizona-Mexico	4-6	.400	28	7	2	0	85	114	75	60	44	37	6.35
MAJOR LEAGUE TOTALS		0-1	.000	13	1	0	0	27	26	23	20	28	6	6.67
MINOR LEAGUE TOTALS		39-48	.448	138	—	44	5	675.2	702	424	327	349	345	4.36

gloves popping. I'd *hear* these. I'd actually *hear* it. And I'd go, 'What in the world?' Then I'd go back to drawing again, working, and I would hear these 'bats' and 'balls' on the first warm sunny day after the winter.

"I went two years that way. And then it kinda faded out."

* * *

When Bill Koski reflects now on the lack of instruction he received during his career, his tone is more incredulous than bitter.

"I never did have a curveball. I threw so hard, the ball didn't have time to break. I really discovered that *after*. If somebody'd said to me, 'Take something off the curveball, slow down.' That's what I do now with a kid who throws hard, but I had to learn that on my own through time and experience. Back then, no one around could tell me. I didn't know *why* I threw harder than everyone else. Now I can take a kid who throws fairly hard and make him throw harder by giving him a little instruction, cause I know *why* now. I can add a few things, make changes in him.

"I do the same thing in hitting. Now I know *why* you hit the ball better. If you want to be a good pitcher, you study hitting. What do hitters think about? When this situation comes about, you put yourself in the hitter's position. I learned this from talking to great hitters like Pete Reiser and Ralph Kiner.

"When you think you know everything about this game, you don't. You'll never know. If anyone ever tells you, 'I know everything there is about this position or that position,' he's full of baloney. Every year I learn at least three to four things. Now Dick Windemuth got me on the right track. He says, 'Anytime an old guy comes up to you...it's gonna happen...some guy's gonna come up to you and say, "I used to throw this pitch back in the Midwestern League," Dick says, 'Listen to him, because he may come up with something you can use.'"

If you pin Koski down, he will admit that coaching in a Rookie League would be his dream job. He finds working with young players rewarding, and relishes the opportunity to experiment with different theories and solutions to "baseball problems." He works each year at Jose Canseco's baseball camp and in addition to his job at the county, serves as pitching coach for California State University, Stanislaus in Turlock, California.

Koski also enjoys the aspect of working with youngsters referred to him by parents or friends of parents. Nancy Koski believes that her husband should have pursued coaching as a vocation 30 years ago. Bill feels differently. "Going through Babe Ruth League and Sunday baseball has really helped me. I couldn't have done this thirty years ago."

Whatever the case, one has the feeling that only now is Bill Koski beginning to realize his life's calling. Ironically, he is inspired by those who were coaching and probably should have been doing something else.

ED SANICKI

Outfielder, 1949, 1951 Philadelphia Phillies

*Ed Sawyer was a quiet manager. Ed Sawyer never said "Boo."
He'd never give you any advice. I'm not bitter towards him... I'd
just like to face him and say, "Why? Why didn't you let me be at
bat fifty times?" I'd love to talk to him about that.*

*In fact, I went to a memorabilia show in Trevose, Pennsylvania, two weeks ago—and then this month, Ed Sawyer's comin' in
from New York State and he's gonna be the guest. And I don't
know whether to go approach him or not. Just ask him, you
know, "Skip, what the hell happened?"*
—Ed Sanicki

For all sad words of tongue or pen,
The saddest are these: "It might have been!"
—John Greenleaf Whittier

Ed Sanicki was never one to waste time introducing himself to pitchers. He homered in his first ever exhibition at bat. He homered in his first official at bat as a professional. He homered in his first major league at bat and later for good measure, in his first game before the home crowd in Philadelphia. Each of the right-handed slugger's first three major league hits left the park and even more incredibly they were a major part of his grand total of only 17 major league plate appearances, all with Philadelphia in the two seasons sandwiched around the Phillies' only World Series in a 65-year span — a pennant race Sanicki missed by a cruel twist.

In those 17 at bats, the five-foot-ten, 175-pound outfielder collected five hits; including three home runs and a double, eight RBIs and a Ruthian slugging average of .882, especially impressive for a player primarily used as a defensive replacement.

Following his retirement from baseball in the early 1950s, Sanicki completed his education at Seton Hall University where he earned his teaching credential, leading to the most rewarding phase of his life: three decades of work with severely handicapped high school children in the New Jersey school system. In 1956 Sanicki was a physical education instructor when approached by the school's principal and asked if he would be willing to organize a P.E. class for handicapped children. Sanicki remembers the principal adding the warning to "be careful, because they're gonna catch cold from too much activity and they're gonna get sick and then the parents are *really* on us."

For the former Phillie outfielder, the assignment opened up a whole new world.

"I found out after awhile that, although limited, these kids are as normal as anybody else as far as physical ability is concerned. And they're *great* kids.

"They were sheltered at home and school got them for the first time sometimes when they were fifteen and sixteen. They were just babies all their lives. And a lot of the parents overprotected the kids an awful lot, which you could understand. You'd try to get hold of the parents and say, 'You're too motherly with them. *Yell* at them once in awhile. They want to be talked to just like their brothers and sisters.'

"I had them in Special Olympics, I had 'em in tournaments. I was also their swimming instructor. I taught so many kids how to swim — I would say a hundred Down's syndrome children, and that *is* different.

They move their arms and their legs and they breathe. They understand those three fundamentals. To see a kid swim across a lake or dive into the water with a big smile when he comes up, that's rewarding."

* * *

Eddie Sanicki first became a rabid follower of the national pastime as a young boy growing up in New Jersey. He would sit in his room playing a baseball board game, rolling dice and looking up the results on cards, all the while managing Dizzy Dean, Carl Hubbell, and Hal Schumacher. He played a 100-game schedule culminating in a World Series and fantasized that one day he might play in one for real.

Sanicki's older brother was an amateur boxer who encouraged Ed's interest in the game and also recruited the 11-year-old to help him with his road work. Each day he enlisted his kid brother to run with him a mile and back to the country store near their home. For his efforts Ed earned a nickel. The Sanicki boys also punched a heavy bag and a speed bag each day before breakfast and Ed would swing his Louisville Slugger at small pebbles to improve his bat speed. Sanicki credits his brother for instilling in him the good work habits and discipline that stay with him to this day.

Unable to play organized baseball until high school since the Clifton, New Jersey, area where he lived had no Little League or American Legion program, Sanicki made the freshman baseball team at Clifton High at the same time his brother was captain of the school's varsity squad. He was soon playing almost every evening after Clifton High's games. Doubleheaders occupied his Saturdays and Sundays.

When not playing in organized contests, Sanicki and his friends practiced two or three hours at a time, hitting on a diamond featuring a short right-field fence. The most important ground rule adhered to was that batters had to steer clear of the temptation to hit a ball over the short fence, which separated the field from two homes. This rule was not adopted in the interest of fairness. Rather it was due to the discovery that any ball hit into the yard beyond the fence was confiscated by the woman living there.

"Later on, believe it or not, one of my big faults in the major leagues was not spreading the ball around," says Sanicki. "I was known as a pull hitter. The majority of the home runs I hit out in left field or left center."

The work habits and discipline instilled in him at an early age, and the realization that he had some talent, helped Sanicki shine as a player in high school. He was All-State in New Jersey for two years and began attracting the attention of scouts by his junior year. Eventually he received an invitation to work out with Jersey City, the top minor league team of the New York Giants.

"They were coached by a fellow named Tony Cuccinello, a former major leaguer. He wanted me to sign in the worst way. He sent me to the Polo Grounds and I hit a couple out there and I came back, reported to him and I said, 'Well no, I'm not ready to go away to professional ball.' Cuccinello said, 'Well, whatever you do when you're ready to sign up for baseball, let me know.'"

Prior to his workout with the Giants, Sanicki had been followed closely by a Brooklyn Dodger scout. Already set to enter Georgetown on a football scholarship, the scout told Sanicki to forget about the gridiron and lined up a baseball scholarship for him at Seton Hall University. A year and a half later, the Japanese bombed Pearl Harbor and changed Sanicki's immediate plans.

Nearing his 23rd birthday after seeing two years action aboard ship in the North Atlantic, Sanicki was offered a contract by the Philadelphia Phillies, including a $2,000 signing bonus. He was ready to play, having kept in shape while at sea through a continuation of his strict workout regimen as well as boxing. It was the Dodgers, however, not the Phillies, that owned Sanicki's heart.

During the late 1930s Sanicki would ride in to Brooklyn with his brother and arrive at Ebbets Field at nine-thirty in the morning. There they would wait in the hallway for the ticket booth to open. As they stood in the corridor killing time until they could purchase their bleacher seats, many of the Dodger players would arrive: Cookie Lavagetto, Freddie Fitzsimmons, Dolph Camilli, Van Lingle Mungo. Babe Ruth, a coach for the Dodgers, would pass through handing out little cards he had autographed beforehand. Those visits to Ebbets Field were among the most cherished memories of his youth.

Sanicki loved the Dodgers, had grown up with them, and that was the team he wanted to play for. With the $2,000 offer from the Phillies in his back pocket, Sanicki went to the Dodger offices to keep an appointment with Branch Rickey. (It was Larry MacPhail who had been in charge of the Dodgers before the war and he had approved the arrangement of Sanicki's baseball scholarship to Seton Hall. Rickey had replaced his former protégé when MacPhail had resigned to join the Army; after the war MacPhail would return to the baseball world with the New York Yankees.)

Arriving at Ebbets Field, Sanicki came to the stadium this time in hopes of becoming one of the Dodgers rather than watching them.

"I went in [Rickey's] office, he was a very polite gentleman, and I told him, 'Look, the Phillies are willing to give me $2,000. If you can make it $2,500, I'd be very happy to sign with you people.'

"He says, 'Well, we *can't* do that, but we'll give you $2,500 if you go to Vero Beach and make the team.'

"I said, 'Well I can't afford that.' I was just out of the service and I was already married. 'The Phillies are giving me [$2,000], it's money right in my pocket. They're willing to take a chance.'

"He wished me luck, gave me a little cigarette lighter...and I signed with the Phillies instead.

"You know, one of the saddest things, is when I finally did make it with the Phillies and when we went to Cincinnati and I was on the ball field, Mr. Cuccinello came right up to me and gave me a good boot right in the rear. He told me, 'Why in the hell didn't you look me up when the war ended?'

"So it coulda gone either way. I coulda signed with the Dodgers, or I coulda had Tony Cuccinello lookin' out for me...which meant *so* much at that time. Someone pushin' you and sayin', 'Hey, I found that kid and I'm gonna follow him all the way.' So you say you missed the boat there too.

"But I would've given my right arm to play for the Dodgers. *Jesus Christ*...I just loved them so much."

* * *

After receiving the cigarette lighter from Branch Rickey, Ed Sanicki went to Philadelphia scout Ben Marmo and agreed to a contract with the Phillies. Officially he was signed by Chuck Ward, who had signed Robin Roberts and was the top New Jersey scout., (and ironically an old-time Brooklyn Dodger infielder). According to Sanicki, Marmo was sort of a "bird dog" for Ward, alerting him to prospects like Sanicki he happened to find. Sanicki quickly discovered that Ward was no Tony Cuccinello; his distaste for front office politics left the young outfielder with the prospect of climbing through the Phillie organization without an important ally and booster.

Signed to a Utica, New York, contract at $175 a month, Sanicki was reassigned to class "B" Wilmington, Delaware, shortly after his arrival. Wilmington was the home of Phillie owner Robert Carpenter's father, who would attend almost every evening home game. Occasionally, the younger Carpenter would join his father in the stands. Sanicki must have impressed them both as he hit 30 home runs and drove in 144, leading the league in both categories. He scored 113 runs, batted .307 and even stole 19 bases.

Of course he didn't impress them enough to make salary negotiations any easier. Sanicki remembers going to Philadelphia minor league director Joe Reardon after the season and asking for a $75 a month raise to $250. He remembers Reardon turning around and saying, "Instead of two-fifty...we'll give you two and a quarter. Come back and have a good year." He was returned to Wilmington.

In 1947 Sanicki tore up the Interstate League once again with an even better year, hitting .320 with 37 home runs and 109 RBIs. Named the league's Most Valuable Player, he also drew 109 walks, scored 127 runs and boasted a .600 slugging average. In the spring he got his $250.

The next season Sanicki was jumped all the way to Triple A, joining Toronto in the International League. The upgrade in competition had an effect on his offense: His home run total dropped to 20 and his batting average slid to .236. On the other hand, he led the league in RBIs with 107 and set a record for outfielders with 29 assists.

Sanicki remained in the International League in 1949, increasing both his power and batting average, socking 33 home runs while batting .268. He once again topped 100 runs batted in, the fourth time in his four-year career he had achieved that mark. In mid-September, at the conclusion of the minor league season, the 26-year-old outfielder was one of several Toronto farmhands brought to Philadelphia for a trial.

He arrived at the Schenley Hotel in Pittsburgh on September 14 and discovered his teammates were already at Forbes Field playing the Pirates. After getting settled in his room, the rookie headed to the ballpark where the afternoon game was in the third inning.

After shaking hands and introducing himself to the rest of the Phillie team, manager Ed Sawyer said to the new arrival, "Go out in the bullpen Eddie and warm up."

"So I went out in the bullpen and I was warmin' up there with a few other guys, Ken Silvestri and a few others, and about the seventh inning I get the signal. *I'm in the ballgame.*

"We're winning about 9-4 and I relieved Bill 'Swish' Nicholson [in left field]. First thing you know, I caught a ball or two, and then we got a rally goin' in the top of the ninth. I found myself at bat [against Pittsburgh's Rip Sewell] with two men on base. I didn't know what the hell bat to use, so I picked up an Andy Seminick bat, which was a thin handle and a heavy barrel. So, I don't know, it was two and two or whatever it was, and I just swung and *boom*...this thing *just* lofted over 'Greenberg Gardens,' which because of Hank Greenberg, they shortened the field, otherwise it wouldn't have made it.

"And I remember having a difficult time trying to get the ball from Jim Konstanty. He wanted to keep it! He had a sports shop and he wanted to keep it!

"He said, 'I'll give you *another* ball, Eddie.' I said, 'No, no. Let me have *that* ball.' Well, the teammates say, '*Christ*, give it to him for crying out loud!' So he gave it to me, finally.

"So... I hit a home run in my first major league at bat, and then someone knew I hit a home run in my first at bat in organized ball...and then you know, I had some reporters around me. So that was a thrill that evening. That was quite a thrill, to be exposed the way I was, just gettin' off the train six hours before."

* * *

Ed Sanicki was making his debut in the shadow of two classic pennant races in 1949, both of which would go down to the final day of the season. In the American League, the Boston Red Sox and New York Yankees were staging their epic battle immortalized in David Halberstam's *The Summer of '49*. The National League was providing an equally entertaining race between the St. Louis Cardinals and Brooklyn Dodgers, from which the "Bums" would eventually emerge victorious.

On September 19, five days into Ed's major league career, the Phillies were at Sportsman Park in St. Louis, taking on the Cards, who were two games ahead of Brooklyn in the standings. St. Louis had slaughtered Philadelphia the previous day by a count of 15-3, a game highlighted by umpire George Barr's ejection of four Phillies, including Sanicki's roommate Bill Glynn who was tossed out for arguing balls and strikes — in his first major league at bat. The Cardinals were sending their ace, Howie Pollet, to the mound in search of his twentieth victory of the season. The Phillies countered with three rookies in their lineup: second baseman Ed Goliat, right fielder Ed Sanicki, and a left-handed sinkerball pitcher named Jocko Thompson, a heavily decorated veteran of World War II with one career victory to his credit. The Brooklyn faithful, led by Manager Burt Shotton, began to complain that while their team was straining to catch the Cardinals, the Phillies weren't putting their best team on the field against the league leaders. Sanicki remembers Shotton not being happy he was in the lineup as he said, "How the hell can they use a rookie, and use a pitcher named Jocko Thompson? We're fighting for a pennant, why doesn't he use his *best* players?"

Ed Sawyer retorted, "Let Brooklyn run its own club and I'll run mine."

Shotton would have little to say after this game. While Thompson was shutting out the Cardinals over the first six innings, Sanicki blasted a two-run homer in the fourth and added a sacrifice fly in the sixth off Pollet, the latter of which proved the end for the St. Louis left-hander. Philadelphia added another run in the seventh via Granny Hamner's single off Al Brazle, scoring Goliat, the Phillies' third rookie in the lineup. Thompson then held on to win 4-3, retiring Stan Musial on a weak infield roller with runners at first and third to end the contest.

"I hope Jocko's work convinced the Brooklyn loudmouths that we are not bringing up 'Patsys' from the minors," said an indignant Sawyer after the game. "We don't have 'Patsys' on our ballclub."

Sanicki had now driven in six runs in his first week in the majors. Furthermore, he had played a significant role in aiding his childhood heroes in their quest for the pennant; without this victory over the Cardinals, St. Louis and Brooklyn would have ended the 1949 campaign in a tie, forcing a play-off. It was the first of three straight years that the Dodgers took the pennant race down to the final day of the season.

As the schedule neared its end, Philadelphia solidified their hold on third place. On September 28, Sanicki followed Del Ennis' second-inning home run with a smash of his own into the upper deck in the seventh inning off the Giants' Sheldon Jones. Those two blows represented the game's entire scoring. The victory was the Phils' eightieth of the season, ensuring their best record in 32 years; since the days when Babe Ruth was plying his trade as a left-handed pitcher in Fenway Park and Grover Cleveland Alexander and Eppa Rixey were the stalwarts of the Philadelphia starting rotation. With only their third first-division finish in 34 years, the 1949 season also foreshadowed the success of the Phillies' "Whiz Kids" in 1950. Good times also seemed to be on the horizon for Sanicki. His final 1949 totals included three hits in 13 at bats, three home runs and seven RBIs in seven games to go with his 33 home runs in the International League.

Sanicki had generated a lot of attention for his September fireworks and was rated to have a shot at beating out third-year man Richie Ashburn in center field. After starting out slowly the next spring training, Sawyer replaced Sanicki with the 23-year-old Nebraska native with the white hair and he caught fire. Sanicki remembers simply that, "You *couldn't* get Ashburn out. You couldn't get him out *at all.*"

Sanicki remained with the Phillies through the spring and as the team barnstormed its way back North. As soon as the squad arrived in Philadelphia, he was informed of his being demoted to Toronto, where he would be given instruction on spraying the ball around rather than pulling every pitch that came his way. After four stellar minor league seasons and a sensational major league debut, he was being told to change his approach at the plate. Sanicki argued, "How can you in *four years* not say a word and I had all these great years? All of a sudden, I'm up in the major leagues and (now) you tell me I gotta change my style?"

"So I get down to Toronto and sure enough one fella comes down there and works with me for three days, 'This is the way you do it.' And then he leaves town and then two weeks later, in comes another instructor. He says, 'To hell with what *he* says, do it *this* way.'

"First thing you know you're all messed up. You try to get back to your old stance, the newspapers are riding you because you hit 33 home runs the year before and now you got about seven and the season's half finished. So I had a terrible year."

In mid-July Sanicki was travelling with the ballclub on the train to Rochester when the Toronto manager called him to his compartment. He told Sanicki, "Eddie, the Phillies are fighting for the pennant. After we get through with this Rochester series, you'll be joining the Phillies as a defensive outfielder relieving [Dick] Sisler in late innings."

Elated, the outfielder took the field the next day in Rochester when the unthinkable happened. Rushing in to make an attempt at catching a bloop single just beyond the infielders, Sanicki turned to reach back as he failed to get to the ball before it fell safely. As he twisted awkwardly, his knee gave out. Having torn several ligaments he was carried off the field by his teammates. It was July 18, his wedding anniversary.

The Phillies promoted Jackie Mayo instead and Sanicki watched the 1950 World Series from the stands.

* * *

If the success of 1949 had foreshadowed even greater success for the Phillies in 1950, then 1950 definitely foreshadowed their next serious run at the pennant: the collapse of 1964, when the team blew a six and a half game lead with 12 games to play. The Whiz Kids had a nine-game lead over Brooklyn in mid-September, only to see it all but evaporate to a single game on the final day of the season — a game against the Dodgers that the Phillies had to win in order to avoid a play-off. Due to injuries and 17-game winner Curt Simmons' induction into military service, Robin Roberts was forced to take the mound for Philadelphia for the third time in five days. The Phillies took the deciding contest, thanks to a great performance by Roberts (who pitched out of a nail-biting ninth inning bases-loaded jam) and the heroics of Richie Ashburn and Dick Sisler. Ashburn, who had one of the most notoriously weak throwing arms in baseball, erased the Dodgers' Cal Abrams at the plate in the ninth inning with a perfect toss to keep the game tied. Sisler's tenth-inning three-run homer then clinched the victory and the pennant. For the Dodgers it was a controversial loss. Arguments raged as to the proper assigning of blame. One camp argued that Abrams had made too wide a turn at third while others questioned the wisdom of third base coach Milt Stock sending him at all. It was a crushing disappointment, but it would pale in comparison to what was coming the next year after a game at the Polo Grounds.

The game secured Ashburn's place in both Phillie and Dodger history. Always a competitor (Sanicki remembers, "If he had two hits, he wanted three...if he had three hits, he wanted four"), any doubts among his teammates regarding his ability were erased by his throw to the plate in that most crucial situation.

For the Phillies it was a high point in franchise history, especially needed for a team that had precious few great moments in its past.

One of the rare icons in Phillies history, the great Grover Cleveland Alexander, was in attendance at the World Series that fall. At that time the only man to have ever won a post-season game for the Phillies, it was one of his last public appearances coming only a month before his death at the age of 63. His presence brought no luck for the Phils, however, and at the end of the four-game sweep at the hands of the New York Yankees, Alexander remained the only vestige of post-season success in Phillies history.

Actually, it was a much closer series than one might remember: The first three games were low-scoring affairs, each decided by one run. Surprise starter Jim Konstanty was beaten 1-0 by Vic Raschi in the first game. (The announcement of the Phillies reliever's assignment caught everyone unaware; the photographers had just gathered the Philadelphia starting rotation together for the traditional World Series photograph when the news was broken by a reporter. He suddenly asked why Konstanty wasn't in the picture since he was the opening game starter. No one looked more surprised than those four Philadelphia pitchers.) Game Two featured a classic pitcher's duel between Robin Roberts and Allie Reynolds, a 2-1 game decided by a tenth-inning home run off the bat of Joe DiMaggio. Game Three went the Yankees' way, 3-2, on a ninth-inning single by Jerry Coleman. Even in Game Four, when the Phils lost 5-2 against a rookie left-hander named Edward "Whitey" Ford, they had the tying run at the plate with two out in the ninth. But in the end, the Whiz Kids were history and the Yankees rolled on, as always.

The Phillies had gone into the series as one of the youngest teams in the history of the fall classic. The oldest starter in their rotation was 26. The infielders, with the exception of 31-year-old Eddie Waitkus, were 25 or younger. Outfielders Del Ennis and Richie Ashburn were 25 and 23, respectively. The future seemed bright indeed.

The team's offensive leaders were Ashburn at the top of the lineup and Del Ennis in the heart of the order. Ennis led the team in home runs and the league in RBIs while hitting .311. A quiet, always pleasant guy who usually kept to himself, he was also as Sanicki remembers, "As strong as an ox. You get up there and think you're a home run hitter until you look at *his* muscles."

Power was also provided by third baseman Willie "Puddin'

Head" Jones and catcher Andy Seminick. Outfielder Dick Sisler and shortstop Granville "Granny" Hamner both drove in more than 80 runs. Hamner, one of the real characters on the team, first joined the Phillies in 1944 at the age of 17. After his career as an infielder waned, he attempted a comeback as a knuckleball pitcher. Judging by his 48 errors in 1950, he might have been throwing a few from shortstop as well. Later a three-time All-Star, Hamner was a highly regarded hitter in the clutch and one of the few Philadelphia players to hit the ball well in the 1950 World Series.

The steadying influence on the infield was provided by veteran first baseman Eddie Waitkus, who was making a comeback after becoming a real life model for *The Natural*, courtesy of one Ruth Ann Steinhagen.

The pitching staff was led by Robin Roberts, the military bound Curt Simmons, and the first relief pitcher ever to be named his league's Most Valuable Player, Jim Konstanty. After bouncing around for a decade, the bespectacled right-hander developed a palm ball and rode the pitch to stardom. At 33 he was the oldest player on the team to see significant service, save for 35-year-old spot-starter Ken Heintzelman.

The team was young, talented and seemed like it would be a contender for the rest of the decade, but even though nine of the mainstays from the Whiz Kid team would still be on the Phillies as late as 1956, this was the team's only shot at a championship. They never finished closer than nine games from the lead during that time.

In the spring of 1951, as the Phillies launched the defense of their first National League title in 35 years, Sanicki was in the minor league camp with Baltimore, Philadelphia's new Triple-A affiliate.

"We're going to play Miami Beach in a minor league exhibition game, and I heard on the radio that I'm going up to Philadelphia [for the start of the season]...and I said, '*Wow!*' So I get up there, very happy to see the guys and everything else...and here I had a *job*! I'm in the ballgame in the seventh inning, defensively. [The next day] I'm in the ballgame in the seventh inning *again*. I said, 'Hey, I got a job here!' I was at bat four times and had two hits in about 18 games. And the first thing you know, it came down to cut-down date.

"I had struck out in the Polo Grounds and then right after the ballgame, we got on a sleeper and headed for St. Louis. They brought me all the way into St. Louis to tell me the next day that I was leaving. And I was going to 'A' ball, which is sort of a slap in the face, too.

"I asked, 'Why can't I go to Baltimore, the highest farm club?' They said, 'They got enough outfielders already,' and they wanted Schenectady to win the pennant, and so forth and so on.

"They sent me to Schenectady. And that really took the bottom out. You know, I went from the major leagues down to 'A' ball. And I went down there, hit twenty home runs and was having a mediocre season. I was really down. And Sawyer came into town and I asked him what were his plans for me. And he said he had no plans."

* * *

At the end of the 1951 season, Sanicki was left unprotected by the Phillies in the winter draft and selected by Tulsa of the Texas League. Two months into the 1952 season he was sold to Houston. Having to be in Texas the next day, he packed up his family, loaded all their belongings into a station wagon and started out on the 500-mile trip from Tulsa to the Gulf Coast. Sanicki always remembers that trip for a statement made by one of his sons.

"Everyone's sleeping and the sun is starting to come up...and one of my sons...he was about six or seven, he says, 'Dad, I'm glad you're not a good ball player.' I said, 'What? *Why*, whattya mean?' He said, 'This way, we get to see so much of the country.'"

Sanicki finished the 1952 season with Houston, after sending his family back to New Jersey in the middle of the season when a polio epidemic broke out, leaving Texas an unpleasant memory for all concerned. It was not a cause for celebration when he was faced with the prospect of returning there in 1953. In talking it over with his wife, Sanicki recalls her saying, "Well, if you go down there again, our marriage is gonna be...kinda risky." He thought about buying out his contract and making a deal for himself as a free agent, but that would have cost $6,500. His wife finally made the suggestion that he return to Seton Hall and earn his degree which he did, graduating later that year.

For Sanicki, leaving the game he had loved all his life was hard. "It *was* a tough adjustment, 'cause each year I would be doing the same thing, working out. I'd work out with Gene Woodling [and] Danny O'Connell at the YMCA, and then I just didn't have [that desire to play] anymore. I just didn't have any more *zing*. You can

ED SANICKI

Born July 7, 1923, Wallington, New Jersey
Ht. 5'9" Wt. 185   BR TR

MAJOR AND MINOR LEAGUE CAREER

Year	Team, League	G	AB	R	H	2B	3B	HR	RBI	BA	SA	BB	SO	SB
1946	Wilmington, Interstate	141	537	113	165	22	4	30	144	.307	.531	71	62	19
1947	Wilmington, Interstate	140	510	127	163	26	3	37	109	.320	.600	109	72	6
1948	Toronto, International	154	526	82	124	19	4	21	107	.236	.407	81	87	3
1949	Toronto, International	153	571	105	153	19	2	33	102	.268	.482	77	70	1
	PHILADELPHIA, National	7	13	4	3	0	0	3	7	.231	.923	1	4	0
1950	Toronto, International	100	303	44	64	8	0	10	42	.211	.337	57	47	6
1951	PHILADELPHIA, National	13	4	1	2	1	0	0	1	.500	.750	1	1	1
	Schenectady, Eastern	116	397	59	99	17	0	20	70	.249	.443	65	41	1
1952	Tulsa-Houston, Texas	146	463	55	110	20	2	9	48	.238	.348	78	38	1
	MAJOR LEAGUE TOTALS	20	17	5	5	1	0	3	8	.294	.882	2	5	1
	MINOR LEAGUE TOTALS	950	3307	585	878	131	15	160	622	.265	.459	538	417	37

1946—Led Interstate League Outfielders in PO (314).
1947—Led Interstate League in Total Bases (306); Led Outfielders in Fielding (.991) and PO (306).
1948—Led International League Outfielders in Assists (29) and DP (6).

Italics in boldface type indicate led league

give just so much and then…but yet I still missed it. I think another year would've been sufficient, to see what would've happened."

* * *

Forty years have passed since Ed Sanicki last laced up his spikes and he's amazed at the surge in popularity baseball has enjoyed, particularly in the last decade, as evidenced by the number of people who still remember his month of big league fame.

"I get these little letters and I show 'em to my grandchildren and I show 'em to my kids. It's quite a thrill. Some letters I got say, 'How the heck can this happen to a guy like you? How come you didn't get a shot?' Some people send pictures that I posed for way back in Toronto in '48, and they want it autographed. I just had a 74-year-old man write me a letter saying he'd seen me at a memorabilia show and was glad to have had the chance to meet me. Just little things like that. I enjoy getting those letters.

"I think about it, it's a *long* time ago. I just got a notice yesterday, my high school is having their fiftieth reunion. Class of '41. Things are *really* [going by fast]…but I feel good. I still have my sneakers and shorts and get my suntan. I read two newspapers in the morning and then I head for the swimming. I go swimming every morning at eleven except weekends. In the afternoon, the Mrs. and I, either we go to the Atlantic City casinos or we go to the race track. We're into gardening. We love it. We've got six grandchildren and all my sons and daughters are within a twelve-mile radius, so if they need a painter or a baby-sitter, why, we're right here.

"I was a high school umpire for 25 years. I had a 40-game schedule, and I just gave that up this year because the kids are on my back and saying, 'Dad, go out and do some fishing down the shore.' And I think I'm ready for it too."

Through teaching, umpiring, and dealing with children in general over the years, Sanicki has seen changes in the priority of the student-athlete.

"In my time, I think every kid's dream was to be a big league ball player. Right now, I would say it's about 50 percent in high school. There's too many activities, too many cars, too many jobs to be had, to be concentrating on practicing and playing baseball six months out of the year. But there's some good ballplayers."

Now retired after more than three decades of teaching, Sanicki has also seen changes in the attitude of the public toward the severely handicapped.

"They're accepted. Right now, they're being mainstreamed. I went to visit my co-workers last week and it's the first time we ever had [handicapped] kids at the [regular] high school, 'cause they're 17, 18 years old with the mentality of about a five- or six-year-old. They're big, they're ungainly, but they put them in high school because they're goin' according to age group. And these kids are walking down the hallway saying, 'Hi ya!' and the regular kids say, 'Hi John...Hi Jenn.' And they'd say hello to these kids. They won't turn around like in the old days and say, 'What the hell is *that* passing by?' TV exposure has helped an awful lot. The Special Olympics has helped an awful lot. They're accepted...They give the 'regular' kids an education.

"I've had big league ball players refuse to come to my class. I thought they were real good pals of mine, and they'd refuse to come in. It took me, I think, three times to get Larry Doby into one of my cerebral palsy classes. He wouldn't come the first two times. 'C'mon Larry, these kids aren't retarded, they're *normal* kids with handicaps.'

"And he came the third time and the kids *loved* him. They interviewed him. They asked him questions and he *loved* it."

While it is fair to say that Sanicki may have indeed suffered disappointment in his baseball career as well as a lack of resolution to it, it is equally fair to say that he has much justifiable pride in his achievements in the classroom. And while it is tempting to ponder the past and dwell on what might have been, it is more reasonable, and of greater importance, that we realize what might have been for a group of special education pupils in the New Jersey school system if Ed Sanicki had not been there to take over a physical education class one day many years ago.

"I fell into the field of special education and I loved it. Just talking with kids and listening...anything you've got to say, they'll just suck right in. They'll just *remember*. And I found out they're just the greatest kids in the world.

"You talk about baseball, I only had seven years of it. But working with those handicapped boys and girls, the Down's syndrome kids...*that* I've had for thirty years. That was my reward. I don't even *think* about baseball when I think of those kids."

JOE STANKA

Pitcher, 1959 Chicago White Sox

Along come a baby boy and we went on a railroad strike. I needed some money and something to do. So I remembered that $750 bonus, which would pay for the baby.

So I signed with the Dodgers, really just intendin' to play that summer, just that one year. I can't really say that I was too awful interested in baseball at that time. It was kinda somethin' to do.

—Joe Stanka

These struggling tides of life that seem
In wayward, aimless course to tend
Are eddies of the mighty stream
That rolls to its appointed end.

—William Cullen Bryant
The Crowded Street (1843)

Joe Stanka's baseball career lasted somewhat past the summer of 1950. In fact, before his "summer job" ended some *17 years* later, he had pitched for nearly a dozen teams on three continents, been a member of pennant-winning teams on both sides of the Pacific Ocean and recorded 100 victories in Japan, more than any former major league pitcher.

The Waynoka, Oklahoma, native played in three Japan Series (the Japanese equivalent to the World Series), hurling shutouts on *consecutive* days to clinch the 1964 Series for the Nankai Hawks. This performance capped a season in which he won 26 games (in a 147-game schedule) and became one of the few Americans to win a Most Valuable Player award in Japan.

Prior to his arrival in the Far East, Stanka had ricocheted around the minor leagues for ten seasons in three different organizations beginning with the Brooklyn Dodgers. They had shown interest in the big right-hander while he was at Oklahoma A&M, offering him a small bonus. Stanka had declined, opting instead for the steady pay and more certain future offered by the railroad. With a child on the way, the railroad workers went on strike and Stanka needed some way to feed his family. He decided to contact the Dodgers and take them up on their earlier offer, intending only to play until the strike was settled.

Splitting the season between Ponca City and Shawnee, class D teams located in his home state of Oklahoma, Stanka's performance seemed to make his decision of going back to the railroad an easy one. He walked a batter an inning and won only two out of 13.

The strike was eventually settled, but Stanka's mind was not. He went back to his job and quickly realized that baseball was somewhat more enjoyable than rail work. The Dodgers had seen potential in his arm and took him back, assigning him once again to Ponca City.

Stanka returned in 1951 determined to throw hard and throw strikes and let the chips fall where they may. With improved control came success; he finished the season with a record of 16-5 and a 2.53 ERA.

Drafted a year later by the Chicago Cubs, Stanka had three solid seasons in their organization, leading the Three I League in ERA for 1953 and following that year with 33 victories over the next two campaigns.

During the winter of 1955 Stanka was traded to the Sacramento

Solons of the Pacific Coast League where he spent the next four seasons. After flirting with the idea of going to Japan during the spring of 1959, Stanka was having his best year for Sacramento and decided if he didn't reach the majors in this, his tenth professional season, it would signal that he should retire from baseball.

The Chicago White Sox gave Stanka's career a reprieve that August, purchasing his contract from the Solons. After a decade in the minor leagues, playing in Oklahoma, Iowa, Colorado, and California — it seemed like the end of an odyssey. It would prove to be only the beginning.

* * *

At the time of Stanka's arrival in Chicago on September 1, the White Sox and Cleveland Indians were battling for the right to end the New York Yankees' stranglehold on the American League. New York had represented the junior circuit in the World Series nine of the past ten years and, after this one year hiatus, would participate in five *more* in a row. Over the previous decade, the Bronx Bombers had fallen short of the mark only in 1954 when, despite winning 103 games, they were bested by the Indians, managed then by current White Sox skipper Al Lopez. (In respect for Cleveland Indian fans everywhere, the events of the 1954 World Series will not be mentioned here.)

Stanka was bought by the White Sox as bullpen insurance for the stretch run and was nearly called on to enter a game on the day of his arrival. Tired from his travels, Stanka pulled his groin muscle while warming up and was thankful that the Sox pitcher got out of the inning and he wasn't brought into the game. Stanka remembers feeling extremely nervous, saying, "I thank the good Lord, He didn't let me get in that game 'cause I don't know that I could've found the mound."

The next day he *was* summoned to the mound and, despite the excitement of pitching before a crowd of over 43,000, he had no trouble finding it. He remembers feeling "no more nervous than I would've been coming in against Portland."

Stanka's first major league performance came in relief of Barry Latman during the fifth inning of the second game of a doubleheader against the Detroit Tigers. Chicago trailed 3-0 but before he knew it,

Stanka had an eight-run lead with which to work after the White Sox clubbed three Detroit Tiger pitchers for 11 runs in the bottom of the inning. Stanka even joined in the hit parade himself with a run scoring single, his only major league hit in three at bats.

"Batting .333 lifetime...you might underline that three or four times. It was a high hop and a hard run. The ball didn't even get to third base."

Stanka pitched into the eighth inning, allowing only one hit and one run over three and a third innings to earn a victory in his major league debut. Stanka's groin injury began acting up in the eighth inning, causing his pitches to sail out of the strike zone, so veteran Gerry Staley took the mound to retire the final four batters.

Three days later, Stanka entered a game in the eighth inning against the Cleveland Indians with the White Sox trailing 5-2. Cleveland shortstop Woody Held greeted the 28-year-old rookie with a 450-foot home run, but he retired the final six batters in a row and nearly picked up his second victory in as many appearances when the White Sox rallied for three runs in the bottom of the ninth, only to fall short by a score of 6-5. The newest White Sox pitcher was becoming a human rally cap.

The one run defeat didn't damage the White Sox all that much; their lead was at five and a half games over the Indians with only three weeks remaining in the season. Meanwhile, despite pitching well, Stanka's groin injury was showing no improvement. He decided to ask the White Sox trainer for advice in dealing with the injury.

"I went to the trainer and asked, 'What do I do about this groin muscle?'

"He said, 'Well, whattya *wanta* do?'

"I said, 'What *I* want to do is get over it as quick as I can so I can get back in.' I was very excited about playing and it looked like Lopez was gonna give me a good shot.

"He said, 'Well, the best thing is rest.'

"I said, 'Should *I* tell Lopez?'

"He said, 'No, I'll take care of it.'

"Well he didn't. [The trainer] told me not to even come to the park if I didn't want to. Quite a bit later I found that not only did Lopez not know about it, he called down to the bullpen for me to warm up and [the bullpen coach] says I wasn't there, that I didn't want to pitch.

"I never did get back in a game. Never did even warm up. I never even did warm up after that."

* * *

The Chicago White Sox won the 1959 American League pennant, their first in 40 years, and earned the right to face the Los Angeles Dodgers in the first World Series to be played on the West Coast.

Although he had not been called on since September 5, Stanka had no inkling of his having taken up residence in the manager's doghouse; he assumed that Al Lopez knew of his injury and was unaware of the White Sox skipper's mistaken impression that he had refused to pitch.

"When the series came around, of course I expected tickets. [He was not eligible to play in the World Series according to major league rules because of his joining the White Sox after the August 31 deadline.]

"One of the guys had asked for tickets and I said, 'I won't be using all of mine. You can have them.' I asked him later if he got 'em, he said, 'They said you didn't have any.'

"I hit the front office stairs about eight at a time and talked to [Hank] Greenberg [Chicago's general manager], and he said, 'I didn't know. But of course you can have your share of tickets.'

"I was *mad*. It had embarrassed me. I was also mad because I had taken a cut [in salary] to come to the White Sox from Sacramento, and I hadn't said anything about it when I got there because I only had a month and it didn't make much difference. I told Greenberg about that. After we got through talking, he was walking away and he turned around and said, 'You got a lotta guts asking for more money when you refused to pitch.' That's when I found out what happened.

"I said, 'I don't have any idea what you're talking about.'

"He told me then about Lopez calling and [the bullpen coach] saying I didn't want to pitch. I don't know whether he ever accepted my explanation of what happened or not...*yes* he did. I guess he said, 'We didn't know about [the difference in salary]. When we asked [Sacramento] what you were making, they told us.'

"[I told Greenberg] some of what I was getting from Sacramento was 'expenses,' which was illegal.

"Greenberg said, 'They *couldn't* tell us about it. So we didn't know about that. We figured we'd given you a little *raise*. I will make it up on the next payday.' Which, as far as I know, he did."

Despite apparently convincing Greenberg of his innocence in the great refusal to pitch incident, and being invited to throw batting practice to the White Sox hitters during the World Series, it became obvious during the winter that the trainer's miscommunication regarding Stanka's physical condition had left a lasting impression on Lopez, and it was not a favorable one.

"I went down to play winter ball in Venezuela...I was reading *The Sporting News* and I saw Lopez was saying they had traded for two or three pitchers and said, 'This will be my pitching staff next year.'

"He named eight that were definitely *in*...but with him not liking me anyway because I 'wouldn't pitch,' there was no way I was gonna be that ninth pitcher.

"I said, 'To heck with this, I'm going to the Far East.'"

* * *

While Joe Stanka was pitching batting practice during the 1959 World Series, his future teammates on the Nankai Hawks were playing against the Yomiuri Giants in the Japan Series. The ace pitcher of the Hawks, 23-year-old Tadashi Sugiura, had helped carry his team to the Pacific League pennant, compiling a record of 38-4 and a 1.40 ERA in 371 innings. As related by Yaichi Nagata and John Holway in their article for *Total Baseball*, over the final two months of the regular season Sugiura won 17 of 18 decisions while pitching almost every other day. He clinched the pennant for the Hawks in his last start of the season, down the stretch compiling an ERA of 0.10 while striking out 95 and walking only four.

With catcher Katsuya Nomura, Sugiura formed the most formidable battery in Japan. Second only to the legendary Sadaharu Oh as a home run hitter, with a career total of 657, Nomura played an incredible 27 years, catching an equally incredible 2,918 games. Tutored early in his career by Roy Campanella, Nomura was reputed to be an intelligent receiver, as well as an iron man second to none. He caught *every inning* the Hawks played one season, six times caught every game on the schedule, and retired with a career batting average 100 points higher in second games of doubleheaders than in first games. (Nomura's son Dan formerly ran the Salinas Spurs of the California League.)

The Hawks had participated in the Japan Series four times previously, and had been defeated by the Yomiuri Giants of the Central League each time. In 1959, the Giants were once again to provide the opposition, and the obstacle, between the Nankai Hawks and their first championship. It seemed that the best chance to finally topple the Giants was for the Hawks to pitch their 38-game winner as often as possible. The model for this strategy had been cast the year before when the Nishitetsu Fukoka Lions used 33-game winner Kazuhisa "Iron Man" Inao in six out of seven games in the 1958 series. With the Lions down to the Giants three games to none, Inao defeated the employees of Yomiuri four straight times, leading one of the most incredible comebacks in the history of professional sports.

Tadashi Sugiura took on the challenge and controlled the Japan Series in 1959, pitching in each of the four games, starting three, and winning all four in a span of *six days*. This would mark the only time that the Hawks got the best of the Giants; in a rivalry reminiscent of that between the New York Yankees and Brooklyn Dodgers, these two teams met in the Japan Series *nine* times through 1987, the Giants emerging victorious every time, with the exception of 1959.

Although the Hawks had finally defeated the Giants, and in fact swept them in the process, the victory was far from effortless for Sugiura. He struggled for eight innings in Game One, before winning 10-7. In Game Three of the series, a corn came off Sugiura's pitching hand, leaving the ball bloodied on each pitch, but he continued and won the game in ten innings by a score of 3-2. Despite intense pain in his hand, he once again went to the mound for Game Four after rain had afforded him an additional day of rest and proceeded to shut out the Giants on five hits to clinch the series. It was a textbook example of the "samurai spirit"; the bravado and courage that all Japanese admired and aspired to. It was a performance to rival Inao's and made Tadashi Sugiura a hero.

* * *

When spring next returned to Japan following the Hawks' victory over the Giants, there arrived a six-foot-five, 200-pound American pitcher named Joe Stanka. His first Japanese training camp proved quite a shock.

"I've read several times recently where they said, 'If the Americans would practice like *we* do, they'd become so much better.' They really wear you out. When you get to where you're in a slump because you're worn out, well what they'd say is, 'You're out of shape.' So they'd work you twice as hard to get you in shape.

"They really do put you through a horrible spring training. We were running up hills with people on our backs. I had a bad back and bad knees ever since I was a kid. I could not do some of the exercises. So I just said, 'No, I'm not gonna do it.' Not in a bad way, but just, 'I can't do it.'"

The Japanese strategy in handling a pitching staff has changed some over the past 20 years, the result of witnessing a tragic number of strong and talented arms blow out over the years. At the time Stanka played in Japan, the starting rotation was handled in a way startlingly reminiscent of American baseball late in the 19th century.

"They had what they called the 'ace' pitcher, and he was gonna start every third or fourth day. If the score was tied or they were ahead [when the ace wasn't starting], he was gonna come in [in] relief and close the game. A lot of them did a good job doing it. I don't know how."

If Stanka was shocked by the theories and training methods of the Japanese, it is fair to say that the Japanese must have been taken aback by the fiery American pitcher. He was not shy in dusting off a batter when he felt it warranted, and frequently displayed his temper on the mound. He once made headlines back in the States after shoving a rival manager, Kaoru Betto of the Kintetsu Buffaloes, who had the temerity to assert to the home plate umpire that one of Stanka's pitches had nicked one of his batters. The ensuing argument sparked a melee that lasted nearly half an hour and resulted in the dispatch of several dozen of Osaka's finest to bring a halt to the battle.

Stanka earned at least four ejections during his career in the Far East. In fact, he and ex-Baltimore Oriole Chuck Essegian staged possibly the first all-American fight in Japanese baseball history when Essegian took exception to what he viewed as Stanka's efforts to behead him.

These traits did not endear Stanka to his manager or the fans. In a system where players are expected to take off their caps and bow to the umpire and the crowd after disagreements, his outbursts and attitudes were considered rude in Japanese society. It took some time for the American to adapt to the differences in culture.

Part of the problem lay in a misunderstanding. When he first came to Japan, Stanka was under the false impression that he was to act as an unofficial coach; to teach the Hawks how to play baseball American style. What the Hawks wanted from Stanka was his pitching arm and nothing more.

"I was really kind of a hothead to tell you the truth, and I saw a lot of laziness on the field, but they really didn't know any better. You'd think, 'Well you don't have to learn to hustle,' but they did.

"They tried to make me adapt to Japanese ways, like pitching every day, et cetera, and accepting at face value anything and everything. I played for a guy by the name of [Kazuto] Tsuruoka. He was a good manager, especially by Japanese standards, and a super fine person. But he didn't understand [when] I'd raise heck and storm around. I would fuss at the umpires, always did, and that's very anti-Japanese. [Tsuruoka] didn't like that...I would cause *him* embarrassment.

"He wouldn't pitch me any more than he had to. That was one of the ways he didn't have to put up with my nonsense. That just made it worse as far as I was concerned. Then later I decided, 'Hey, just live with it. If he doesn't want you to pitch, just forget it.'"

Since 1950 there have been 12 major league teams in Japan. The teams are divided into two six-team major leagues, the Central and Pacific. Each team carries a 25-man roster, plus one 25-man farm team, which acts as a sort of "taxi squad." Each day, the 25-man roster for a particular game is determined by circling those names out of the 50 players on the two rosters. Occasionally, the roster will change between games of a doubleheader.

"After [Tsuruoka] found out I was not a relief pitcher and that I could only pitch every four or five days, he didn't even circle me [unless] I pitched. [On the other days] I was back at the hotel bar, having a few beers and watching it on TV. I had the greatest job in baseball a couple of those years. It was always that way. For two or three weeks I was the greatest guy in the world, and then there might be a month or two that I wasn't pitching.

"I don't think Tsuruoka *disliked* me. I really never did feel that. It was his way of not having to mess with me. We have a very close fondness of each other. I believe that. I know I like *him* a lot and when I was over there in '84, he definitely went out of his way to show affection for me. I don't think there was ever any *bad* relationship."

During Stanka's first year in Japan, Tadashi Sugiura continued his dominance on the mound for the Hawks, posting a 31-11 record with a 2.05 ERA. After three seasons, his record stood at 96-27. In 1,003 innings, Sugiura had struck out 868, walked only 180 and compiled an ERA of 1.81.

"Sugiura was one of the best pitchers I've ever seen. He threw submarine and could hit spots at 90 miles an hour or more. I'd say Sugi would've won his fifteen to twenty games [in the United States] every year."

By 1962, Tadashi Sugiura was no longer dominant, having suffered the same type of elbow injury that temporarily derailed the career of Tommy John. While John was able to recover, his was an experimental surgery more than a decade away and by then it would be too late for the Hawks' ace.

He suffered through back-to-back losing seasons in 1962 and 1963 before bouncing back briefly with a 20-15 record in 1964. After that, Sugiura was washed up at the age of 29. He won only 23 more games before his career permanently came to an end.

In 1964, the Hawks found a new "ace," an American named Joe Stanka.

*   *   *

Stanka had started the 1964 season pitching in the same pattern Tsuruoka had used in previous years. In mid-June, the ex-White Sox hurler had won six games, a typical figure for him at that point in the season. His innings pitched had declined each year since 1960, from a high of 240 to 187 in 1963.

Injuries forced Tsuruoka's hand; Sugiura could no longer carry the burden and when the Hawks' manager turned to Stanka, the American pitched the best baseball of his life. He won 20 games over the last two-thirds of the schedule, basically overpowering the Pacific League hitters. Stanka struck out 172 while allowing just over seven hits for every nine innings pitched. The league batted under .210 against him for the year. During the final month of 1964, he was pitching almost every other day, his final record standing at 26 victories against only seven defeats over 278 innings pitched. It was a performance the likes of which the 33-year-old pitcher never had before, and never would again. He is left with no logical explanation for his phenomenal success that year.

"I guess if I was real truthful I would've won fifteen to twenty games here. I believe that. But I also am truthful when I say I wasn't a major league pitcher. With my lack of control and lack of breaking stuff, I was not a major league pitcher. I didn't have any style more than throwing the ball ninety miles an hour or more. You get on a good hitting ballclub as I was, and you throw the ball that hard, you're gonna win some ballgames. It's really that simple.

"I think God was setting me up for something, because I lost my son in '65 [fifteen-year-old Joey, who died in an accident at home]. I 100 percent believe that God planned somehow that I should go to Japan. I don't know why. As the Bible says, 'Who knows the mind of God?' I don't.

"Too many things happened. For instance, the last part of the season I was the *only* pitcher to win a ballgame. I won the last eight ballgames that we won in about a fifteen to twenty game stretch. That's not reasonable.

"Then to pitch three shutouts in the series? All my life I could not lift my arm the day after I pitched. Talk to any manager I ever played for, they'd tell you, 'Joe is no good if you don't give him four days' rest. If he pitches in between, he is no good.' How do you [explain that within] twenty-four hours I pitch two shutouts?

"The next year, I had a pretty good year but nothing like *that*. [Tsuruoka] didn't pitch me as much, but just all in all, the split-finger wasn't there and the fastball wasn't quite as fast. It wasn't overwork from the year before, I just didn't have the stuff. God just wanted me to have a great year in '64. For whatever reason. I believe that as much as I'm sitting here. I *know* that. But I don't know *why*."

* * *

Japanese baseball has gained a reputation for playing unfairly when a foreigner is doing well, especially at the expense of a Japanese player. There have been some blatant examples of "Gaijin's Complaint"; in 1965, Stanka's teammate, Katsuya Nomura, won the Pacific League Triple Crown in part because of the absolute refusal of several teams to throw a pitch anywhere near the plate to ex-New York and San Francisco Giant infielder Daryl Spencer, who was challenging Nomura for the home run title. Spencer even came to the plate holding his bat from the wrong end and wasn't thrown a strike.

In 1971, George Altman, an ex-Chicago Cub outfielder, was in a

battle for a batting title with teammate Shinichi Eto, when he began
to notice that whenever Eto came to the plate, the opposition left the
right side of the infield wide open.

Recent American imports Leron Lee, Randy Bass, and Bob Horner have all advanced the opinion that the strike zone magically
expands when they are on a hot streak.

Of course, there are parallels to these incidents found over the
course of American major league history. Debate still surfaces occasionally, among those with nothing better to do, regarding the 1910
American League batti g race between the popular Napoleon Lajoie
and the hated Ty Cobb. With Cobb holding a slim advantage over
Lajoie going into the final day of the season, the St. Louis Browns kept
their third baseman back on the edge of the outfield grass, enabling
Lajoie to bunt for base hits at will with the hope that he could overtake
Cobb. While the Browns may be criticized for their actions, it must be
noted that Lajoie was not above picking up a bunt base hit or two...or
six.

Some 66 years later, Kansas City Royals teammates George Brett
and Hal McRae were also fighting for the American League batting
title going to the final day of the season, in a game against the
Minnesota Twins. When the game was over, Brett had won the race by
a single point and McRae, a black, made the accusation that
Minnesota's white left fielder, Steve Brye, allowed a fly ball to drop in
front of him so that McRae's white teammate would win the batting
championship. The charge was never substantiated, but it illustrates
that claims of creative sportsmanship know no color, creed, or nation-
ality.

As the 1964 season wore on and Joe Stanka's success grew, he
discovered that foreign pitchers encountered the opposite problem of
foreign hitters.

"The strike zone *shrinks* when you're a pitcher. I could never get a
called strike hardly, certainly a third [strike] is out of the question on
Oh and Nagashima and some of those guys.

"But it's the same way here. DiMaggio and Williams and those
guys had the same thing going. That was some of it...and you had
some umpires that were for a particular *team*. I think it was more
accentuated there than it is here.

"Plus the fact that no matter what they say, they're not really that
fond of *any* foreigner. It's not particularly America. I mean there're

countries they dislike a *lot* more than they dislike America. I can't say in all honesty that they're *fond* of America, but what country are *you* fond of? Canada? Do you like Canadians just because they're Canadian? Or Irish or British or Germans?

"If you really stop and think about it, what country just on the face of it, are you really fond of?

* * *

The Hawks defeated the Hanshin Tigers four games to three in the 1964 Japan Series, and Stanka was named Most Valuable Player of the series. He also captured the MVP trophy for the regular season, becoming the first non-Japanese in the history of the Pacific League to win the award, and points to this as evidence that Americans don't always receive the short end of things in Japan.

"I had a good relationship with the team, and they wanted to win so bad and I was able to help in that respect. It made me feel good. The year I won the MVP in the league, I really felt Hirose shoulda been the MVP. There's no question I shoulda been the MVP of the Japan Series...I pitched three shutouts. Shutouts in the sixth and seventh games. Wasn't even close for MVP of the series.

"But for the league that year, Hirose was great. He played every day. He hit .340, .350, stole a lot of bases, was a good outfielder...a *great* outfielder. I was surprised when they gave me MVP of the league. It should have been Hirose."

Stanka's third shutout clinched the Hawks' first Japan Series victory since the heroics of Sugiura five years before. The next season, he returned to his former role of pitching only when his manager had no alternative. With Sugiura hurting, the pitching burden was spread more evenly ("They didn't have a choice...there wasn't another Sugi"), with pitchers named Minagawa and Miura joining Stanka in leading the Hawks to the pennant in 1965, this time against the powerful Yomiuri Giants.

Led by the "O-N Cannons," Sadaharu Oh and Shigeo Nagashima, the Giants were, and are, the glamour team of Japanese baseball. They took the 1965 series in five games to begin a streak of *nine straight* Japan Series titles.

Sadaharu Oh is, of course, the most recognizable Japanese player to American baseball fans. During his career, he hit 868 home runs from his distinctive one-legged stance. He won nine MVP awards, 15 home run titles, and led the Central League in Runs Scored *and* RBIs for *13* consecutive years. He also won five batting titles and back-to-back Triple Crowns. On top of that, he was awarded nine Diamond Gloves for fielding excellence.

As impressive as Oh's accomplishments were, he was not the greatest star in the eyes of Japanese fans. That honor went to Nagashima, the Giants' third baseman. Perhaps no sports hero has ever been as idolized in any country as Shigeo Nagashima in Japan.

Compared to Ron Santo by American players who had seen both, Nagashima was a star even before turning professional, and he cemented his legend with a "Sayonara Home Run" (a game-ending round-tripper) to win the greatest game in Japanese baseball history, the first professional contest attended by the Emperor and Empress of Japan.

Nagashima led the league in home runs his first two seasons, and won five MVP awards and six batting titles during his career. Batting behind Oh in the order one year, he drew an incredible 89 intentional walks. The country ground to a halt for his wedding in 1964 and, in a manner befitting his heroic image, he hit his 444th, and final, home run in his last game.

Stanka feels that both Oh and Nagashima were great ball players and while they might not have had the same impact on the American major leagues, he does feel that they would have been stars here.

"Oh was such a home run hitter. It was amazing how a guy could stand on that one leg like he did. It was just amazing. The guy really didn't have any glaring weaknesses. He really didn't. He hit all pitches, (and) he was a great first baseman.

"Nagashima was known more to have it all. You know, the arm, the speed, and the glove, and the power. All around, Nagashima shone more. And he was Japanese and Oh was Chinese. And he was a good looking devil. So I mean, [Nagashima] had everything in the world going for him."

* * *

The death of Stanka's eldest son Joey in 1965 was a tremendous blow. He had been the little boy who came along back in 1950, inadvertently starting his father's baseball career. The fifteen-year-old had asphyxiated at home in Japan when the flame on a bathroom heater went out while he was taking a shower. After the tragedy,

Stanka's first reaction was to return home to Oklahoma and quit baseball. It just hurt too much to put on a uniform since his son had so loved the game. Later, he and his wife realized that their pain would be with them wherever they were and after talking things over, Stanka decided to accept an offer with the Taiyo Whales and play another year. It would be wonderful to say that Stanka capped off his years in Japan with his greatest performance, but the emotional burden was simply too much.

"It was a horrible year. I did have some good friends there, but I was totally out of shape mentally and physically. Going to a new team...it takes awhile for them to get to know you, especially when you can't talk to them. After that season I just knew I was not gonna get back in shape and I felt I was stealing."

Turning down an opportunity to stay on as a coach in 1967, Stanka decided instead to call it quits. The "summer job" was over.

"I'd just had enough. I'm very thankful that I could play 17 years, but I never really looked forward with fear or dread to the time I would quit. I kinda looked *forward* to quitting. I was just ready to go on to other things.

"I felt like I could come back and conquer the business world here. Boy, did I get a surprise. I had prepared for the life insurance business and really liked it. It didn't like me. I found out that I had a great deal more pride than I thought I did, and people were very friendly until they found out I was a life insurance agent, and then they'd run away fast.

"I couldn't handle that, so I bought a franchised employment agency here in Houston. That didn't go as well as I'd hoped it would, due to my lack of business expertise, so I sold that business and went into selling home study courses."

Stanka watched as two companies folded out from under him during that venture, so he joined with a son to form a duty drawback enterprise based in Houston. The function of the organization is to recover duty paid on imports by foreign countries that are used in products later exported by the United States.

"So I'm still working with the Japanese. Some of our clients are the big major league companies, such as Mitsubishi, Mitsui, C. Itoh, and some of the Japanese trading companies. We have clients that aren't Japanese, but the Japanese got us started."

Working closely with trade and the Japanese in this country,

JOE STANKA

Born July 23, 1931, Hammon, Oklahoma
Ht. 6'5" Wt. 200   BR TR

MAJOR AND MINOR LEAGUE CAREER

Year	Team, League	W-L	Pct	G	GS	CG	SHO	IP	H	R	ER	BB	SO	ERA
1950	Ponca City, K-O-M	1-3	.250	5	—	2	—	28	24	16	11	22	28	3.54
	Shawnee, Sooner State	1-8	.111	16	9	4	0	62	76	77	60	69	35	8.72
1951	Ponca City, K-O-M	16-5	.762	33	—	17	3	196	164	74	55	88	132	2.53
1952	Pueblo, Western	7-11	.389	37	—	10	1	172	180	113	91	140	102	4.76
1953	Los Angeles, Pacific Coast	0-0	—	1	0	0	0	2	1	1	1	2	1	4.50
	Des Moines, Western	1-3	.250	6	—	2	—	28.1	23	20	19	23	17	6.04
	Cedar Rapids, I.I.I.	12-8	.600	23	20	17	3	180	131	59	47	87	155	2.35
1954	Los Angeles, Pacific Coast	0-0	—	2	0	0	0	4	1	0	0	2	1	0.00
	Macon, South Atlantic	16-5	.762	26	26	15	5	192.1	192	72	64	99	135	2.99
1955	Los Angeles, Pacific Coast	0-0	—	2	1	0	0	4	8	4	4	2	2	9.00
	Des Moines, I.I.I.	17-9	.654	29	28	17	3	210	199	100	80	74	148	3.43
1956	Sacramento, Pacific Coast	5-14	.263	31	24	6	0	173.1	156	87	83	84	108	4.31
1957	Sacramento, Pacific Coast	10-14	.417	33	25	16	3	202.2	192	94	79	88	133	3.51
1958	Sacramento, Pacific Coast	10-14	.417	30	28	7	2	195	173	95	79	91	113	3.65
1959	Sacramento, Pacific Coast	12-12	.500	29	29	12	3	204	206	92	74	67	104	3.26
	CHICAGO, American	1-0	1.000	2	0	0	0	5.1	2	2	2	4	3	3.38
1960	Nankai Hawks, Japan Pacific	17-12	.586	38	—	—	4	240	186	84	66	95	174	2.48
1961	Nankai Hawks, Japan Pacific	15-11	.577	41	—	—	2	231.2	208	93	85	74	176	3.30
1962	Nankai Hawks, Japan Pacific	8-10	.444	38	—	—	0	206.2	186	98	83	72	131	3.61

1963	Nankai Hawks, Japan Pacific	14-7	.667	34	—	—	4	187	154	63	53	60	89	2.55
1964	Nankai Hawks, Japan Pacific	26-7	.788	47	—	—	6	278	221	93	74	80	172	2.40
1965	Nankai Hawks, Japan Pacific	14-12	.538	34	—	—	2	173	172	69	63	57	76	3.28
1966	Taiyo Whales, Japan Central	6-13	.316	32	—	—	0	145	153	75	67	44	69	4.16
MAJOR LEAGUE TOTALS		1-0	1.000	2	0	0	0	5.1	2	2	2	3	3	3.38
MINOR LEAGUE TOTALS		108-106	.505	303	—	125	23	1853.1	1726	904	747	938	1214	3.63
JAPAN LEAGUE TOTALS		100-72	.581	264	—	—	18	1460.1	1280	575	491	482	887	3.03

Italics in boldface type indicate led league

Stanka has noticed the coolness in America's attitude toward Japan and the controversy over foreign domination of American markets.

"I truly *love* Japan, and I truly love the Japanese. And I hate to see the controversy.

"What you get is what you read in the papers. Well who's saying it? Somebody that's got an axe to grind. We have trade barriers that our people don't know about [and] they have trade barriers their people don't know about. Sure they have some problems, but that's the way they run their country.

"But you can trust them. I wouldn't be scared to deal with [the Japanese] on an unsigned agreement if I was introduced properly."

In 1984, Joe Stanka returned to Japan for the first time in 18 years. The occasion was a celebration marking the 20th anniversary of the Nankai Hawks' championship.

"It was just fantastic. Indescribable. We were treated *so* well, I mean it was almost to the point of being too much. But it was great seeing all the old guys. There's something about a championship team. I was lucky enough to play on several...and there's a closeness that develops that's really *lasting* on a team like that.

"Just having played ball, professional baseball, there's a closeness that develops. I still have a real real close friend, Roger Osenbaugh, that was my roommate for four years there in Sacramento. We talk a couple times a week and we'd do anything in the world for each other. It's just a bond there.

"The competition...it's something you'd have to experience to really fully understand, but professional sports will build a friendship more than if you were in a company...or an accounting firm."

Or working on a railroad.

BILL ROHR

Pitcher, 1967 Boston Red Sox; 1968 Cleveland Indians

I had no idea at the time that nobody'd ever done that before. I really didn't have any idea that it was that big a deal. It took me awhile to come to the realization that this was as big a deal as it was. I think, for one reason, growing up on the West Coast, a sporting event wasn't that big a deal. Back in New York and New England, it's a different story. I mean, the Red Sox and the Celtics and the Yankees and the Jets...those things are institutions. Those things are ways of life. I'm not sure that's anything that I had ever realized had existed.

I got back to the hotel Saturday after the game, and there was a note there from some guy. It said he was an agent and that he wanted me to be on "The Ed Sullivan Show."

And I said, "Yeah, right." It's my teammates jerking my chain, right? I get back in the room and the little light's blinking that says you got a message and sure enough, it's this guy that wants me to go on "The Ed Sullivan Show" Sunday night.

The next day, I rode out to the ballpark in a cab with Russ Gibson and, I think, Mike Andrews and maybe Jim Lonborg ...and the cab driver picked us up and he did not know who we were. And this cab driver couldn't stop talking about that kid from Boston. I'm sitting in the back seat and Russ Gibson says, "Cabbie, do you know who this kid is?" I could see this cab driver and see his eyes looking in the rearview mirror. And he turns around, and I mean this guy didn't slow down one mile an hour. He just turned around and stared and kept going down the street. He says, "Holy shit, it's Billy Rohr!"

—Bill Rohr

Fame is a bee.
It has a song —
It has a sting —
Ah, too, it has a wing.
                    — Emily Dickinson

On October 15, 1892, Charles "Bumpus" Jones tossed a no-hitter in his major league debut for Cincinnati of the National League, beating Pittsburgh by a score of 7-1. The next year, the pitcher's rubber was moved back ten and a half feet to its present location and whether or not by coincidence, the career of "Bumpus" Jones was shortened as the distance to the batter was lengthened — his major league days ending during the 1893 season after seven appearances and an ERA of 10.19.

Later, Leon "Red" Ames tossed a five-inning no-hitter in his first game for the New York Giants in 1905, and in 1953, Alva "Bobo" Holloman of the St. Louis Browns threw nothing but blanks in his first start, although it was not his first appearance. As of April 1967, no one in baseball's modern era had ever made his bow in the big leagues with a nine-inning no-hit, no-run game.

As Bill Rohr stood on the mound at Yankee Stadium on a Friday afternoon in mid-April, staring in at Red Sox catcher Russ Gibson to receive the sign for a 3-2 pitch to Elston Howard with two out in the bottom of the ninth, this 21-year-old left-hander was one pitch away from doing just that. If he got this one pitch past the Yankee veteran, his name would go into the record books. Rohr was one pitch away from immortality, and one pitch away from foreshadowing "The Impossible Dream" season of the 1967 Boston Red Sox.

*   *   *

Now more than two decades removed from his moment in the spotlight, Bill Rohr is an attorney practicing personal injury and product liability law as a partner in an Orange County, California, firm, working the defense side "90 percent of the time." Rohr's original intention when entering law school, however, was to pursue a career in law enforcement, preferably with the FBI. He now laughingly insists that he went to law school with every intention of never practicing law, but rather "chasing bad guys." Instead, he says, "I am one."

While quite satisfied with his current career, Rohr's goal as a youngster growing up in Southern California during the 1950s had always been to play baseball; among his early heroes were slugger Steve Bilko and other stars of the Pacific Coast League, and later, after the major leagues moved West, a stylish fellow southpaw by the name of Sandy Koufax.

Like most boys, he played hours upon hours of catch with his father in the backyard, but that ended around the time Rohr was in the eighth grade. It seemed his fastball began developing some movement and a couple of tosses shot past his father's mitt and into his ribs, causing a couple of fractures.

Limiting himself to throwing the ball to those better protected, Rohr continued playing, starring at Bellflower High School and eventually signing a contract with the Pittsburgh Pirates in 1963. The 18-year-old then fell victim to a change in rules, and a resulting manipulation by the Pirates to get around those rules, that kept him on the bench during his entire first season.

The draft rules had been changed in the early 1960s as part of an effort to discourage the six-figure signing bonuses that were becoming far too common in the eyes of some major league executives. The idea was to expose these players to the draft, forcing teams to protect the "bonus babies" at the risk of losing players who were more established. The Pirates' plan to combat this obstacle was to "hide" Rohr and three other pitchers from the winter draft by signing them to bonuses and then placing them on the disabled list, claiming they had sore arms. This would make them less desirable to other teams at the winter draft.

The Pirates made one major miscalculation, however. The team assigned the four pitchers to their rookie team in Kingsport, Tennessee, where they worked out before the games in uniform and then sat in the stands in their street clothes to watch the game.

"So guess who we sat next to all summer?" says Rohr. "Every scout from every organization in baseball. We would sit next to them, and they found out who we were fairly soon, and they would say things like, 'What's the matter with your arm?' And I would say, 'There's nothing the matter with my arm.' And we'd talk to them very freely 'cause I didn't have anything to hide and I didn't realize at the time that the Pirates did either, frankly."

As one might surmise, the other scouts got the idea something was amiss and as a result Rohr was drafted the following winter by the Boston Red Sox and was elated by his change in fortune. Far from being forgotten, he saw a situation where everyone was treated fairly and valued by the organization. The coaching at the minor league level, including Bots Nekola, Mace Brown, and "Broadway" Charlie Wagner was first-rate. In short, the Red Sox reflected the image of their owner Tom Yawkey who prided himself on being a "player's owner," often working out with the team in full uniform at Fenway Park.

Of course, another reason for the young left-hander's enthusiasm was the realization that he would now get to wear a uniform *during* games, instead of playing games in the stands.

Rohr's life with the Red Sox got off to an interesting start with an invitation to the big league training camp. At six-foot-three and all of 150 pounds, the stringbean teenager found his locker strategically placed between the two largest players on the team, Dick "The Monster" Radatz and Earl Wilson. Six-foot-six, 230 pounds and six-three, 220 pounds, respectively, the two Boston pitchers spent spring training asking who this was between their lockers and why didn't someone get him something to eat?

It was during this training camp that Rohr accidentally nailed slugger Dick Stuart with a pitch during batting practice. "Dr. Strangeglove" as he was known, enjoyed hitting the long ball more than anything or anybody. He had hit 42 home runs the season before, reputedly refusing to go to first base once when hit by a pitch because it would deprive him of the chance to smack one out of the park. He then proceeded to strike out. Stuart was not one who had the reputation of being a team player, and did not take kindly to this green kid plunking him instead of tossing up a lollipop for him to crush.

"I didn't realize it was some kind of a carnal sin. I hit him in the butt or something which, as I recall, comprised a good percentage of Dick's anatomy. But I was trying to throw batting practice and Bob Turley was the pitching coach, and that son of a bitch decided it'd be a good idea to give me a chew of tobacco.

"This chewing tobacco starts running down the back of my throat and I start getting goofy. I mean, I don't know whether I'm sick or drunk. I can't figure out what's going on, but I don't feel good at all. And now, Dick Stuart's in there yelling at me to, 'Get that shit over the plate.' So I accidentally, but prophetically enough, hit him right in the ass.

"Now Turley can't stop laughing because I'm sick. Stuart's throwing shit at me. He's storming out of the batting cage, yelling and screaming at [Johnny] Pesky to, 'Get this goddam kid off the mound, and get him out of the organization!' Everybody else thinks it's funny. I just wanted to die. I just wanted to go home and go to junior college and have these people leave me alone."

Rohr was sent to Wellsville, New York, in the Class A New York-Pennsylvania League, an assignment unrelated to the Stuart incident. It was a great place for a teenager beginning his adventure in the "glamorous" world of professional sports. He loved the town, the fans, and the small ballpark with its outfield fences so cozily placed "that you could spit over the fence." There were only two showers in the locker room, one of which consisted of a pipe coming out of the wall with no shower head. The limited availability of hot water meant that if a pitcher was knocked out of the box early, the rest of the team faced the very real possibility of receiving a brisk surprise when the water worked its way out of the plumbing.

Rohr struck out 185 batters in 168 innings at Wellsville while winning 11 of 20 decisions. Despite some control problems, he completed eight games and showed great poise for a 19-year-old.

As he looks back on that season today, Rohr considers it one of his most cherished memories. Even the road trips, where the manager/bus driver would have to floor the old rickety bus on a downhill run in order to get it up the other side. Life really got exciting when late at night the ground fog would develop and two dozen young men would go careening into the darkness without being able to see where they were going.

Says Rohr today of that year, "I wouldn't trade that [experience] in for anything. That was as much fun as a bunch of kids can ever have."

* * *

Promoted to Winston-Salem of the Carolina League, which was a Class A League for more experienced players, Rohr dropped his first three decisions before reeling off seven straight victories. Without notice, he received a phone call telling him to report to Toronto right away. He was to pitch for Boston's Triple A affiliate that Saturday night. All of a sudden Bill Rohr, not yet 20 years old, was at the threshold of the major leagues.

Nervous and worried that he didn't know what he was doing out there on the mound, he pitched very well under the circumstances, compiling a 2.73 ERA and allowing only 89 hits in 122 innings to offset his hard-luck 6-10 record.

That first season in Toronto also served as Rohr's introduction to the management stylings of Dick Williams, then a rookie manager who had just finished his playing career the year before as a utility player for the Red Sox. Rohr found that Williams' approach to managing was always the same.

"That's the one thing you can say about Dick, he was consistent. He expected you to just win. If you got beat 1-0, it was not altogether different than getting beat 20-0. You either won or you didn't. And if you didn't, you were in Dick's doghouse. It was the easiest doghouse to get into that I've ever seen. Ever. And not the easiest to get out of.

"I think Dick Williams is one of the best managers I've ever known or heard of. I enjoyed playing for him 'cause I enjoyed playing the game and he was my manager. I didn't particularly *like* Dick. I could've probably liked playing for Saddam Hussein, just because of where I was and what was going on."

Toronto finished third during the regular season and then won the 1965 International League play-offs, losing just one game in two best-of-seven series. Rohr returned to Toronto in 1966, along with his manager, and the team won the International League play-offs once again, as a group of young players began to emerge who would help lead the Red Sox out of two decades of futility. Among the players on the Toronto roster were future Boston starters Joe Foy, Mike Andrews, and Reggie Smith.

Of this group, Smith was the most talented. Originally signed by the Minnesota Twins, Smith had played for Wytheville in the Appalachian League the year that Rohr was in the same league sitting in the stands with the scouts. He had gone from being a shortstop who, according to Rohr, "could throw a ball into the second deck with the best of them" (he made 41 errors in 66 games his first season), to International League batting champion in 1966.

A teammate of Rohr's that season, Smith was also passionate about his beliefs and was especially affected by the Watts riots. At one point the young infielder was planning to jump the club and go to Los Angeles to fight what he considered to be *his* war. Unable to deter him, the Red Sox activated team scout Billy Harrell whose job was to room with Smith and keep him from going AWOL. Harrell was successful and Smith starred, hitting .320 with 18 home runs and 80 RBIs. He was called up to Boston at the end of the year.

Meanwhile, Rohr fashioned another strong season in Toronto, winning 14 games, completing ten and striking out 161. His best outing came against Toledo, the Yankees' farm team, when he gave up his only base hit of the game with two out in the ninth, falling short when Mike Ferraro singled on a 2-2 pitch.

As the season came to an end, Billy Herman was fired as manager of the Boston Red Sox and through the grapevine filtered word that interim manager Pete Runnels was not to be the permanent successor. The new manager of the Boston Red Sox was to be Dick Williams. He was being brought in to shake things up. With his attitude would come a number of young, hungry ball players who had a taste of winning. What a wild ride it would be.

* * *

Going into the 1967 season, the Boston Red Sox had not enjoyed a winning record since Ted Williams' last batting title nine years before. Worse, the perception was that the players didn't care. Tom Yawkey treated his charges well and most of the players felt they could flaunt the rules and do as they wished regardless of the endless entreaties made by Pinky Higgins, Johnny Pesky, Billy Herman, or anyone else for that matter. So, the team floundered for a decade despite a cadre of talented players including Carl Yastrzemski, Tony Conigliaro, Dick Stuart, Dick Radatz, Earl Wilson, Frank Malzone, and Bill Monbouquette. True, the Red Sox had finally finished ahead of their hated rivals from New York in 1966 (for the first time since 1948), but so had everybody else in the American League. After finishing next to last, the Sox were more than two decades removed from their last World Series appearance and entered the season as 100-1 longshots to capture the flag. These developments had spurred the thorough housecleaning during the off-season as the organization injected younger players into the lineup and a new manager who was bringing with him a different attitude to the clubhouse.

Dick Williams had played with many of the Red Sox in 1963 and

1964 and had witnessed the attitude of the athletes first-hand. He was having none of this "country club" atmosphere the team was famous for. He knew what was happening and worked quickly to send a message: Dick Williams was the boss and his word was final.

Bill Rohr was attending his fourth big league training camp that spring and immediately noticed the change.

"The biggest difference was when Dick told some player to do something, he did it. Pinky [Higgins] would tell Dick Stuart to do something, or Pinky would tell Bill Monbouquette to do something, and they would say, 'I'll do it if I feel like it.' Nobody *ever* said that to Dick."

True to his word, Williams brought several players with him from Triple A to the major leagues, including a skinny left-handed pitcher from Southern California who earned the third spot in the starting rotation.

"It was absolutely mind-boggling. I mean, when we finally had opening day...and Lonborg was gonna pitch against the White Sox...and somebody throws out the first ball and somebody plays the national anthem and there *you* are. Anybody that tells you that doesn't make the hair stand on the back of their neck either is lying to you, or they didn't have any business being there in the first place."

The Red Sox opener had been pushed back a day due to cold weather, so Rohr, who was to have pitched the final game of the series at Fenway against Chicago, was instead to face the Yankees in their home opener on Friday.

The night before his first major league start, Rohr was more than a little nervous about his impending debut and switched roommates in order to spend time with staff ace Jim Lonborg.

Just three days shy of his 25th birthday, Lonborg was already the recognized ace of the staff. Like Rohr a native Southern Californian, Lonborg had the natural ability, movie-star good looks, and approachable personality perfectly suited to achieving stardom in a rabid baseball city like Boston. In only his third major league season, the Red Sox would ride Lonborg's strong right arm and Yastrzemski's superhuman performance to the seventh game of the 1967 World Series.

The rookie southpaw picked Lonborg's brain for the better part of four hours over dinner that night, going over each hitter in the Yankee lineup. Looking back, Rohr remembers, "That's a lot of time per hitter when you've only got two pitches."

Yankee Stadium had been refurbished over the winter, and although the crowd the next day was small, it was chock full of luminaries. Among the 14,000 in attendance were Mayor John Lindsay (who threw out the first ball), current and former Commissioners of Baseball William Eckert and Ford Frick, U.S. Senator Jacob Javitz, American League President Joe Cronin, and CBS Chairman William Paley. Also attending the game were Jacqueline Kennedy and her young son, John-John, who clutched a Red Sox pennant throughout the contest.

While Mickey Mantle was not in the starting lineup this day, Rohr's opponent on the mound was the legendary Whitey Ford. The 38-year-old pitcher was attempting a comeback after two shoulder operations and was appearing in what would be his last Yankee home opener. In fact, he would make only six more starts, including a shutout, before retiring.

Things started shakily for the veteran as Reggie Smith touched him for a lead-off home run. Ford then settled down and allowed only two more hits, one a bunt single, through seven innings. Normally, the Yankee star's performance would have been the story of the game, but Boston's rookie pitcher was stealing his thunder by flirting with the unthinkable. He retired the first ten batters of the game before Bill Robinson drew a walk. One out later, Joe Pepitone also walked but Rohr escaped further trouble when Elston Howard lined out to George Thomas in center.

In the sixth, Rohr retired Horace Clarke on a sinking liner to left that Yastrzemski sprinted in and caught at his knee. Once again, up to the plate stepped Robinson. The Yankee rookie promptly lined one off Rohr's leg, the ball rocketing to Joe Foy at third base, who threw out Robinson.

Rohr was convinced that Robinson's line shot had broken his leg. He limped around the mound feeling as if a bowling ball had ricocheted off his shin. Dick Williams and Red Sox trainer Buddy LeRoux rushed to the mound to offer aid and after a few heart-stopping moments, it was determined that the pitcher was all right and could continue.

After walking the next batter, the rookie shook off the effects of Robinson's "routine" 1-5-3 ground out and retired five more batters in a row. At the end of seven innings, Boston led 1-0 and the Yankees were still without a hit.

In the Boston half of the eighth, Russ Gibson singled off Ford to start the inning and two outs later Foy smacked a slider over the fence to provide Boston a three-run cushion and their rookie pitcher some breathing room. Rohr was now only six outs away from history.

In New York's half of the eighth, Rohr had turned his back to home plate to watch a pop-up hit toward center field and following the catch heard an ovation slowly build from the Yankee Stadium faithful until the small crowd sounded like a packed house. Puzzled, he turned back to the plate, walked to the top of the mound and stared in at Gibson for the sign. Standing in the right side of the batter's box was New York's next hitter. It was Number Seven.

"Now that'll make the hair stand up. I will never forget just looking down there at Gibby and seeing [Mickey] Mantle stand there...he had arms that looked like telephone poles. I got him out, he hit the first pitch. He hit it 400 feet, but it was 200 feet straight up and 200 feet straight down."

Rohr needed only three more outs.

In the bottom of the ninth, the Yankees' Tom Tresh led off the inning with a screamer over the head of Yastrzemski in left field that seemed destined for extra bases. Somehow, Yaz caught up with the ball and made a spectacular, leaping, somersaulting catch for the first out. Many called it one of the finest catches they had ever seen. After that effort, Rohr knew he *had* to pitch a no-hitter. He now owed it to the Red Sox left fielder.

The next batter, Joe Pepitone, hit a lazy fly ball caught by right fielder Tony Conigliaro for the second out, and Elston Howard then stepped to the plate representing the Yankees' last hope. Suddenly, time was called and Williams went to the mound to talk to his young pitcher. It was a move the rookie couldn't understand.

"He didn't tell me anything about how to pitch to Elston. He came out and said, 'Take it easy, it's still a three-run game. You've got to get these people out and just relax.'

"The one thing I can remember thinking is, 'Why the hell is he out here? I may have needed him before...I don't need him now. Leave me alone and let's get this thing over with.'"

Williams' recollections of the conversation differ. In his autobiography, *No More Mr. Nice Guy*, Williams claims that he tried to tell the rookie how to pitch to Howard but that he was "too excited to listen."

Williams does agree that he shouldn't have gone to the mound. In his book, he recounts an incident he had witnessed some years before when in the same situation, Bobby Bragan had gone out for a conference with his hurler. The pitcher, his concentration broken, gave up a base hit to the next batter and lost his no-hitter. Williams vowed he would never duplicate what Bragan had done that day, yet there he was. As the Red Sox manager said later, "What do they say about those who ignore history? That they're doomed to repeat it?"

After Williams returned to the dugout, Rohr's first pitch was a curveball in the dirt. Howard swung and missed. Then came a ball and a called strike. With the count one and two, Rohr fired a fastball headed for the outside corner. For an instant he thought he had done it. It looked like strike three. He saw Gibson start to rise out of his crouch. Howard took a half-step as if to cross the plate and head to the dugout. Home plate umpire Cal Drummond's arm seemed to come about half-way up, but then he stopped and said, "Ball two."

Rohr's next pitch missed the mark leaving the count full. With the crowd standing and cheering wildly, he delivered a curve that didn't, and Howard hit a line drive over second baseman Reggie Smith's head for a clean single amid a chorus of boos. Charlie Smith then flied out to right and the game was over, a 3-0 one-hit shutout for a rookie playing in his first major league game.

"The three-two pitch was just a badly thrown curveball and it hung. Just flat as a pancake and he reached out and smacked it. If he'd have taken it, it woulda been ball four. It wasn't a strike."

After the game, Howard was quoted as saying, "It was the only time I ever got a base hit and was booed in New York."

When told after the game of Howard's reaction to the crowd's disappointment, Rohr jokingly said, "I'm not one of his fans either."

* * *

As Rohr headed into the tunnel that led to the visitors' clubhouse, he felt an arm on his and turned to see a man in a dark suit urging him to stop for a moment. Slowly, he came to realize that he was a Secret Service agent and had been sent by Jacqueline Kennedy to get an autographed baseball for her son. Today he wishes he had thought to give a baseball to John-John and asked *him* to sign it.

Rohr squinted into the glare of the cameras and banks of microphones, answering all the requisite questions, and a three-

picture sequence of his delivering of the fateful pitch to Elston
Howard, his cap falling off on his follow-through, was spread across
the sports pages of the *New York Times*. Leonard Koppett, covering
the game for the *Times* predicted a long and successful career for the
young pitcher who had been known previously only for his being part
Cherokee Indian. His performance brought to Koppett's mind the
feat of "Bobo" Holloman some 14 years before, and he recalled that
Holloman had ended that season in the minor leagues, never to
return. Koppett was not ready, however, to relegate Rohr to the
dustbin of history as he wrote, "No one who watched Rohr yesterday...expects glory to be so brief for him. He displayed a good fastball
(called "sneaky" by the Yankees), a good curve, a good change of pace
and plenty of poise and courage."

The furor was far more than the 21-year-old could have imagined. "The Ed Sullivan Show" booked him for an appearance. Yet,
it still hadn't sunk in that he had become an instant celebrity.

He suddenly remembered giving Rico Petrocelli a roll of film
prior to the game. Rico was to give it to his brother, a New York
policeman on duty at the stadium, so that Rohr would have some
photographs from his major league debut. When he finally tracked
down Rico's brother, Rohr discovered that there were no pictures of
him anywhere on the roll. It seemed that Rico had neglected to tell his
brother whom the film was for, so he had taken pictures of the
ballpark and Rico's friends, ignoring Rohr entirely. It wasn't until
about the sixth inning that anyone realized the importance of the
occasion and by then the entire roll of film had been used.

While he had no snapshots of his feat, Rohr did get to appear on
"The Ed Sullivan Show," although he was afraid for a time he might
miss the opportunity. Scheduled for two days after his one-hitter, he
had to receive special permission to stay over in New York Sunday
night while the team flew on to Chicago, an arrangement only
reluctantly agreed to by Dick Williams.

Boston's newest celebrity spent the day relaxing on the bench,
knowing he wouldn't be playing but grew anxious as the game went
into extra innings. The tenth inning went by, and the 11th, and the
12th. It was getting later and later but Rohr couldn't leave the bench
without permission. And he wasn't about to go up to Williams in the
middle of a tight ballgame and ask if he could leave. Finally, Williams
walked over to him and said, "If you're gonna go on that goddamned

television show, you better get dressed." The game eventually went 18 innings.

While his teammates played on, Rohr arrived at the studio, met Ed Sullivan and called his parents from the dressing room (they were not aware he was to appear on the program). Sullivan showed the audience highlights of the rookie's performance and then introduced him. It was a nice day, topped off by his meeting Tony Bennett and Count Basie, who were guest stars on the program that evening.

As Rohr rejoined his teammates on the road trip, he was the pre-game guest on all the home team radio and television broadcasts, which in addition to the notoriety helped greatly expand his wardrobe and watch collection. In fact he received so many different gift certificates, he was never able to cash in all of them.

When the Red Sox returned to Boston, a large crowd was there to greet the team. To Rohr's surprise, the majority were there to greet *him*.

"It was *nuts*. There must've been 5,000 people at the airport and I, for the life of me, I couldn't figure out why. I had no idea they were there to see *me*. And they were."

A week after his debut, Rohr was to pitch against the Yankees again, this time in a rematch at Fenway Park. Despite a severe cold snap, more than 25,000 attended the night game and through seven innings Rohr enjoyed a 6-0 lead and was attempting once again to make baseball history. He was four outs away from becoming only the fourth man to begin his American League career with back-to-back shutouts. Then, Elston Howard struck again, lining a hit off the "Green Monster" that drove in a run.

"I thought the crowd was gonna come out and string him up. They started throwing those cushions that you rent when you go to a ballgame."

He settled for a 6-1 victory, and another near-miss at making history. But the disappointment was slight indeed when he looked at the end results of his two starts in the big leagues. He had bested a legend, Whitey Ford, and the Yankees' best pitcher, Mel Stottlemyre, in two pitcher's duels. Over his first 18 major league innings, Rohr had been touched for only one run and nine hits and was 2-0 with a 0.50 ERA. What no one could foresee is that with that second triumph, Rohr had also picked up the next to last victory of his big league career, and his last for the Red Sox.

* * *

Rohr's third major league start didn't go quite a smoothly as his first two. After holding the Kansas City Athletics scoreless for two innings, he took a 2-0 lead into the third when everything unraveled. It began when the Red Sox southpaw hit the A's speedy shortstop Bert Campaneris in the foot.

"I didn't hit him very hard. He went down like he'd been shot. Jesus Christ, he's rolling on the ground and I thought they were gonna have to put the little bastard to sleep.

"Gibby comes out and he says, '*Bullshit*, Bill. I'll guarantee you he's gonna steal on the first pitch. Pick his ass off.'

"I didn't have a very good move, but I picked him off from here to the Charles River. Tony Horton was our first baseman...your basic slow white kid...sort of a young man's Dick Stuart as it were. Tony decided it would be a good idea, for reasons I will never understand, to *chase* Campaneris. Now, Tony Horton chasing Bert Campaneris is not a good idea.

"Rico [Petrocelli] was standing on the bag *begging* Tony to throw him the ball. Campaneris runs into second base standing up. Horton dives after him, falls down, drops the ball. By the time Campaneris got to second base, I think he was starting to laugh. He's being chased by this...this rhinoceros, who couldn't have caught him in a Corvette. But there he was.

"[Soon, I have] the bases loaded and two out, Campaneris would have been the third out, and who hits one in the cheap seats but Dick Green. Puts one up in the net."

Rohr soon exited that game, and two more in succession, enduring a ghastly streak where he allowed 12 runs in seven and two-thirds innings over three starts. He was rapidly heading for Dick Williams' doghouse, and his manager's only advice was for him to get his act together or he'd be back in the minors. He found even less help from Boston pitching coach Sal Maglie.

"I have never understood how Dick ended up with Sal. I don't think Dick had a whole lot of use for Sal. Sal was of very little use, quite frankly. And I don't mean that to be mean or derogatory at all about Sal, he's a nice enough fellow. But he was not a pitching coach. He had no idea how to coach anybody at anything. If you were a good pitcher, then Sal would be your pitching coach and get his picture taken with you while he told you how he used to pitch to Willie Mays. And that was the extent of his ability to coach.

"One of my dearest recollections about the near no-hitter was actually something I read in the paper the next day. There was a quote from Sal and the quote was something like, 'Gee, I told that kid not to throw Howard any curveballs.' And I asked Sal if he said that and he says, 'Oh…well sure.' And I said, 'You know Sal, I really am sorry I gave up a hit. I'll see if I can do better next time.' Can you believe that?"

At the beginning of June, while still in his slump, Rohr reported for a two-week stint in the Army Reserve and during his absence, the Red Sox traded Tony Horton and Don Demeter to Cleveland for starting pitcher Gary Bell. It was a deal that contributed greatly to the Sox winning the pennant and essentially ended Rohr's participation in the starting rotation. Not wanting to use him out of the bullpen, the Sox assigned him to Toronto, later bringing him back for the September stretch run. He pitched only once after his return, allowing four runs in one inning against Baltimore in an 11-0 loss. His final record for Boston stood at 2-3 with a 5.10 ERA.

Offered a chance to be on Boston's World Series roster, he declined preferring instead to try and iron out his problems in winter ball. Although he never said anything, Rohr felt his decision probably angered Dick Williams — in part because Williams never said anything to him. Ever again.

Meanwhile, the Red Sox came within one game of the World Championship, losing to Bob Gibson (who tossed a three-hitter and socked a home run to boot) in Game Seven. They had, like Rohr, almost pulled off a miracle, and also, like their rookie pitcher, had fallen just short.

The next spring Rohr was optioned to Louisville and after one start, and one year and 12 days after his celebrated debut, he was sold to the Cleveland Indians.

* * *

Cleveland's Municipal Stadium was definitely light years away from the ambience and magic of Fenway Park. It was foggy, windy, cold, and often empty — so empty that on many occasions, Rohr could distinctly hear the announcer's play-by-play description echoing through the cavernous stadium while he was on the mound.

The Cleveland Indians had not won a pennant since 1954, but the franchise was far from bereft of talent. They featured arguably the deepest starting rotation in the American League with Sam McDowell, Luis Tiant, Sonny Siebert, Steve Hargan, and Stan Williams heading up a staff that led the junior circuit in strikeouts, shutouts, and ERA (2.66). McDowell struck out 40 over three consecutive games and Tiant amassed a string of 41 consecutive scoreless innings. Both averaged more than a strikeout per inning and they finished one-two in earned run average, McDowell at 1.81 and Tiant recording a 1.60 ERA — the lowest in the American League since 1919.

It was a colorful team, loaded with personalities guaranteed to provide Manager Alvin Dark with ulcers the size of the Great Lakes. Dark, a mild-mannered, decent man known for having a lineup card in one pocket and a New Testament in the other, was no match for this group. McDowell, who now serves as a lecturer and counselor to other athletes facing the problem of substance abuse was at that time the last person you'd ever think would counsel anyone. In the grips of his battle with the bottle, McDowell, as Rohr recalls, was in constant trouble.

"Sam had too much talent. He had more talent than any one person ought to, and bless his heart, he had problems to go with it. He was an adventure. It got to the point a few times where certain municipal officials would call Alvin in the middle of the night. Alvin wouldn't even respond. He'd just call Jack Sanford [Cleveland's pitching coach], and he'd say, 'Jack, they got Sam again, go get him. I ain't going. I don't care if he stays there forever.'

"Jack'd go get him. Sam'd be at the park the next day like nothing ever happened."

Other players stumbled into mischief, somewhat more innocently but just as likely to make Dark cringe. Jose Cardenal was always "armed and dangerous." Luis Tiant always tended to do things that made Stan Williams angry, which was not a wise practice.

"They used to have some of the all-time great poker games with Luis Tiant. Luis Tiant didn't know a poker game from a ham sandwich. And he'd get in there and some of the guys would just fleece him. He'd let them get away with it, or they were getting away with it, and Stan Williams would get angry and when Stan got angry, everybody paid attention. It got interesting, especially on those little-bitty airplanes where there's no place to hide.

"My whole career would have been much poorer had I not been able to play a round of golf with Luis Tiant and Stan Williams. There was one course over in Arizona...with a lot of big, high shrubs. I mean, fifteen, twenty feet high and just as thick as they were high. If a ball went in them, forget it. Don't even bother going in there.

"Tiant would hit a ball in there and he'd take a club and he'd go in there after it. Now you know damn good and well he was never gonna find the ball, but he'd be in there for awhile. Pretty soon, you'd hear him in that little squeaky voice say that he'd found it, and the next thing you know, you'd hear him taking that golf club, whack it against the bush and he'd throw the ball out. And just get madder than hell if anybody accused him of cheating. It was pretty funny stuff and I enjoyed it."

With Rohr's acquisition, Dark envisioned him coming out of the bullpen rather than starting, and sent him to work with Jack Sanford.

Sanford helped smooth out Rohr's delivery, which was somewhat "herky-jerky" as he describes it, and worked to slow him down and refine his mechanics. Initially the efforts met with a great deal of success.

In Rohr's first eight appearances he was scored on on only one occasion, when Hal Kurtz gave up a Curt Motton home run that scored two runners he had inherited from Rohr. From that point, things didn't go quite as well, a pattern similar to his experience the year before in Boston. The Indians finished third in 1968, exactly one-half game ahead of the Boston Red Sox, but Rohr wasn't around for the end of the season. After the great start, he allowed 12 runs in his last nine times to the mound and in July he was sent to the minor leagues, never to return.

After spending the remainder of 1968 and all of 1969 with the Portland Beavers, Rohr began the 1970 season with Wichita, Cleveland's new Triple A affiliate, until he was traded in mid-season to the Detroit Tigers, who in turn assigned him to their Triple A team in Toledo.

"That's really when it all ended. That's when I should've just come home, but I didn't. That Detroit outfit was a mistake from the get-go. I shouldn't have gone and I shouldn't have stayed once I got there. I don't know why they bothered to trade for me; the manager didn't know I was coming when I got there. Didn't have a clue. And he didn't give a damn, which was all well and good, but what was I doing in Toledo? That Detroit organization I have no use for.

"I actually came back in '71 for reasons I…I just don't know why I did. I guess I was twenty-five years old and I was afraid to get on with my life. And lo and behold, I made the All-Star team and was the winning pitcher in the All-Star game and guess who we beat? The New York Yankees. Can you believe that? The game was in Rochester, New York, and the score was like 16-16 or something, but I pitched one inning and the International League All-Stars happened to score a bunch of runs after that inning. I didn't know till I looked at the boxscore the next day that I was the winning pitcher.

"In '72, I wound up with Montreal's Triple A outfit in Peninsula, down around Tidewater [Virginia]. I think they won me in a raffle. I was twenty-six, and July the fifteenth, I went home. That was the end of it.

"I drove from Virginia to California, hoping I'd never get to California 'cause I didn't know what I was gonna do when I got there. I mean, I was twenty-six and pretty much felt like my life was over. I couldn't imagine anything I could possibly go do that would be as meaningful as what I had just done which, in retrospect, wasn't much. But it was all I had, so it was all I had to relate to. Now, where do the hell do you go for your next standing ovation? Most folks out here don't give them.

"I just feel extremely fortunate and blessed that I had some people that were encouraging me and that, for reasons that I'll never quite understand, I found my way to law school and I've been given an opportunity for another career. So far, it's okay, 'cause I know a whole lot of fellows didn't end up with a second chance."

* * *

The year 1967 was definitely a highlight for both the players and the fans of the Boston Red Sox, and that team holds a special place in the memory of all who experienced the magic of that summer, including Bill Rohr.

"It was the most incredible thing I've ever seen in my life. We'd go into a game and if we were down less than four runs going into the seventh, we figured we had them right where we wanted them.

"Dick [Williams] is an incredibly shrewd and intelligent person and I think Dick subtly performed a few maneuvers in the course of that season that were genuinely little tiny minor strokes of genius. I mean, we're not talking about changing world events, we're just talking about managing a baseball team. But Dick did some things that were the right thing to do, and I think therein is really the mark of the brilliant baseball people. And fortunately, it doesn't have anything to do with personalities. If Dick could've just been a little nicer guy, I think the world would've probably built a shrine to him."

Two months after becoming a villain in both New York and Boston, Elston Howard was acquired by the Boston Red Sox, and the two men who had shared the spotlight were in the same clubhouse. It was at first a strange experience for Boston fans to root for the veteran catcher who had been their enemy in pinstripes for so long.

"When everybody was out at batting practice or what have you, why, the newspaper guys couldn't get enough pictures of Ellie and me together. And the people kind of warmed up to the idea that he was being very friendly about it and that he and I were getting on really well. So I don't think they were as hard on him as they might've otherwise been, 'cause he was such a gentleman and I think most baseball fans knew that.

"We talked about his breaking up the no-hitter. And he told me exactly the truth. He said, 'You can't throw a pitch like that and expect somebody not to hit it.' And he was absolutely right."

Looking back a quarter of a century later, it is apparent that the 1967 Boston Red Sox were an intriguing group of individuals. There were the magnificent performances of Jim Lonborg and Carl Yastrzemski, who seemed to win every game with his hitting or fielding. During the final two months of that season, Yastrzemski always seemed to be up at bat in clutch situations and he delivered every time.

There were the funny players. George Scott, who *lived* in Dick Williams' doghouse because of one thing or another. Usually it was one thing—his weight. But he was so likeable, not even Williams could stay mad at him forever. Also there was Rico Petrocelli, who, according to Rohr, was so afraid of flying that he'd get sick when they passed out the meal money because he knew it meant a road trip was coming.

Then there were the tragic figures. Tony Conigliaro, whose great career for all intents and purposes ended on that August night when a Jack Hamilton spitter crashed into his head. Disappointment dogged him the rest of his life and a catastrophic heart attack left him an invalid in his final years. Joe Foy battled and overcame drug addiction

BILL ROHR

Born July 1, 1945, San Diego, California
Ht. 6'3" Wt. 192 BL TL

MAJOR AND MINOR LEAGUE CAREER

Year	Team, League	W-L	Pct	G	GS	CG	SHO	IP	H	R	ER	BB	SO	ERA
1963	Kingsport, Appalachian			DID NOT PLAY										
1964	Wellsville, NY-Penn	11-9	.550	26	22	8	0	168	158	109	86	98	185	4.61
1965	Winston-Salem, Carolina	7-3	.700	12	12	8	0	89	73	37	29	45	81	2.93
	Toronto, International	6-10	.375	19	17	6	1	122	89	48	37	54	88	2.73
1966	Toronto, International	14-10	.583	29	29	10	3	198	180	87	78	78	161	3.55
1967	BOSTON, American	2-3	.400	10	8	2	1	42.1	43	27	24	22	16	5.10
	Toronto, International	3-5	.375	17	15	1	0	103	105	47	40	43	70	3.50
1968	Louisville, International	1-0	1.000	1	1	1	0	9	9	3	3	2	6	3.00
	CLEVELAND, American	1-0	1.000	17	0	0	0	18.1	18	16	14	10	5	6.87
	Portland, Pacific Coast	7-5	.583	16	15	2	1	105	118	48	38	38	72	3.26
1969	Portland, Pacific Coast	11-9	.550	23	21	6	1	132	158	70	60	49	59	4.09
1970	Wichita, American Assn	1-6	.143	7	7	0	0	33	45	23	16	16	27	4.36
	Toledo, International	3-9	.250	23	14	2	0	90	93	66	53	56	62	5.30
1971	Toledo, International	3-7	.300	59	0	0	0	70	74	44	34	42	59	4.37
	Montgomery, Southern	1-0	1.000	4	0	0	0	5	7	2	1	6	5	1.80
1972	Quebec, Eastern	0-0	—	1	0	0	0	4	2	6	3	3	3	6.75
	Peninsula, International	0-2	.000	12	0	0	0	11	17	9	8	13	11	6.55
MAJOR LEAGUE TOTALS		3-3	.500	27	8	2	1	60.2	61	43	38	32	21	5.64
MINOR LEAGUE TOTALS		68-75	.476	249	153	44	6	1139	1128	599	486	543	889	3.84

1964—Led NY-Penn League Pitchers in Assists (43).

that most surely shortened his career, but not before taking its toll. Old before his time, his recovery did not enable him to forestall an early death in 1989 at the age of 46.

It was an amazing team that in its triumphs and tragedies holds a special place in the hearts of Boston's baseball fans because in the end, it was the only Red Sox team since the days of Babe Ruth that hadn't left its fans feeling disappointed at the end of the season.

Despite his all too brief moment of celebrity, and the disappointment that followed, Rohr retains a lot of pleasant memories of his time in the game. After all, few ball players gain the kind of recognition he earned in April 1967. Or play on a special team that people remember. Not everyone is asked to appear on "The Ed Sullivan Show," or enjoy the feeling of having crowds gather for a glimpse of them. Looking back on his nine years in baseball, he has few complaints, and maybe only one regret.

"The Red Sox had the best pitching coaches I've ever seen in their minor league system…Mace Brown in particular. I have often wondered if Mace Brown had been the pitching coach in '67, that things could have been different. I don't have a teaspoonful of hard evidence to support that. It's just a thought. What I do know is, that when I did get out of the groove in Boston, Sal Maglie did not spend fifteen minutes with me all year. Ever. There was no pitching coach in Boston in '67."

But in the end, the memories are pleasant, almost without exception. Especially those revolving around the camaraderie of the sport.

"Hell, I wouldn't trade those bus rides in Wellsville for four years at Stanford. And I got to play against Mantle and Killebrew, and Rod Carew and Boog Powell and Frank and Brooks Robinson. Reggie Jackson hit a homer off me in Cleveland that would have been eight dollars in a cab. I was fortunate in getting to face and play against some real great ball players that are gonna be remembered by my grandkids. Certainly, I'm not going to be remembered by theirs, but that's all right."

AL AUTRY

Pitcher, 1976 Atlanta Braves

Our plans miscarry because they have no aim. When a man does not know what harbor he is making for, no wind is the right wind.

— Seneca

It's a great game, it's a lot of fun. I never had a bad day at the ballpark. Oh, there were days I wish I were fishing and those kinda things. But, sitting in the bullpen and playing grab ass, and giving a hot foot, and eating hot dogs and peanuts while the game was going on, knowing you weren't gonna play 'cause you were a starting pitcher...that's a great life. And if you can make big money doing it, that's really neat.

— Al Autry

Baseball has been characterized by those not enamored of the game as an island of activity lost in a sea of statistics, and with continual debate over which newspaper prints the better box score or which book provides the most complete statistical analyses, even the most stalwart fan sometimes feels the need for a degree in mathematics.

However, once in awhile among the cavalcade of the obscure and the inane, there comes along a statistical oddity that catches one's eye.

Since the days of National League pioneers George Wright and Frank Pearce, more than 600 professional players have pitched in only one major league game. Some were position players, such as Ted Williams and Stan Musial, taking the mound as a publicity stunt or because a team saw no reason to waste a pitcher in a lopsided contest. Cesar Tovar and Bert Campaneris toed the rubber in order to play nine positions in one game. The most interesting of these one-time hurlers, however, are not those who appeared for publicity's sake, but rather those who were career-long pitchers.

Most of these phantoms came away without leaving any kind of impression, while more than 130 left the big leagues with a mark on the wrong side of the ledger.

Of the 600 "one-game wonders," 31 actually came away victorious. Of the latter group only two, Earl Huckleberry of the 1935 Philadelphia Athletics and Al Autry of the 1976 Atlanta Braves, have achieved their moment of perfection since the close of World War I.

What makes Al Autry's sole major league appearance most intriguing is its timing: a starting assignment some three weeks before the end of the season for a team buried deep in the National League West cellar and, after winning the game, receiving as his reward a seat at the end of the bench.

As Autry stood on the mound in Atlanta on a muggy September evening in 1976, his appearance represented the culmination of a seven-year journey through Winnipeg and Waterloo and Jacksonville and Omaha and a thousand great times and a thousand hardships. Autry had begun to doubt that this day would ever arrive. His wife had vowed not to set foot in a major league stadium until her husband was a participant. Paula Autry had a reserved seat this evening.

A mere 970 people were scattered throughout the stands, a mediocre-sized minor league crowd lost in a cavernous major league stadium. The gathering was witness to Autry's entire major league career during the second game of a doubleheader versus the Houston Astros; a team that, like Atlanta, was playing out the string, as teams tended to do in the National League West when Cincinnati's Big Red Machine was at its peak. The season for these two teams had effectively ended sometime back in June, but that made no difference to the young man on the mound. At 24 years of age, Autry was a big league pitcher, albeit as he remembers, a nervous one.

"I started to warm up and I did not feel good. My rhythm was not there, *nothing* was there. I hadn't touched a ball in eight or nine days. To be honest it helped my nerves because I thought, 'God, I feel bad, and let's just see what happens.'"

Five innings later, Autry had surrendered home runs to Astro outfielders Cesar Cedeno and Jose Cruz, but was leading 4-3 (the eventual final score), courtesy of a Willie Montanez three-run homer.

"I was pretty relaxed, didn't feel too bad, and when I came in after the fifth inning [Atlanta Manager Dave] Bristol said, 'Hey, good performance rookie, that's all we need ya for. Take a shower.' I sat around in the dugout till about the seventh. Then I moseyed back in the clubhouse. They had a TV in there and it wasn't until maybe about an out or two in the eighth where I started thinking, 'Hey, I could *win* this game!' I hadn't really thought about the win. I just thought, 'Hey, I'd had a decent performance.'

"So that was on, I don't know the date, I would guess it was about September tenth [actually 15th]. So by rights, I was going to end the season with them October third or fourth...in about three weeks. I would figure to get about three or four starts. Well, a couple of weird things happened."

* * *

Only 16 when the Davis High School baseball season began in his senior year, Autry was the kind of pitcher with a great arm whose coaches would shake their heads and tell him, "If you'd ever get smart, you could make a million dollars, but you're always trying to do it your own way." His way was to strike people out and his fastball had already attracted the attention of the Astros and Braves, ironically the same teams eventually involved in his only major league appearance. Both Atlanta and Houston had sent scouts to observe him and Al anticipated being drafted that summer by one of those teams, but it was instead the expansion Kansas City Royals that made him their fourth choice of the 1969 summer draft. He signed for a modest bonus, plus an $8,000 college scholarship, and reported to the Winnipeg Gold Eyes of the Northern League. His first two minor league seasons, which also included stops at Billings, Montana, and Waterloo, Iowa, were typical of a young pitcher learning the ropes. He didn't win very often.

"I was one of those guys who threw real, real, real hard and they didn't care if I won or lost. They just kept saying, 'Well hell, he's only 17. Well hell, he's only 18. Jeez, he's only 19.' Just thinking it was gonna come."

Jack McKeon, who was later to become manager of the Kansas City Royals, was in charge of the Royals' winter camp at the time. He told a reporter that Autry showed great promise; he had talent, threw hard and he could see a real possibility of Autry joining the Royals' starting rotation in the future.

Autry understandably felt very good about McKeon's assessment. It amounted to his sticking his neck out on behalf of a young pitcher who had won only three games in a year and a half. Autry recalls McKeon making the statement that his success was, "Just a matter of maturity, getting his control and learning how to pitch." It was an evaluation with which Autry had no disagreement.

"I didn't really know how to pitch, and it was a lot *my* fault because I liked to throw hard, and it was a lot *their* fault because nobody was telling me, 'Hey, let's learn how to pitch.' They kept thinking, 'He's young, he's young.' That kinda thing."

While Autry may not have studied the art of pitching, he did major in the art of enjoying minor league life. He was assigned to San Jose of the Class A California League in 1971, affording him and his wife the opportunity to visit family and friends in Modesto (75 miles east of San Jose) after Sunday afternoon home games. The two of them didn't have to be back in San Jose until Tuesday...Monday was always an off day for the team because the local roller derby franchise had priority use of the stadium.

The season in San Jose proved a turning point for the young pitcher. The raw talent that McKeon had spotted the previous winter surfaced in the California League and Autry began to win some games. He shut out Modesto on two hits. He struck out 14 in six innings versus Visalia. He seemed to be on the verge of living up to his potential, that often over-used label that is more often curse than compliment. During the winter, the Royals placed him on their 40-man roster.

Despite his new-found success, Autry discovered that everyone was more or less socially equal in the low minors. There were no prima donnas; everyone was friendly, teammates were close, the atmosphere was much like that of a college dorm. The boredom of the road was often combated through pranks: throwing a television set into a hotel pool, fire extinguisher fights in the hallway, bricking teammates into their rooms, flooding the baseball field to avoid playing the next day.

There were also moments on the field that could only occur in the minor leagues. One night in Modesto an outfielder lost a fly ball in the lights that hit him on the head and bounced 30 feet back and *over* the fence for a home run. Another teammate once suffered the indignity of having his leg wedged in an outfield fence while attempting to chase down a line drive up the alley. In the Southern League, Autry pitched against Denny McLain, the one-time 30-game winner, whose efforts to hang on in baseball had reduced him to plying his trade, somewhat ineffectively, in a Class AA league. Pitching a complete game, Autry lost 4-3 to the two-time Cy Young Award winner after allowing three home runs.

Of course, along with the fun, minor league life carries with it an inevitable downside. Many of Autry's teammates were left behind as others moved up. Some were traded...the less fortunate were released. It would usually happen in a very cold way. Often a player would find his name on the clubhouse bulletin board with instructions to see the manager. Everyone knew what that meant and it was there for all to see. Occasionally, someone would forget to put the name on the board and the unfortunate team member would be summoned over the loudspeaker. Once in awhile, a player would go to his locker and find his uniform missing, eliciting the comment, "Well I thought they told you."

As he moved closer to the majors, Autry realized that teammates were no longer equal; the atmosphere being in direct correlation to the proximity of the big leagues.

"The higher you get, the more dog eat dog it becomes...the more competitive it is, the more secrets there are, the less somebody wants to help you throw that curveball. The less sorry they feel for you when you didn't do good. I never wanted anybody to do bad, but face it, the guy higher than you on the list to go to the big leagues...the better he was doing...the worse it was for me. That's competition, that's fair. As my wife and I look back and recall, we had the greatest times back in A ball, when everybody was so damn far from the big leagues, it didn't matter what everybody did."

* * *

While in the Royals organization, Al Autry played with the core of what became a championship major league team. At various times his minor league teammates included Al Cowens, U. L. Washington, Frank White, John Wathan, Mark Littell, Steve Busby, Lou Piniella, Hal McRae, and George Brett.

"Lou Piniella was one of the *last* guys I would've ever thought to become a manager. One day in spring training, he struck out and when he came back, he took his bat and smashed every light fixture in the dugout. And this was an exhibition game.

"One of the best hitters I ever saw was Hal McRae. Kansas City had just acquired Hal and he was in Sarasota, Florida, for winter ball. I can remember him intentionally fouling off five or six pitches to avoid walking...and, as it should be, lining a double when he got the pitch he wanted.

"George Brett was one of the purest hitters I've ever played with. Although he never really hit as well in the minors for average, you could tell that one day he would become a great hitter. You know, line drives off the left center field wall, inside-out smashes down third base."

Brett and Autry were attending the Royals' major league training camp in Fort Myers, Florida, one spring. It was the young pitcher's first major league spring training—he and Brett had roomed together previously in Sarasota while attending the minor league camp and had become good friends. The two of them decided to head for the ocean one day, driving to their destination in Autry's brand new convertible. After reaching the beach, they decided to enjoy the sun while wading in the surf. Suddenly, Autry felt a sharp pain in his foot, courtesy of an angered stingray. His foot swelled instantly and, certain he was dying, Autry begged Brett to rush him to a hospital. According to Autry, as he lay delirious in the front seat of his new car, Brett took the long way around to the hospital, test driving the automobile, all the while assuring his friend that yes, he'd take care of Paula. In the end the wound was treated simply by soaking the foot in a bucket of warm water, which proved enormously entertaining to their teammates.

By 1975, Autry discovered that playing in a talent-laden farm system had its drawbacks. While placement on the Royals' winter roster protected the organization from losing his services, he was stranded in the American Association with no options as it became apparent that he was to move no further toward the big leagues. Free agency was still in the future; he could not take his talents elsewhere. After compiling a record of 11-13 with 173 strikeouts and a 3.33 ERA for Double A Jacksonville in 1972, the Royals assigned him to Omaha in 1973, back to Jacksonville in 1974, and then once again to Omaha. Autry was in his seventh season of professional baseball and couldn't seem to make that last jump to the major leagues, at least with Kansas City.

Having been on the 40-man major league roster for four years, his frustration with the low pay of the minor leagues and inability to play for another team began to surface.

"The first year they gave me a rookie contract. The next year I made $550 [a month], the next year I made $625, the fourth year, I was on a major league contract and I made $3,800...I made $640 a month for six months. [Autry once returned his contract with a note asking where the food stamps were.]

"That's a real problem the major leagues have with their minor league systems. When they put you on that forty-man roster, that means nobody else can draft you to a higher level. So they *own* you for that year. And the next year I was on one, and the next year I was on one, and the next year. I wasn't playing in the big leagues and I wasn't making any money either. Yet I'm good enough to be protected on the big league roster."

On June 30, 1975, Ray Sadecki was traded by the Atlanta Braves to the Kansas City Royals for veteran relief pitcher Bruce Dal Canton and "players to be named later." Two months later, Autry was one of those named (along with a close friend, pitcher Norm Angelini), and he became a Brave. He was driving home to California from Omaha at the conclusion of the American Association season when the transaction was completed. When he got home, he telephoned the Braves and they invited him to travel with the team on their West Coast trip in September. He threw batting practice and got a chance to feel a part of the organization as the Braves swung their way through San

Francisco, Los Angeles, and San Diego. It left him with a good feeling about his change in fortune. He felt he had a new start.

The Braves assigned Autry to Richmond, Atlanta's Triple A minor league team, and who was the manager there but Jack McKeon. Autry was not necessarily glad to see his old booster; he felt McKeon hadn't gone to bat for him when he was in a position to do something about Autry's entrapment within the Royals' minor league system.

"I got there and he was pretty friendly to me and he decided I was gonna be another Goose Gossage. So the first two or three games he brought me in I threw hard, but I was wild…I'd walk a run in, get us in a jam…so he pretty much just had it with me. I rode the bench quite a bit and that was the first time in my life I hadn't started every fifth day. Johnny Sain was the pitching coach that year and he just kept saying, 'Be ready, be ready.'

"So I threw and I threw and I threw. And…we had a lot of rainouts. Every pitcher on the staff, including the left-handed short reliever, got starts because we had doubleheader, doubleheader, doubleheader. And I still hadn't started. They pitched me a couple of times in long relief and I threw real well, so I finally got my start and I never looked back. I never had a bad game from June on."

By the end of the season, Autry was the best pitcher on the team. Historically a streaky performer, he had catapulted himself from oblivion to ace of the staff, compiling an earned run average of 2.11 in his 18 starts after being moved into the rotation. His final record stood at 9-6, but if not for Scott McGregor (who defeated Autry twice by the score of 1-0 and once 2-1 in ten innings), he could have easily finished at 12-3. The major difference was a change-up he had learned from Atlanta pitcher Andy Messersmith during spring training. In baseball parlance, he had crossed the threshold from thrower to pitcher.

Autry felt that Johnny Sain had noticed the difference as well.

"When I'd come in and pitch a shutout and had only three strikeouts, Sain would always make sure to say, 'Hey, I told you that you could throw eighty-five and beat them.' That helped me, 'cause it made me think about it."

Richmond made the International League play-offs but was eliminated in the first round and Autry was recalled by Atlanta. The Braves were away on a road trip at the time, so he was instructed to report when the team returned in a week and a half. In the meantime,

Autry stayed with pitcher Rick Camp, who was to report from Richmond as well, at Camp's farm just outside of Atlanta.

While there they celebrated by dove hunting (bruising their arms shooting), and went more than a week without picking up a baseball. When the Braves returned, Autry went to the stadium early to sign his contract. It was an exciting day. His wife had been a minor league wife for six years and they now had a daughter who was nearly two years old. It had been a tough ride, but now the sacrifice seemed more than worth it.

Autry met with Bill Lucas, the Braves' director of player personnel to sign his contract. Lucas chatted with him a bit, inquiring about his wife and child as Lucas always did, and congratulated him on making it to the major leagues.

As Autry turned to leave Lucas' office, the Braves executive said, "By the way, you're pitching the second game against Houston tonight."

* * *

Following his successful major league debut, Autry waited with anticipation for his next start. Dave Bristol had given no hints regarding the date of Autry's next turn on the mound, leaving the rookie to mark time and enjoy life as a big leaguer. He enjoyed himself right into Bristol's doghouse.

"I was a rookie and I got myself into a couple of things where I could understand Bristol being mad, but not hold a grudge. Camp had a bad game. I'll never forget it, Rick was gonna pick a man off first base and when he turned and threw, he absolutely *launched* it. I mean like *two hundred feet*, into the bleachers. It wasn't like a bad throw to first, it wasn't even *close*. So they take him out and we're walking off to the clubhouse and we got talking about it and we got tickled. We were chuckling and laughing and when we got to the top of the runway, just to go into the clubhouse, Bristol was standing there and he looked at us and he said, 'It wasn't that fucking funny.'"

Autry warmed up in the bullpen a couple of times after that incident but was never called into a game. He sat on the bench as San Francisco's John Montefusco no-hit the Braves on September 29, and four days later the season was over.

Considering his success at Richmond and his victory for the big league club, Autry couldn't understand how one incident could explain his inactivity at the end of the year and wondered about his future in the organization. He went to the front office to see Bill Lucas. He told Lucas, "I really don't understand anything that's happened this year. I finally come up to the big leagues, I pitch my first game and I win. I don't get the ball for three weeks. You don't want me to go to winter ball. What's going on?'"

Autry was assured by Lucas that changes were going to be made; that he should go home and rest up for next year. The Braves had recently announced Lucas' promotion to general manager, so Autry trusted Atlanta's new boss would see to it that things worked out.

"I thought, 'Well, what the hell. Big leagues. Won my first game, I'm on my way. Things are gonna happen for me.'"

Autry received his contract that winter calling for a salary above the major league minimum. It was a "one-way" contract, remaining in force even if Atlanta sent him to the minor leagues. He took this as a sign that the Braves definitely had him in their plans for 1977 and, considering the evident weakness of Atlanta's pitching staff, he was sure he had an excellent opportunity to break into the starting rotation.

In December he was invited to travel in the Braves winter caravan, where players and management tour the hot stove league, spouting enthusiastic predictions about the upcoming season and promoting goodwill and season tickets. The group made a stopover in Plains, Georgia, for a softball game and dinner with President-elect Jimmy Carter. Everything went well; Bristol was cordial during the trip.

Once spring training began, the atmosphere once again grew cold. Soon, the team had gone through the rotation twice and Autry hadn't even touched the resin bag.

"At that time, I had gotten to know Messersmith a little bit. I sat down in the locker room one day and both Messersmith and [Phil] Niekro were there, and I talked to them and I told them what happened. Both of them pretty much said, 'You should go talk to Bristol and tell him just what you told us. How you feel; that you want to pitch, you wanna make this club. And you think you deserve the chance to make it and you don't think you're getting a fair shot.'

"And so I did.

"It was a big mistake.

"He blew up. He really did. He told me he was running the club and he'd run it how he saw fit and I would pitch when he was damn ready to pitch me."

After appearing in a couple of "B" squad games outside of Bristol's presence, Autry was optioned to Richmond. The one-way contract he had signed, which had seemed such an advantage a few months before, now worked against him. Because of that document, he could not be recalled by the Braves without first passing through waivers, a process that made it difficult for Atlanta to bring him back. And Bill Lucas couldn't help. He had suffered a fatal heart attack.

Also packed off to Richmond at the same time was a promising catcher by the name of Dale Murphy. The year before, appearing in only his third major league game, Murphy was behind the plate when Autry pitched against the Astros. He had caught Autry at Richmond the previous season as well. Seemingly a lock to make the team, the young receiver was being sent to the International League to regain his confidence, which had been shattered during a tumultuous spring.

"He was one of those guys that hit your mistake pitch out to right field. So you could just tell he was gonna be good. Same way when I played with Brett, you could just tell. Murph had it all going for him. So we went to spring training and Murph was the biggest thing since Johnny Bench. He had the size, the power, the arm, the youth, the good looks. He was a churchgoer, the all-American guy. *Sports Illustrated*...they were all there and they were on him like flies, bad. All around his locker and Murph this and Murph that, and the phenom that's gonna bail Atlanta out. I think he just absolutely got so much pressure put on him that he cracked. And the way he cracked was in his throwing. He couldn't throw the ball. If he was trying to throw to second, he might throw it five feet in front of the mound or he might throw it in the air to the center fielder."

In recognition of his impressive season the previous year, Autry was awarded the honor of starting on opening day for Richmond in 1977. Dale Murphy was behind the plate.

"First guy on base, first situation, I'm in the stretch, throw it, turn and duck like a pitcher does. The guy takes off...Murph drills me in the back. After a couple of months, they got him out of there to the outfield."

* * *

The remainder of Al Autry's career resembled a roller coaster

AL AUTRY

Born February 29, 1952, Modesto, California
Ht. 6'5" Wt. 225 BR TR

MAJOR AND MINOR LEAGUE CAREER

Year	Team, League	W-L	Pct	G	GS	CG	SHO	IP	H	R	ER	BB	SO	ERA
1969	Winnipeg, Northern	0-5	.000	8	7	0	0	30	43	34	30	28	40	9.00
1970	Waterloo, Midwest	1-0	1.000	3	3	0	0	11	13	8	6	10	15	4.91
	Billings, Pioneer	2-5	.286	7	7	2	1	43	41	40	30	42	49	6.28
1971	Waterloo, Midwest	1-2	.333	3	3	1	0	20	11	6	2	12	28	0.90
	San Jose, California	8-11	.421	22	22	6	1	134	116	84	61	85	149	4.10
1972	Jacksonville, Southern	11-13	.458	29	29	7	1	184	152	79	68	76	173	3.33
1973	Omaha, American Assn	9-11	.450	28	28	7	1	153	161	114	104	104	136	6.12
1974	Jacksonville, Southern	10-5	.667	19	19	5	1	137	104	57	44	66	124	2.89
	Omaha, American Assn	2-4	.333	8	8	1	0	46	52	25	23	33	22	4.50
1975	Omaha, American Assn	9-7	.563	23	23	5	0	137	140	73	60	63	81	3.94
1976	Richmond, International	9-6	.600	32	18	8	2	161	142	58	51	77	109	2.85
	ATLANTA, National	1-0	1.000	1	1	0	0	5	4	3	3	3	3	5.40
1977	Richmond, International	6-6	.500	18	15	5	0	106	108	60	53	53	56	4.50
	New Orleans, Amer Assn	4-6	.400	12	11	1	1	58	60	40	32	37	43	4.97
1978	Springfield, Amer Assn	3-2	.600	25	4	0	0	77	68	53	45	62	66	5.26
MAJOR LEAGUE TOTALS		1-0	1.000	1	1	0	0	5	4	3	3	3	3	5.40
MINOR LEAGUE TOTALS		75-83	.475	237	197	48	8	1297	1211	731	609	748	1091	4.23

ride, with all the thrills and twists and turns and near-misses that leave you at first excited, but ultimately wanting to throw up at the end.

He lost his first six decisions for Richmond in 1977 before quickly turning things around, winning six straight to even his record. The Braves then attempted to recall him to the majors but were blocked by the St. Louis Cardinals, who claimed the pitcher on waivers and subsequently bought his contract from Atlanta after he was withdrawn from the waiver wire.

Autry was assigned by St. Louis to the American Association, having just missed a return to the big leagues with Atlanta. (In fact, if St. Louis had been allowed to take him on waivers rather than purchasing him in a separate transaction, they would have been required to bring him to the big leagues.)

The move to the Cardinals eventually brought Autry's career to an end. At one point he developed a wicked sidearm delivery that when coupled with the velocity of his pitches proved an effective combination, but he was unable to impress the St. Louis scouts. Soon, his pitching mechanics and his psyche fell apart. A knee injury that had to be repaired surgically ended his season and during the winter Autry discovered he'd lost his desire to play. After a year and a half in Triple A, only one frustrating step from the major leagues, he reported to spring training in 1979 only at the urging of a friend, and was soon faced with the reality that he would not reach the big leagues again.

"When I was called in to be released, I knew it would happen. I even knew the day. I expected it. It was almost negotiated. It was more of a bowing out than a cold-cut release. It wasn't hard for me. I was looking forward to it. I had already made up my mind...that's the way it should be."

* * *

Today, Al Autry is the display advertising manager for the *Modesto Bee*, the daily newspaper published back in his hometown, where his duties include supervising a staff of 16 and overseeing all print advertising. He frequently makes sales calls and finds he is still remembered in the community; his baseball career usually proving an advantage in his relationship with clients. He seems happy with his job, feels fortunate to be working for a good company, and takes pride in his family which now includes his wife Paula and their three children: Monica, age 17; Paul, age 14; and Jared, better known as "Bear," who is 8 years old.

Playing when he did, at the infancy of free agency, Autry missed out on the opportunity to earn big money. But he doesn't begrudge the current group of players who have been fortunate.

"People need to realize truly how much a player pays for the opportunity to get his free agency and to earn that million dollars. People say they're overpaid. That's not true. You're a commodity. You're one that was not given the opportunity of free enterprise. You earned what you got. You earned it because you started when you were seven years old and you played every day, and you stayed after school and played. Sure you *liked* it, maybe even *loved* it. But you *paid*, like the piano player that took lessons all those years. You play all those years and finally earn the free agency status or the opportunity to make money.

"On the other hand, a ball player should never forget to take the time out to sign an autograph, to tip his hat; and when he doesn't have time to sign, to make damn sure that he apologizes for the reason that he doesn't. Not to just walk by, or not do it. Without the fans, they don't make a million. They make a million not because they're good, but because people want to see them."

Autry admits it still bothers him that he never received a full shot at the big leagues.

"I'd always said, 'Just give me the damn ball. Let me start eight or ten games. If I'm good enough, keep me. If I'm not, I'll go home.'

"In retrospect, everything I got out of baseball was through pure, raw talent. Not good coaching and not good ambition. And not from the love of the game or the drive of it. I never was a baseball fan, I'm not a very good baseball fan now. I don't follow it closely, I didn't follow it when I played. I didn't work at it very hard. I only went to winter ball the first three or four years and then said, 'To hell with it, I'd rather not.' The majority of the fault lies with me and I've accepted that. It just wasn't my dream. And most people have a difficult time with that, 'cause they can't imagine it *not* being their dream.

"I approach my job here [at the newspaper] with a fun-loving attitude, but more aggressive than I did in baseball...I *learned* that from baseball. I've got a good company and a good job and I figure I won't let this one get away quite as easily as I did the other one."

JOE BROVIA
Outfielder, 1955 Cincinnati Reds

> The whole art of war consists in getting at what is on the
> other side of the hill, or, in other words, in learning what we do
> not know from what we do.
> —Duke of Wellington

*I'll tell you what was tough. When I used to play with the
San Francisco Seals, [Manager Lefty] O'Doul would play me
against right-handers and he'd play Dino Restelli against left-
handers. So then Portland finally bought me, right? Bill Sweeney
[Portland's manager], an old Irish guy, said, "Joe, listen, I
brought you here to play everyday, against left- and right-handed
[pitchers]."*

*So I got a young left-handed pitcher to come out there,
okay? I never hit left-handers well. I'd go out there and I'd make
this guy throw to me, throw to me, throw to me. Till my damn
hands would bleed. Well, I got to hitting them. You know, the
first sixteen home runs I hit...right...twelve of them against left-
handers.*

*Left-handers come inside and they hit me in the ribs, right?
I'd get hit maybe fifteen, sixteen times a year in the ribs from
left-handers. The ball'd take off inside. And I wouldn't give them
bastards an inch, hear me? And I stood up there, "You
sumbitches, you ain't getting me out and that's it." That's the
way I was. There's no fear at all, hey, "You sumbitches, I'm
gonna get you or you gonna get me." And that's the way I was up
at the plate.*

*What makes a good hitter? Good concentration. And you
can't think of the people bothering you in the stands, or what
you're gonna do tonight. You got to concentrate on that pitcher.
"Hey, you goddam SOB, you're trying to take my living away*

*from me and I'm gonna take it away from you, kid. It's you and
me, right?"*

*When a guy's out there pitching, hey, I'd sit there and watch
him. Everybody'd be up there in the clubhouse...I liked to go up
and change after outfield practice. I'd watch how their guy's
throwing; is he gonna throw three-quarters, sidearm, or overhand? I'd go watch this guy throw; try to pick the ball off, try to
pick it up when it leaves his hand. Mental, 100 percent, hear me?
And concentration, 100 percent. You gotta have that confidence,
"Hey, I'm gonna hit you, you son of a bitch." I hated pitchers,
that's what made me concentrate. That's the way I was.*
                                        —Joe Brovia

Joe Brovia was one of the Pacific Coast League's most feared
hitters. Ex-New York Giant hurler Roger Bowman called him one of
the three toughest hitters he had ever faced. George Bamberger, who
played against him for six years in the Coast League, feels Brovia
would be a top hitter in the big leagues today. Over his career he
battered PCL pitchers to the tune of a .305 lifetime average. In his 12
years in the league, he smashed 174 home runs and drove in more
than 800 runs.

If competitive athletics is the closest thing to war, this six-foot-
four, 210-pound outfielder personified it every time he stepped into
the batter's box and fixed his gaze toward the pitcher standing on that
hill a scant 20 yards away. His 35-inch, 35-ounce bat was his weapon,
and it was always loaded. The left-handed slugger faced the pitcher,
cap pulled down over his eyes, hands at his belt close to his body with
the bat held straight up, always uncoiling at the last possible moment
to attack the ball with a fury matched only by his hatred for opposing
hurlers. He was known for his fearless nature; never backing off the
plate regardless of the number of inside fastballs hurtling toward his
mid-section. Cal McLish and Gene Mauch both recall the time Brovia
was decked twice by their teammate, Eddie Chandler of the Los
Angeles Angels. With his teammates urging him to charge the
mound, according to both men, Brovia turned and yelled, "If he
wasn't so good to hit at, I'd go out and get him." He promptly lined
the next pitch off the scoreboard for a double.

Brovia took every at bat personally. Should a pitcher have the
audacity to get the best of him, especially with "slow stuff," he would
curse at the offending hurler on his way back to the dugout. Aggres-

sive, but nonetheless difficult to strike out (only once did Brovia fan more than 50 times in one season), he always *seemed* to impress opposing managers, such as Connie Mack, when the Seals would play against big league teams in exhibition contests, but he never got the call. It made him wonder if he had a bad reputation. Despite his ferocity and slugging ability, Joe Brovia was 33 years old before receiving his one shot at the big leagues, five weeks as a pinch hitter for the Cincinnati Reds in 1955.

One of the more popular players among fans in the PCL during the league's glory days of the 1940s and 1950s, when he first joined the San Francisco Seals prior to World War II, daily "Brovia Bulletins" were posted in the newspaper back home. There Brovia was known as "The Davenport Destroyer," a moniker bestowed on the only professional player to come out of the small town situated ten miles north of Santa Cruz on the Northern California coast. He holds the distinction of belting the longest home run in the history of Seals Stadium, variously estimated as having travelled anywhere between 500 and 565 feet. (After the New York Giants moved West to inhabit Seals Stadium, the spot where Brovia's blast landed was pointed out to Willie Mays who gasped, "That's a ten dollar cab ride!") When he was exiled to Portland by the Seals following the 1948 season, partially in response to a series of contract disputes, the San Francisco newspapers assailed the team and lamented the loss of the fiery slugger.

Brovia went on to delight fans in the Northwest. He took aim on the old foundry roof outside the right field wall of Vaughn Street Park, home of the Portland Beavers, slugging 39 home runs in 1950 and adding 32 more in 1951 while driving in 133. He also delighted area restauranteurs. Few articles of the time failed to mention his various adventures with knife and fork. Joe Brovia attacked food as he attacked pitchers. Among other feats, he once inhaled nine hamburgers in one sitting. Another time he dined at a restaurant that featured a free 48-ounce steak, provided the customer could consume it in one sitting. He topped off the steak with dessert.

Brovia definitely lived life to the fullest, as they say, but by the mid-1970s, this man who never gave up on the baseball diamond had pretty much given up on life after being disabled by a work-related injury.

"I hurt my back delivering [beer] kegs. I had surgery in 1961 and I came back in 1970 and I tore six discs apart.

"I went to Stanford clinic. I was up at Stanford...all over the hospital. I started tripping over curbs, lost the use of my legs on account of...all the surgery on my back. Then I had to have the hips replaced. I went to twelve different doctors, they couldn't pick it up. So finally, I saw a doctor in San Jose, California, a top bone...orthopedic man. I was in a wheelchair, my wife pushed me in the wheelchair. They spread my legs apart and hey, the doctor says, 'You got hip problems, you got no hips.' They x-rayed. No hips.

"The sad thing is I weighed 270 pounds, now I'm down to 200. I had to lose all that weight. 'Cause I laid in bed for four years and drank and I didn't give a shit what in the hell was going on, hear me?"

* * *

As a boy, Joe Brovia followed baseball in front of the family radio, listening intently to broadcasts of the San Francisco Seals and taking note of the latest exploits of his heroes, Vince DiMaggio and Al Wright. He was raised on a farm during the Great Depression and, growing up in a traditional Italian family, he was expected to work as long as the sun was visible. While it may sound cliche, it was true that in the Brovia household if you didn't work, you didn't eat. The family tables and chairs were handmade by Joe's father. The family was poor but pooled whatever resources they had, as many families did in those hard times, and survived.

When the San Francisco Seals offered the Santa Cruz High School student a $65 a month contract to play baseball in 1940, he was in heaven. Signed as a pitcher ("I didn't have a curveball, only a wrinkle," he recalls), Manager Lefty O'Doul watched hitters continually launch the teenager's offerings into an olive grove beyond the fence at the Seals' spring training complex at Boyes Hot Springs (located in the wine country north of San Francisco), and came to a decision.

O'Doul went up to the teenager and said, "Kid, take your toe plate off. I'm gonna make you an outfielder."

Brovia could not have had a better mentor when it came to striking bat against ball. O'Doul was a two-time National League batting champion and still shares, with Hall of Famer Bill Terry, the league record of 254 base hits in one season.

O'Doul was a great manager, both in handling players and in teaching. He is one of the rare baseball helmsmen whose virtues are extolled by hitters and pitchers alike, perhaps in part because he had been a pitcher for several years before arm problems sent him to the outfield. O'Doul managed in the Pacific Coast League for 23 years, most of those with the San Francisco Seals and also gained a great reputation in Japan during his annual visits there as a goodwill ambassador for baseball during the 1930s.

Superb at spotting and developing talent, if not for his excellent salary and ties to San Francisco, O'Doul might very well have gone down as one of the great major league managers.

When Brovia joined the Seals early in O'Doul's managerial career, the San Francisco skipper had already gained a great deal of notoriety for his ability to coach hitters. Among his more apt pupils were Joe Marty, the DiMaggios, Joe and Dom, and Ted Williams, who became a disciple of O'Doul and refers to him frequently in his own classic book, *The Science of Hitting*. Brovia was all ears when listening to the legendary O'Doul discuss batting theory.

"I coulda listened to him talk about hitting twenty-four hours a day. He told me, 'You got to wait back on the ball. You gotta use your wrists. Hitting's from the elbow down to your wrists. It's hips and wrists. And don't stride over three inches, hey, you're a dead pigeon if they change up on you. And look for one pitch—the fastball—at all times.' That's what O'Doul taught me. And I went to his theory and I had good luck hitting."

At the end of his first spring training, the Seals sent Brovia to El Paso of the Arizona-Texas league to gain experience, which he did, driving in a league leading 103 runs in 104 games while ripping 19 triples and using his .383 batting average to inflate more than a few earned run averages along the way. After a season with the Seals and another in Tacoma, his contract was purchased by the Chicago White Sox for 1943. One month later, Uncle Sam intervened and Joe Brovia traded in his pinstripes for olive drab. The deal with Chicago was canceled and it would be 13 years before his next big league opportunity.

After two years of combat duty in Europe, Brovia came back to the States and found himself so out of practice he declared, "I couldn't hit my house!" Optioned by the Seals at the end of spring training 1946 to Salt Lake City, their farm team in the Pioneer League, Brovia's batting eye showed no signs of improvement. By his reckoning he began the season hitless in his first 39 at bats. The drought continued until at his roommate's suggestion, the two of them went out and got drunk to relieve the stress. That night, Brovia slammed a home run and a double and began a 27-game hitting streak and never looked back. From August 6 to September 3, Brovia hit .439 (47 for 107) and then topped off the season with a 16 for 22 performance in the play-offs.

He returned to the Seals for nine games at the end of that season and spent the next two years platooning in the San Francisco outfield. It was in April 1947 during a game against the Seattle Rainiers that he smashed one of the longest home runs in Pacific Coast League history, an enormous shot marked at Seals Stadium up until the day of its demolition by a star located at the point where the ball passed over the fence. The victim of the prodigious blast was ex-St. Louis Brown pitcher Sig Jakucki.

"Only time in my career that this happened. I hit the ball and you know something, the goddam bat *gave*. I could feel the bat *give*, hear me? And I snapped at it, it was a 3-2 pitch, fastball high and away, and I went after it and the bat just *gave*. I mean, I said, 'I musta *hit* this.' And the fog was blowing in and I didn't even know it was over the center field fence. I got to second, and the umpire said, 'Hey, Joe, it's over the fence.'

"I got to third base, and you know what O'Doul says? 'Hey Brovia, you got muscles in your *shit!*' And the people there stood for fifteen minutes. For a month, I couldn't buy a meal or a beer in San Francisco. Everything was on the house."

Paul Fagan, whose family made its fortune in the San Francisco banking community, became part-owner of the Seals in 1945 and immediately set out to establish his as the preeminent franchise in the Pacific Coast League, which was lobbying hard for recognition as a third major league at that time. He paid his players better than many major league teams; some even refused big league offers because they represented a cut in salary. Fagan tried to persuade other owners in the league to eliminate working agreements and end the practice of selling their best players to the majors. His efforts resulted in one of the best minor league teams of the era, the 1946 Seals, featuring 30-game winner Larry Jansen and infielder Hugh Luby, as well as future and former major leaguers such as Ferris Fain and Cliff Melton. Because of Brovia's talent and popularity, Fagan's success in convincing the league to hold onto its better players ultimately hurt the slugger's chances of making the majors. While a player of Joe Brovia's ability might be traded within the league, the feeling was that the PCL as a whole had to retain its talent base in order to have a chance to go big league.

Fagan was a "hands-on" owner who often made suggestions to his players with an idea toward improving team image or fan support. Brovia was not always appreciative of the "advice."

"He didn't like the way I wore my pants. I copied Ted Williams, remember how he wore his pant legs low? Fagan used to tell me, 'You got to bring them up around your knees.'

"I said, 'I'm not bringing them up around my knees.'

"Then he wanted me to carry a handkerchief in my pocket. [Seals Manager Lefty O'Doul carried a handkerchief which he would wave to help rally the crowd behind the team. It became a popular symbol, picked up by the fans and Fagan decided he wanted each player to carry a "rally handkerchief."]

"I said, 'I ain't carrying a handkerchief in my pocket. Hey, I feel the way I'm gonna feel. I want nothing in my pocket. And I feel comfortable where I'm at hitting the ball.'

"They sold me to Portland."

* * *

Sold to the Beavers prior to the 1949 season, Brovia finally received the chance to play everyday after platooning for two years, and he flourished. Between 1947 and 1954, he was a model of consistency, posting batting averages of .309, .322, .313, .280, .303, .290, .314, and .302 in a league many felt was competitively comparable to the majors. Yet the idea of playing in the "big time" seemed a distant dream. The Pacific Coast League was successful in gaining an "open" classification status in 1952, a major step toward achieving its goal. Teams in the league voided all major league affiliations, made their players ineligible to be chosen by the major leagues in the winter draft and held on to their fans' favorites. (One exception was the Los Angeles franchise which remained closely tied to the Chicago Cubs, since the Wrigley family owned both ballclubs.) After a couple of years financial reality set in, and the teams re-established their ties to the major leagues. The final death-knell for the concept was sounded when the Dodgers and Giants moved West, taking away the Pacific Coast League's two most attractive markets.

In 1955, Brovia joined Oakland and was reunited with O'Doul, now managing the Oaks. A notoriously slow starter, Brovia was ablaze from opening day and at the end of June was hitting well above .300 with power. Suddenly, major league teams were interested. It had been 16 years since he had signed his first professional contract.

"I was in Seattle when the news hit. 'Hey Joe, you're sold to the Reds. Go out and pick up your stuff.' And all of a sudden, I was sold, and me, I was the happiest damn guy in the world."

He stepped right off the plane and up to the plate to pinch-hit, striking out against Warren Spahn in the ninth inning of a game against the Milwaukee Braves. Brovia was a major league ball player at last, but his achievement would be short-lived. Occasionally, a team will bring in a player only to put him in a difficult or unfamiliar role, nearly ensuring his failure. Brovia arrived in Cincinnati under the impression he was to get a shot at playing right field for the Reds, but instead was informed by Reds president Gabe Paul that he had been acquired to fill the difficult role of pinch hitter.

He played only one game in the outfield while with the Reds, in an exhibition game during the All-Star break against the Detroit Tigers. Hitting a double and a home run in that contest, his performance had no influence on his role with the club. He was used exclusively as a pinch hitter in league play. Brovia *was* burdened with the reputation of being a bad defensive outfielder, a characterization he felt was undeserved. Many former teammates and opponents comment on his lack of defensive acumen but Bob Hunter, who covered the Coast League with the *Los Angeles Examiner* for many years feels that while he wasn't the best, "He wasn't the worst either. That's been exaggerated. Maybe his hitting overshadowed everything else." Others feel Brovia's defense suffered *because* he always wanted to hit instead of working with the glove. Whatever the reason, perception often becomes reality and he was left with the tag of liability on defense. While Brovia now admits to wishing he'd worked harder on his defense and throwing arm, he is sensitive to suggestions that he was a poor defensive player. He feels his reputation with the glove dated back to a game with the Seals early in his career, a game in which he went three for four at the plate and oh for four in the field. Following the four-error debacle, which received a lot of play in the press, Brovia was quoted as saying Seals first baseman Ferris Fain refused to speak to him for three weeks.

The team Brovia joined in Cincinnati during the summer of 1955 featured four .300 hitters and only one regular who batted below .268. Ted Kluszewski, Gus Bell, and Wally Post each drove in more than 100 runs. The pitching staff led the National League in shutouts. Yet the Reds finished below .500, 23 and a half games out of first place.

It is often said that much of a team's success comes from its "chemistry." This elusive and usually transitory ingredient is often cited as the most important factor in a team's vault into contention, or a talented team's struggle onto the heap of chronic underachievers. Good players play better in comfortable surroundings. Brovia felt trapped in an uncomfortable role and in an uncomfortable atmosphere.

He feels things would have been different had he been with the team beginning in spring training. That way he feels he would have had the chance to fit in better and make more friends. The truth was that outside of Roy McMillan (the man for whom Brovia pinch-hit in his first game), Gus Bell, and Ray Jablonski, the team generally ignored the fiery veteran. The Reds lack of success translated into frustrations among the sporting press and the 33-year-old pinch hitter became a natural target for those impatient with the team's progress.

"The sportswriters in Cincinnati didn't like me. I run down to first, they called me 'Waddle Butt.' I wasn't the fastest runner. They said, 'If you're gonna lose, use your young kids, don't use the guys like Brovia.' So I'm thirty-three, right? At any rate, I was irritated with that. The point is, I didn't get to play. I played in one exhibition game. After awhile, I lost my concentration and timing due to not playing."

After a little more than a month in the major leagues, and two hits and one walk in 21 plate appearances, Brovia was returned to Oakland for the remainder of the 1955 season and then sent to Buffalo, the Reds' Triple A farm team in the International League for 1956.

"I was in the International League. They had hard throwing left-handers and I started backing away from left-handers. I started backing away. I said, 'Hey Joe, time to get your ass outta this game.'"

He returned home to Santa Cruz during the 1956 season and signed to play for the local California League team in San Jose, where he ripped Class C pitching for 22 home runs and 90 RBIs in 72 games.

That winter Brovia travelled to Hermosillo, Mexico, as he had every year since 1950 to play an 80-game winter league schedule. A consistent .300 hitter in a league that over the years featured pitchers like Jim Bunning, Paul Foytack, Red Munger, and other major leaguers, Brovia led the circuit in batting in 1957. He was awarded a large brass belt buckle which he still proudly wears to this day.

He remained in Mexico for the first time through the spring, playing for Veracruz in the Mexican League before finally calling it quits for good.

"I just came home and everybody'd say, 'Hey, how come you work driving a beer truck, Joe? You should do better'n that, you know. You're an ex-big league ball player, you played in the Pacific Coast League.' I say, 'Hey, I didn't have the opportunity to get educated. I come up during the tough days of the Depression years. What the hell I'm gonna do? I'm satisfied. I'm raising my family with a pretty good job,' which it was. Everybody knew me from baseball. I delivered to grocery stores, delivered to liquor stores, delivered to bars. So, what the hell, hey, it didn't cut no damn ice with me. I earned a good living. I got a nice pension out of it."

* * *

The 1970s brought hard times for the Davenport Destroyer.

"I went through nine major surgeries, had four back operations, a pelvic bone shifted eight inches and they straightened that one out. Two hip implants, and what the hell else?

"I couldn't walk for ten years. I was wheelchair bound, bedridden for four of the ten years. I was about ready to commit suicide. People, people come here, to my house, and they'd cry. They saw me in a wheelchair. They saw me in bed. And I was crippled up bad, I mean, hey. I used a bedpan because I couldn't get up to go to the bathroom no more, hey, put yourself in my shoes.

"Well, my wife turned it around for me. They found out the problem, so I finally lost the weight and had the surgery and I was in a lot of pain. I was supposed to exercise forty-five minutes, three times a day, right?

"One night, my wife comes in and I was in so much goddam pain. She says, 'Joe, you gonna do that?' I says, 'Nah, to hell with it Kathy, I'm not gonna exercise.' Poor thing put up with me for a long time, right? With all the problems I had: I couldn't walk, she had to work, and I was on all kinds of medication. I'd call her up and say, 'Hey, I gotta have my medication at noontime.' I says, 'You pick it up and bring it home here.' I was a nasty son of a bitch. When you got problems and you can't walk and you don't see yourself...and especially being an athlete, right? And active all your life.

"'To hell with it,' Kathy slammed the door and said, 'The therapist comes here everyday, Joe. She's trying to help you, and to heck with you.' But she didn't mean it.

"So then, I started exercising myself. Boom. Bang. She could hear me in the next room. I was exercising, exercising, exercising, exercising. So she kept after me. And she'd walk with me, you know, she'd make me walk. And I was walking crooked. 'Get that toe straight out! You're bending your back.' My wife was instrumental to me. Finally, little by little, I got better.

"One morning I got up, and I used to bitch like hell. Kathy has to go to work, she had to be on the job at eight o'clock, and I'd say, 'I feel, ah, I feel like horseshit, goddamit.' But this day, I said, 'You know, Kathy, I feel 100 percent better this morning.'"

"Kathy said, 'Oh my God, first time I heard you say that in twelve years.'

"From that time on, I went to therapy for about a year and a half and I pulled out of it. My back straightened out, I started walking again, and the doctor who did the surgery saw me. He couldn't believe what he saw.

"He was coming down the hall and I was walking towards him. 'Joe, I can't believe what I see. I didn't think you'd ever straighten your back up, or ever walk again.' This doctor threw his arms around me, and I saw tears come down this man's eyes. He threw his arms around me, he says, 'Oh my God,' and he called it a miraculous, incredible recovery. Then he took me out and showed me to the nurses.

"Today, I'm fortunate...very thankful for what happened to me and I can thank my wife for my recovery. Like the doctors said, 'You got a good woman Joe. She's the one that helped you along.' 'Cause I was very bitter, you know. A very bitter guy."

* * *

The Pacific Coast League, as it was prior to 1958, still holds magic for its fans and ex-players. The stars and semi-stars of that league have not been forgotten. Joe Brovia still receives several fan letters a week,

JOE BROVIA

Born February 18, 1922, Davenport, California
Ht. 6'3" Wt. 210   BL TR

MAJOR AND MINOR LEAGUE CAREER

Year	Team, League	G	AB	R	H	2B	3B	HR	RBI	BA	SA	BB	SO	SB
1940	El Paso, Arizona-Texas	104	415	73	159	21	19	3	103	.383	.547	34	39	4
1941	San Francisco, Pacific Coast	92	195	20	62	6	3	0	27	.318	.379	17	19	0
1942	San Francisco, Pacific Coast	24	36	4	6	2	0	0	4	.167	.222	2	2	0
	Tacoma, Western Intl	78	310	54	90	17	3	6	52	.290	.423	36	16	2
1943-45	MILITARY SERVICE													
1946	Salt Lake City, Pioneer	47	183	30	62	16	5	2	27	.339	.514	13	20	3
1947	San Francisco, Pacific Coast	9	9	0	1	0	0	0	1	.111	.111	—	—	—
1948	San Francisco, Pacific Coast	114	359	45	111	29	4	10	63	.309	.496	34	35	1
1949	Portland, Pacific Coast	127	444	53	143	28	4	9	89	.322	.464	40	37	0
1950	Portland, Pacific Coast	117	364	59	114	21	2	11	51	.313	.473	43	29	2
1951	Portland, Pacific Coast	193	649	88	182	28	0	39	114	.280	.504	77	56	1
1952	Portland, Pacific Coast	161	574	76	174	25	2	32	133	.303	.521	77	50	2
1953	Sacramento, Pacific Coast	170	551	78	160	25	1	21	85	.290	.454	*109*	46	0
1954	Sacramento, Pacific Coast	165	525	76	165	36	1	20	97	.314	.501	*105*	32	1
1955	Sacramento, Pacific Coast	149	504	59	152	32	0	13	91	.302	.442	67	40	0
	Oakland, Pacific Coast	114	372	59	121	19	4	19	73	.325	.551	54	41	0
	CINCINNATI, National	21	18	0	2	0	0	0	4	.111	.111	1	6	0
1956	Buffalo, International	46	122	12	28	7	0	6	28	.230	.434	17	23	0

1957													
San Jose, California	72	252	67	91	18	0	22	90	.361	.694	59	21	0
Veracruz, Mexican	23	80	13	25	6	0	1	16	.313	.425	18	9	1
MAJOR LEAGUE TOTALS	21	18	0	2	0	0	0	4	.111	.111	1	6	0
MINOR LEAGUE TOTALS	1805	5944	866	1846	336	48	214	1144	.311	.491	802	515	17

1952 — Led Pacific Coast League in Hit by Pitches (8).
1953 — Led Pacific Coast League in Hit by Pitches (7).

Italics in boldface type indicate led league

not only from the West Coast but from all over the country. He diligently answers every piece of mail and is constantly surprised when people remember him. He states with considerable pride that, "People never forget that Pacific Coast League. People still talk about it. It was a *good* league."

After his recovery, Brovia was inducted into the Italian Hall of Fame, and was later a guest of honor at a Bay Area fund raiser saluting area baseball stars for their contributions to the game. Other invitees included Joe DiMaggio, Frank Robinson, and Joe Morgan. The owners of both the Oakland A's and San Francisco Giants were in attendance and Brovia was surrounded by many of the stars he had played with and against during his career. He was presented with a replica of the star commemorating his long home run at Seals Stadium (the original had disappeared with the ballpark). One of the highlights of the evening for Brovia was the "The Yankee Clipper" walking up behind him and pinching him, saying as he was leaving, 'See you around, Joe.' When he reflects on these moments, whatever bitterness there is seems to fade from his face.

"I was happy I went to the majors. I wish I'd went up with a different attitude. It wasn't *all* that bad. I gotta blame myself a little bit too. I can't just blame the manager or the ballclub. It wasn't all bad to see Musial hit and Campanella hit and Mays hit.

"I tell you, if I had to do it all over again, I'd play that game again tomorrow, because I met the most beautiful people, and the funniest people, in my life. I *love* the game. I think it's the greatest game in the world.

"What I used to love to do is get up there and hit that ball. I mean man, I couldn't wait to get to that damn plate. I used to just love to walk up there, and man, challenge that pitcher. 'Hey, you son of a bitch. You got to get it over and I'm gonna hit you.' I mean, I was kind of a cocky guy, but you had to be cocky. That's my living, hey. I'm feeding my family. I gotta hit here.

"I just liked to walk up there and hit."

JOHN LEOVICH
Catcher, 1941 Philadelphia Athletics

To tell you the truth, it was the nice people that I met that I enjoyed the most. That to me was something that I'll never forget. The game itself...it's inconsequential. The friends you make, you have friends for life. I think, if you take that out of sports, you've missed something.
—John Leovich

A true friend is that most precious of all possessions and the one we take the least thought about acquiring.
—La Rochefoucauld

When John Leovich speaks of his experience in baseball, you do not hear a rehash of games in which he participated, or a recitation of his statistics, or even how some manager never gave him a chance to play. What you hear instead are memories of treasured acquaintances Leovich made along the way. He tried to treat every person he met as a potential friend and rarely found anyone in which he couldn't find *something* to like.

His formative years were spent around the various ballparks and playing fields of Portland, Oregon, in the early 1930s with his frequent companion, best friend Johnny Paveskovich. The two boys worked each spring and summer at Vaughn Street Park, home of the Pacific Coast League Portland Beavers—young Leovich employed as a clubhouse boy while Paveskovich served as bat boy.

The Portland Beavers have a long and colorful history in the Pacific Coast League, the franchise having been a league member for all but six seasons since 1903. Mickey Cochrane and Jim Thorpe played there, as did future Yankee, Indian, and Senator shortstop Roger Peckinpaugh and baseball's first "30-30" man, St. Louis Browns outfielder Ken Williams.

Hanging around the Portland clubhouse in the early 1930s, Leovich viewed at close range some of the great PCL legends like Oscar "Ox" Eckhardt, the four-time Coast League batting champion who hit .382 in his six seasons in the league. Leovich remembers, "He was a tremendous line-drive hitter; he just *overpowered* the ball." There was Smead Jolley, who once carried a .404 batting average through 191 games on the PCL schedule. Also known for his fielding "ability," of which many of his more dubious feats are still legend in Boston and Chicago where he played major league ball, Jolley could hit any kind of pitching. He hit .305 during his four seasons in the American League and .366 in the minors. He slammed 380 home runs in his professional career in the days when home run sluggers were rare and had over 1,900 runs batted in, twice collecting over 300 hits in a Coast League season. In the days of smaller rosters and less specialization, even a player of Jolley's hitting ability could not make up for his lack of defensive acumen. Young Leovich was especially fond of watching Jolley hit: "Since I was a grade school kid at that time, his long-ball hitting impressed me the most." Other PCL stars included Arnold "Jigger" Statz, who could play center field as well as anyone in the game and Frank Shellenback, a spitball pitcher who was inexplicably left off the list of those grandfathered by baseball as eligible to throw the pitch in the major leagues when the rules were changed in 1920. Shellenback remained in the Coast League through 1938 winning nearly 300 games. He later became Ted Williams' first professional manager and was a major league pitching coach for the Browns, Red Sox, Tigers, and New York Giants.

Among Leovich's other memories of that time is the fact that one of his future Philadelphia teammates, Bob Johnson, played for the Beavers while he was clubhouse boy. He also had the experience of witnessing the exploits of a skinny 17-year-old outfielder with the San Francisco Seals by the name of Joe DiMaggio, who in 1933 began a 61-game hitting streak during the second game of a May double-header in Portland.

It was a fascinating time to be around the Pacific Coast League, which was producing players like Frank Crosetti, Augie Galan, Ernie Lombardi, Gus Suhr, Bobby Doerr, and Dolf Camilli. To the wide-eyed Leovich, this *was* the major leagues.

As summer faded, the leaves fell, and the winter chill set in, Leovich and his best friend headed to the ice rink where they practiced with professional hockey players from the minor league Portland Buckaroos.

If you pressed them, the boys would tell you that they actually enjoyed ice hockey more than any other sport. Paveskovich was an especially good player and Leovich recalls the man who ran the Buckaroos offered both of them professional contracts. With the country in the grips of the Depression, however, there was little money in professional athletics at the time. To Leovich, the prospect of attending college was much more exciting.

He eventually opted for Oregon State University, where he played both baseball and football (playing wide-out on a team that lost only once and played in the Hula Bowl), and received contract offers from both the Detroit Tigers and Philadelphia Athletics in 1941. Yet he was not really interested in pursuing a professional athletic career. Leovich played sports for *fun* and although he eventually did sign a contract with Philadelphia, the reason he did so was ostensibly to provide financial support for his ailing mother who had been widowed when Leovich was five years old.

Reporting directly from the Oregon State campus to Philadelphia after signing his contract, Leovich was installed as the A's third string catcher behind Frankie Hayes and Hal Wagner. On May 1, the Athletics were defeated by the Cleveland Indians, with Bob Feller receiving credit for the victory while hitting a home run and recording his 1,000th career strikeout in the process. The game also served as Leovich's major league debut. Hayes had started the game behind the plate.

"I guess something happened to him and they put me in the game. I was up twice. First time, I lined out to Lou Boudreau and the next time, I hit one to right center for a double."

The double off Bob Feller represented the only base hit of his major league career. Though he remained on Philadelphia's roster much of the season, he appeared in only that one major league boxscore.

"That Hayes, he wouldn't get out of a *doubleheader*. He was a hell of a guy, but that was his job, and he wasn't gonna let anybody else in there. Which, you know, you can understand. He was a competitor."

Leovich spent part of the season in the Interstate League and when with the Athletics, he generally remained in the bullpen and worked with coach Earle Brucker on his catching. His other duties usually involved the warming up of pitchers between innings and in the bullpen. He wasn't in the lineup, but that didn't lessen his enthusiasm for life in the big leagues, or admiration for his manager, the seemingly everlasting Connie Mack.

"He was a great gentleman. That's all you can say. He was *Mister* Mack. He had a nice sparkle in his eyes and he looked right at you when he was talking to you. Anything he told you, you could bet it was right. I really enjoyed having met the man."

The Athletics of the 1940s were well into one of the long down cycles of the Connie Mack era, "The Tall Tactician" having long since sold off his great players from the legendary 1929-1931 teams. While the Athletics may have been low on talent in comparison with the rest of the league, their outfield of Bob Johnson, Wally Moses, and Sam Chapman was second to none, with the possible exception of the Yankees.

"One of the big injustices is Bob Johnson never making the Hall of Fame with the records he achieved," says Leovich with great conviction. "He was the center fielder. He always hit .300, or close to it, and twenty or more home runs a year. Used to hit a lotta doubles and triples." [Johnson also drove in 100 or more runs seven seasons in a row and retired with a career slugging average of .506, a figure higher than that of Ernie Banks, Johnny Bench, or Reggie Jackson.] "He had a great arm, could run like a deer. He did it *all* out there. 'Course, he played for the Athletics...the bottom of the league...no fanfare. He *was* well thought of in those days, but I mean, if he'd a been playing on a *contender*, hell, he'd a gotten a lotta publicity. I thought that was one of the great injustices. 'Cause he could do it all. You name it, he did it."

Warming up pitchers between innings, Leovich often had to contend with the talented but wild Phil Marchildon or the knuckle-ball of Luman Harris. That famous sit-com catcher, Bob Uecker, once joked that the proper technique in catching a knuckler is to pick up the ball *after* it stops rolling. Leovich's attitude toward the pitch was somewhat different. He studied the ball, determining where it would break based on its behavior. That worked most of the time, but not always. Especially if Luman Harris was throwing into a good stiff wind.

"I was out there one day and he threw one that started in about the middle of the plate. It ended up fifteen feet high on the back of the screen, which was quite a ways away [from home plate] at Shibe Park. When he came in after the inning was over, I says, 'What the hell you trying to do, *decapitate* me?' The more wind you had coming in to the mound...*jeez*, that thing'd really duck and dive."

Playing in the American League in 1941 provided Leovich a great vantage point from which to witness baseball history, for instance Ted Williams' .400 season and the second-longest hitting streak of Joe DiMaggio's professional career. While Leovich admired the "Yankee Clipper's" talents, he felt Williams the better and more disciplined hitter. He once witnessed "The Splendid Splinter" hit a foul ball completely out of Shibe Park that landed on Nineteenth Street, a block from the stadium.

"He was a very gracious person. If a person on the other ballclub was having trouble hitting, he'd meet them out at the ball park at ten o'clock and straighten them out. *There* was a side that nobody knew about because he was always fighting with those Boston writers."

An exhibition game provided Leovich with an opportunity to play...and catch the legendary Satchel Paige.

"You just put your glove there and he'd hit it and he had a lot of fun while he was doing it. He'd talk to you before the game and tell

you what he'd like to do. And then, he'd put on a little show with that
[hesitation] pitch. He'd give me the sign when he was gonna take the
step and then throw it later. He knew what he was doing out there all
the time.

"He had tremendous control of his curveball. He'd get two strikes
on you most of the time. Depending on the situation, he'd throw that
curve by them. He'd fool them, you know. He'd dilly-dally around
with half a curve...slow curve...this 'n' that. Then, when he wanted
you outta there, he'd throw one that'd break right off the table. He
could *fire* that ball, when he wanted to. He'd learned to pitch after all
those years. He was a very smart man. He knew what he wanted to do
out there."

* * *

The 1942 season saw Leovich report to spring training with
Philadelphia's Triple A affiliate in the Pacific Coast League—the
Portland Beavers. Far from disappointed, it allowed him to be home
and help out his mother. He served as the team's starting catcher and
often threw batting practice as well. The Pacific Coast League was a
strong and colorful circuit known for its prodigious hitting, pleasant
weather, and players who made the league colorful.

The Beavers finished in last place that season, despite the heroics
of four-time PCL home run king Ted Norbert ("A real gentleman at
all times, a serious hitter and a good sense of humor. He was a credit
to the game"), and an interesting pitching staff highlighted by
extremes in style. The ace of the staff was Ad Liska, who in his
mid-thirties had already played for the Phillies and Senators before
coming to the Coast League. A submariner, Liska played 14 years with
the Beavers, picking up 198 of his 248 career minor league victories for
Portland.

"Ad Liska was a fierce competitor. He hated to lose at anything.
He was a pleasure to catch. It was like sitting in a rocking chair, he was
always on target. His control was perfect and he didn't dilly-dally
around on the mound. Ad pitched fast and you had better be in
position to receive his pitch when you returned the ball to him. He
fired the ball right back, as soon as he got it. Most of his games were
over in an hour and a half. We played a seven-inning game with Ad
pitching and the elapsed time was one hour and seven minutes. In

another *nine*-inning game the elapsed time was one hour and nineteen minutes."

At the opposite end of the pitching spectrum was Joe Orrell, a young, hard throwing pitcher who went on to play in parts of three seasons for the Detroit Tigers.

"You didn't know *where* he was gonna throw the ball, you just had to be set [for anything]. A guy coming up to the plate, you'd say, 'Hey, you better be pretty loose, Bullet Joe Orrell is *wild*.' Catching the knuckleball wasn't as hard as catching *his* fastball."

The Beavers were a team that enjoyed practical jokes and one that involved Orrell without his knowledge occurred on a day when he was especially wild. Unknown to him, the Portland players pointed out their teammate on the mound to their opponents and in an attempt to "warn" them, told the opposition that Orrell was blind in one eye and could barely make out the difference between the catcher and the hitter. Orrell never realized the true reason for his increased effectiveness that day.

Leovich always enjoyed the pranks and stunts that players pulled on each other and his favorite involved Billy Schuster, a shortstop for Los Angeles who later went on to play for the Chicago Cubs. Schuster was notorious and popular for the stunts he pulled over the years. He once "fainted" in shock over an umpire's bad call and was as likely to slide into the pitcher's mound as run to first if he hit a dribbler back to the mound.

The fun began when Schuster, a man evidently not comfortable making enemies, attempted to separate Leovich from the baseball on a play at home plate.

"We had him out by ten feet. He tried to bowl me over. Next thing I know, I got him over my shoulder and he's coming down on his head. And on the way down, he tried to hit me with his cleat and a photographer took a shot of it.

"The next day, Lindsay Brown [Portland's shortstop and Leovich's teammate], took this picture to the batting cage and he was showing it to Schuster. He says, 'Hey Bill, that kid's hot at you. He says the next time you come to the plate, you better be on the goddam ground. That kid's on fire.'

"That was a big lie because, you know, after a ballgame you'd forget those things. Good ol' Lindsay, he *was* an agitator.

"Next day, same thing happens. Schuster's on second...he comes in. This time he started sliding and I hit him with everything. You know, the ball, my knee…and he never got within ten feet of the plate. He started sliding *way* out and I jumped on him on all fours.

"The next day, we're going to the ballpark and we get out in front of the park and Schuster's waiting there. He wanted to talk to me. He says, 'Do you think we could be friends?'

"I says, 'Well *hell*, Bill, what are you talking about?'

"He says, 'You know, that picture.'

"I says, 'Oh, you mean that one Lindsay's talking about? I didn't pay any attention to *that*. After the game's over with, Bill, the next day's a different day.' And then he knew he'd been had. After that we got to be real good friends."

Of course, Leovich now knew how to make Billy Schuster squirm and it didn't take long for an opportunity to arise where he could take advantage. Schuster made the mistake of confiding his dislike for one of Leovich's teammates, pitcher Sid Cohen, to his new friend.

"He's telling me about this 'goddam Cohen.' I said, 'Bill, you don't wanta be farting with him. Sid is known as *Kid Cohen*. He used to be a fighter.'

"And I built it up. And old Lindsay Brown, I told him and *he* built it up. Following day, at the ballpark…same thing. Billy meets Cohen coming outta the cab. He says, 'Hey Sid, how about being friends?'

"'Oh sure Bill, absolutely.' I'd already clued Sid in. And Sid never got over that until the day he died. Every time I'd call him on the phone when I'd pass through El Paso, he says, 'John, you remember that Schuster?' I had Sid built up as the greatest fighter in the country."

* * *

Despite being hampered by injuries, Leovich caught 116 games for Portland in 1942. Various aches and pains affected his hitting but in that era a player didn't want to come out of the lineup, even to heal, because there was always the chance you could lose your job. If you were conscious, you played. He had a serious collision at the plate with Barney Olsen of the Los Angeles Angels. Injuring his shoulder badly while blocking the plate, the young catcher returned, "As soon as it quit throbbing."

"Then another time, I got hit in the head by [Eddie] Stutz, who was a helluva curveballer. He threw a curveball that didn't break. First one he'd thrown in nine years that didn't break. They didn't even give me a pinch runner, I don't know why. So I had to stay in until the game was over. I tell you, I felt that for quite awhile."

Following the 1942 season, Leovich joined the Coast Guard and patrolled the Alaskan coastline during the war. Although he didn't see any action during his three years of duty, he had a lot of friends who did...and a lot of friends who didn't come back. By the time he returned home from his tour of duty, Leovich decided that he really wasn't interested in playing anymore. Two seasons of professional baseball were enough.

"My priorities had changed quite a bit," he says. "I think that when you lose a lot of friends, athletics becomes insignificant..."

Leovich joined his sister and brother-in-law in their tavern business, and later opened restaurants, first in Seattle and then Lincoln City, Oregon, where he now lives. It's a well-known resort area, 90 miles west of Portland on the Oregon coast, far from the fast-paced big city life of which Leovich had grown weary.

Baseball now seems a distant memory for Leovich, and time has dimmed his recall for details of many events that are now some 50 years past. To him, sports was not a major inspirational force in his life. It wasn't all-important. It was fun. But while his memory may be cloudy regarding details of his professional career, Leovich still vividly recalls playing baseball as a youngster.

"We had a double play one time in grade school. Double play went from Leovich to Paveskovich to Stepovich. Michael Stepovich was the first baseman...he was later governor of Alaska."

Leovich's boyhood friend, Johnny Paveskovich, also gained a measure of fame as he too went into professional baseball, although under another appellation. He remembers how his friend earned his new name during a pick-up game at Vaughn Street Park when both boys were employed there.

"Johnny was just a little kid hanging around the ballpark, and L. H. Gregory was the sportswriter at the *Oregonian* [Portland's major daily newspaper]. Gregory loved baseball, he had pitched years before in the Midwest somewhere and he used to bring a team up to play a pick-up game against the kids that worked in the ballpark.

"So Gregory's pitching one day and here comes Paveskovich up to

JOHN LEOVICH

Born May 5, 1918, Portland, Oregon
Ht. 6'1" Wt. 200 BR TR

MAJOR AND MINOR LEAGUE CAREER

Year	Team, League	G	AB	R	H	2B	3B	HR	RBI	BA	SA	BB	SO	SB
1941	PHILADELPHIA, American	1	2	0	1	1	0	0	0	.500	1.000	0	0	0
	Toronto, International			NO RECORD AVAILABLE										
	Wilmington-Lancaster, Interstate	54	158	8	30	1	1	0	16	.190	.209	22	14	2
1942	Portland, Pacific Coast	117	337	16	64	12	1	1	31	.190	.240	22	31	0
1943-45					MILITARY SERVICE									
1946	Bremerton, Western Intl				LESS THAN TEN GAMES									
MAJOR LEAGUE TOTALS		1	2	0	1	1	0	0	0	.500	1.000	0	0	0
MINOR LEAGUE TOTALS		172	495	24	94	13	2	1	47	.190	.230	44	45	2

bat, and the bat was bigger than he was. Gregory called me over and says, 'What's this? How do I throw to this little guy?'

"I says, 'Throw it and duck, Greg.'

"And he didn't quite believe me. Anyway, Johnny hit four terrific line drives and went 4 for 4. After the game Gregory said, 'What's that kid's name?'

"John Michael Paveskovich.

"'*What?*' he says, 'He's a pesky hitter, so his name's Johnny Pesky from now on as far as I'm concerned.'"

* * *

Leovich enjoys travelling. It was his habit to close his restaurant, "Captain John's," for two months each winter to traverse the country and look up old friends. He recently sold the restaurant and now lives a quiet, contented life in his home overlooking the Pacific, where he can see the ocean from every room in his house. He strolls down for breakfast each morning to meet with a group of friends at a local eatery and used to make the trip to Seattle each time the Boston Red Sox came to town when Johnny Pesky still travelled with the team. He remains an avid sports fan, following professional basketball and baseball closely, while refusing to live in the past. His friendships are his memories.

"I never kept any scrapbooks or anything when I was playing...you gotta look ahead. In fact, somebody asked me the other day if I'd ever played for the Athletics and I said, 'God, I'm not sure, it was that long (ago). I'd have to go home and ask my wife.'

"The thing about it, everybody that was playing baseball in those days really enjoyed playing the game for the game itself, and you had a lot of camaraderie that I don't think you have on ballclubs today. I enjoyed being part of it, even if I *was* just sitting there.

"There were a lot of great people that I met in baseball which I cherish. I thought it was great. My proudest memories are that I met a lotta nice people.

"There's an old saying I had up on my bedroom wall when I was a little kid, about what keeps you in perspective. It says, 'Fame is the scentless sunflower with a gaudy crown of gold, but friendship is a breathing rose with sweets in every fold.'"

BERT SHEPARD
Pitcher, 1945 Washington Senators

So I landed in New York and then I went down to Walter Reed Hospital to get a new [artificial] leg. While we're waiting Secretary of War Patterson asked two officers and two enlisted men that just returned from prison camp [in Germany] to come down to his office. So he sent the staff car out and I happened to be one of the prisoners [of war] that was chosen to go.

And so Patterson saw me walking on this crude artificial leg that was made in prison camp. He asked us what we wanted to do and one old farm boy from Arkansas, he says, "All I want to do is go home and get my shotgun and shoot some ducks."

Patterson come to me and I said, "Well, if I can't fly combat, I'd like to play professional baseball."
— Bert Shepard

If you are distressed by anything external, the pain is not due to the thing itself, but to your own estimate of it; and this you have the power to revoke at any moment.
— Marcus Aurelius

Problems are only opportunities in work clothes.
— Henry J. Kaiser

Baseball could no more go unaffected by World War II than any other American business. Signs of the conflict were everywhere: through rationing, travel restrictions, and the daily list of casualties in the newspaper. On the diamond, most of the great players were gone by 1944.

In their stead were men who would never have received the opportunity to play in the major leagues—and a few, like Joe Cronin, Jimmie Foxx, and Pepper Martin, who were able to extend their careers *because* of the war.

By the third year of America's involvement overseas, major league teams were looking everywhere for available manpower, or even boypower. High school sophomore Joe Nuxhall became, at 15, the second youngest player in major league history when he pitched in a game for the Cincinnati Reds. (In 1887, 14-year-old Fred Chapman hurled a complete game for Philadelphia of the major league American Association.) At the other end of the spectrum, the starting outfield for the Detroit Tigers included 40-year-old rookie Chuck Hostetler.

If age was no barrier to the prospective major league player, neither was infirmity. Cleveland outfielder Ken O'Dea was blind in one eye. Dick Sipek, who patrolled the outfield for the Cincinnati Reds, was deaf. Pete Gray was the wondrous one-armed outfielder for the St. Louis Browns.

As he sat in Undersecretary of War Robert Patterson's office on that February day in 1945, Bert Shepard had been released from a German prisoner of war camp only weeks before, following eight months of confinement after his plane had been downed during a strafing mission. The experience had cost him his right leg below the knee. Shepard's request to be offered an opportunity to return to the diamond was not entirely folly; before joining the Army as a flier the 25-year-old had spent three seasons as a minor league pitcher. Incredibly, Shepard's best days as an athlete were still ahead.

Born in Dana, Indiana, on June 28, 1920, Shepard first became interested in baseball during a visit to his grandparents' home, and he recalls listening to their radio as Pepper Martin stole seven bases against the Philadelphia Athletics in the 1931 World Series. He was soon playing baseball at every opportunity. His day would begin with pick-up games involving boys his age, followed by his shagging fly balls for the neighborhood teams.

When he reached the age of 18, Shepard played semi-professional baseball in Clinton, Indiana, where he was spotted and signed by the Chicago White Sox in 1939 and sent to Longview, Texas, for spring training. There he pitched every day out of sheer enthusiasm and inevitably developed a sore arm.

"It's amazing the lack of coaching then. Shoot, they'd let you just pitch every day if you wanted to. Then they answer after you were injured, 'Well, he *said* he was alright.'"

Shepard bounced around for the next two years, playing in Anaheim, Wisconsin Rapids, and Bisbee, Arizona, only to be released at each stop.

"I walked a lot of batters because I didn't have the right coaching and theory. Everybody said, 'Pitch to the corners.' The corner's what, three inches wide? So you're throwing a ball three inches outside. That's still accurate throwing but it caused me to walk a lot of people. As I look back now...I wasn't wild...my problem was where I was trying to throw the ball."

In May 1942, after receiving his fourth outright release in professional baseball, Shepard headed off to war.

* * *

Reporting to Daniel Field in Georgia, Shepard tried out for the base football team, even though he'd never before played, outside of an occasional pick-up game. When asked where he was from the young recruit replied, "Indiana," which was taken to mean Indiana *University*.

"I made first string fullback and all the rest of the team is college players," recalls Shepard. I went behind the barracks that night to practice the Notre Dame shift. I didn't want people to know I didn't know much about it.

"So I played one game against Clemson and got a rib hurt. Then two games later, we played Jacksonville Naval Training Station. They had six of their starting eleven out of the pro league. I intercepted three passes, made eleven clean tackles, and even gained a few yards even though we got the hell beat out of us.

"So I get back and my orders are there to go to Cadets. And the newspaper said, 'Daniel Field will miss the valuable experience of Shepard.' [Laughs.] That's the first whole game I ever played. But you don't tell people all those things. It's a good example of how people often overrate the opponent."

Transferred from Daniel Field to Santa Ana Air Base in California, Shepard was scheduled to begin training as a fighter pilot.

"I'd never been *near* an airplane. Hadn't been within a *mile* of one. So I was studying about flying...I go out with five other students to our instructor...and they've all flown before. The instructor gets to me and he says, 'Have you ever flown?'

"I said, 'This is the closest I've ever been to an airplane.'

"He said, 'Well then, I take you first.'

"You don't know [what to expect]. You're getting into something you don't know anything about. And you say, 'Well, I'm gonna give it a try.' So I see I had some skills as a pilot...I wanted to fly. I wanted to learn it. I wanted to pursue it to the fullest extent and the more I pursued it, well the more I liked it. I enjoyed flying tremendously. You're the boss. You're in a fighter aircraft, a P-38, and in a dive we could get about 525 miles an hour out of it. We could go up to 46,000 feet. And I've rolled it fifty feet off the ground in front of the tower and been grounded for a couple of days." [Laughs.]

On Christmas Eve 1943, Shepard boarded a train in Los Angeles, California, bound for New York on the first leg of a trip overseas and into combat. He was more excited than nervous.

"That's our job...you know it's leading you to combat. That's what you're trained for, and when you go into the unknown, you're anxious to get there. Like if you was taking a trip someplace and you never been there before, you'd be anxious to get there, wouldn't you?"

On January 9, Shepard and the others arrived in Scotland and after an additional six weeks of training, he joined his unit. On his 34th mission, he flew in the first daytime bombing raid over Berlin. As the weather improved, the base decided to organize a baseball team and Shepard volunteered to manage. Their first game was scheduled for May 21, 1944.

"I'd flown four out of the last five days, but on that Sunday...it was a long mission, a lot of strafing...so I figured well, I'd better fly this one because I can get out of something where maybe somebody else couldn't. So I put myself up to fly that day and I never got back for our first game.

"I was going in to strafe an aerodrome and I'm probably a mile or two away...about twenty feet off the ground. When you go in to strafe an aerodrome, they've got a hundred or two hundred automatic weapons, and they're just setting up a crossfire. Some airplanes had already strafed the field and there were some [German] planes burning so I had a good column of smoke to line up on. I didn't have to raise up to see the field.

"I'm probably a mile from the field and they shoot my right foot off. You can just feel the foot coming loose at the ankle. I called the colonel and told him I had a leg shot off and I'd call him back later. In the meantime, I get hit in the chin and that caused me to slump over the controls and the next thing I know, I'm just ready to hit the ground. I pulled back. I can't make it. The airplane crashes at 380 miles per hour, explodes, and burns.

"I wake up in a German hospital, oh hell, I don't know, two or three or four days later. I can never find out. They had the leg amputated and the gunsight had mashed in my skull over my right eye. They had removed about a two inch square piece of the frontal sinus bone over the right eye.

"I woke up fat, dumb, and happy. They talked to me a little bit, gave me a shot, and I went back to sleep."

After recovering from his injuries Shepard spent his time as a prisoner working himself back into shape. He located a book of Abraham Lincoln's letters and a biography of John McGraw.

"You do a lot of thinking [in prison camp]. You realize that when you got shot down, your family got a telegram [saying], 'Your son's missing in action.' Some of the reports might indicate you might be killed since you crashed and burned. You know that they've said some prayers for you. And anyone is happy to answer their mother's prayers, aren't they? And I figured, one of these days, I'm gonna answer her prayers."

While in prison camp, a Canadian prisoner by the name of Don Errey crafted Shepard a crude artificial leg on which he could walk surprisingly well. Shepard and Errey then located an old cricket ball and a glove and the two would play catch every day. Shepard began to test his limits; he pivoted, practiced covering first base and fielding bunts. He quickly discovered he could do a lot more than he had originally thought. The German doctor was so impressed he brought his hospital staff out to watch the American prisoner.

While Shepard was exploring the potential of his new limb, the

Red Cross regularly came through the camp to interview injured detainees and identify those unable to return to combat. Those classified as "D.U." (Definitely Unfit for combat) were made eligible for inclusion in the next trade of POWs between the Allies and the Axis. Shepard was examined by the Red Cross and cleared for repatriation at the beginning of 1945.

"January 23, we made the prisoner exchange down at the Swiss border. The Germans came over on the *Gripsholm* [the Swedish Red Cross ship employed for prisoner exchanges], to Marseille, France, and then a train to Lake Constance, I think. And they got off the train and we got on. Their greeting when they got there was a picture of Hitler and an apple.

"The Germans would try to tell us, 'New York is *kaput*,' and, 'Chicago is *kaput*. We bombed and flattened those places.' Which wasn't quite true.

"We took the train to Marseille and then came home on the *Gripsholm*. An interesting thing is [when] we came up to New York Harbor, the fireboats came out and they got the bands playing and they're escorting the *Gripsholm* in the harbor. And the band is playing the song, "Don't Fence Me In."

"I'm telling everybody, 'Isn't that clever that they wrote a song for us?' not knowing it was number one on the Hit Parade."

* * *

Undersecretary of War Patterson looked at Bert Shepard, this young man walking around on an artificial leg made by a fellow prisoner of war, and remained skeptical of his dream to play professional baseball.

Patterson said, "Well hell, you can't do that on that leg, can you?"

Shepard replied, "As soon as I get a new leg, I'm pretty *sure* I can."

Patterson telephoned Clark Griffith, a friend of his and the owner of the Washington Senators. He told Griffith, "We have a prisoner of war that just came back from Germany and lost his leg. He says that he can play pro ball."

Griffith, perhaps sensing the publicity to be gained replied, "Well after he gets his new leg, have him come out."

Four days after receiving his new artificial leg, Shepard was working out at Walter Reed Hospital when *Washington Post* sportswriter Walter Haight happened by. Haight gave Shepard a ride to the Senators' spring training complex at the University of Maryland, where he was directed to a locker room and provided a uniform. It was only as he was getting dressed that the players and Manager Ossie Bluege realized Shepard was an amputee. As he walked to the mound to throw batting practice, it was nearly impossible to tell he was wearing an artificial leg. The illusion continued as he fired the ball to the plate. He was throwing hard and it was apparent that Shepard was serious about playing and wanted to make it on his own merit, not out of any pity. Word got out that this amputee war veteran was causing a stir in the Senators' training camp and before long reporters and newsreel cameramen clogged the edge of the playing field.

At one point, a Paramount cameraman filming the workout asked Shepard if he could field bunts.

"I can field a bunt. Let me know when you're ready," replied Shepard.

The camera was set up. The Senator players all stopped and silently watched as Shepard delivered the ball to Al Evans, who bunted the ball just in front of the plate. Shepard came in, pounced on the ball, pivoted, and fired the ball to first. Then he did it again for good measure. The Washington players were abuzz. Manager Bluege, in a choked up voice, yelled, "Atta boy, Shep."

The former fighter pilot became an overnight celebrity and his workout was featured in newsreels across the country. He was the hero of Ward 49 at Walter Reed where many other amputees of the war were recovering. In *The Sporting News*, Haight called him, "The baseball man of the hour. Or the afternoon or evening."

Shepard then became a matter of dispute between Griffith and the Yankees' Larry MacPhail.

"I'm over at Secretary Patterson's office, in the afternoon [after the workout], and MacPhail came in, who was on his staff. He says, 'Bert, we got a lotta amputees over at Atlantic City. How about coming over tomorrow and work out with the Yankees? If the Senators don't sign you, I will.'"

Undersecretary Patterson's pilot picked up the war hero and took him to Atlantic City where he worked out with the Yankees. Unknown to Shepard, Griffith had scheduled him to pitch that day. When Griffith discovered where the lieutenant was and with whom, he blew sky-high, screaming, "Larry MacPhail is stealing one of my ball players!"

The War Department in an attempt to defuse the situation told Griffith that the trip had been for the morale of the soldiers and that it had been their idea, not MacPhail's. Satisfied for the moment (one wonders what Griffith would think today with a MacPhail running his old ballclub in Minnesota), the Senators' owner signed Shepard as a coach but gave every indication the war veteran would get a chance to play for the team as a pinch hitter or pitcher during the 1945 season. Griffith was quoted in the *Washington Post* as saying, "We certainly welcome Lieutenant Shepard to the club. This boy is a symbol of the courage of American youths. The same spirit that carried him into combat with our enemies is with him in baseball. He believes in himself and we believe in him." This courage was rewarded later that year when Undersecretary Patterson awarded Shepard with the Distinguished Flying Cross before a Senators game on August 31.

Shepard pitched in several exhibition games during the spring of 1945. The Senators frequently played armed forces teams, whose lineups were often more formidable than those of the wartime big league teams. The ex-fighter pilot was heavily publicized in order to inspire other veterans returning from the war in a situation similar to his.

While most definitely an inspiration, Shepard also performed well. He tossed two innings against Fort Story, giving up a run in the eighth inning before striking out the side in the ninth. He went five innings against New London Naval Base, one of the better armed forces teams, allowing only one run on three hits against a lineup that included Yogi Berra.

When the season began, Shepard served as Washington's batting practice pitcher, a role he discovered helped his control problems and contributed to his confidence in his ability. "I would pitch batting practice to the good hitters and I'd throw the ball right down the middle. They *didn't* get a hit every time. They *didn't* hit it out of the park. And so it gave me confidence in not being afraid to throw the ball over, you see."

Shepard also discovered that his artificial leg didn't seem to drastically affect his play.

"No, because you pitch off your back foot and I was left-handed and my right leg was off. So I was coming down on the right leg. And as far as batting, well I batted left-handed and Mel Ott could've had his right leg off and still hit 510 home runs."

He also allows that not having lost his right knee made a lot of difference in, for example, fielding bunts. Amputation *above* the knee, as was the case with Monty Stratton, would have made the adjustment much more difficult.

Shepard continued working on his game as he waited for the day he might be activated by the Senators. He was anxious to go on the active roster, but wasn't at all disappointed in his role with the team in light of what he'd already accomplished.

"I was so happy to be with a major league ballclub. I was pitching batting practice almost every day so I was gradually developing myself all the time. I used to take infield at first base. After Joe Kuhel would take the first two rounds, I would take the next two. And I've had people tell me that they didn't know when we changed. So that gave me good practice as far as the footwork was concerned. I bided my time. I was just as happy as the devil to be there."

* * *

The Washington Senators had finished in the American League cellar in 1944, and following the season were stripped of their only serious offensive threat when Stan Spence (who had batted .316 with 100 RBIs) went into the military. In an amazing turnaround, the Senators were in 1945 making a bid to become the first team in American League history to go from last place to first in the span of one season. (Their descendants, based in Minneapolis, would eventually be the first to turn the trick in 1991.)

Washington featured one of the most unusual starting rotations in major league history. Four of their starters, Dutch Leonard, Johnny Niggeling, Roger Wolff, and Mickey Haefner, were primarily knuckleball pitchers. Not only did they throw the pitch most of the time, they each employed a different *type* of knuckler (made possible by using different grips to release the ball) which kept Hall of Fame catcher Rick Ferrell hopping all summer. All except Leonard had mediocre careers after the war; Wolff, who went 20-10 in 1945 with an ERA well below three, injured his arm and won only six more games after that season.

The Senators' pennant hopes received a boost in July 1945 when

Buddy Lewis rejoined the team following his stint in the military. Like the Tigers' Hank Greenberg, who had returned earlier that season, Lewis had been drafted prior to Pearl Harbor and his four-year hitch was over before the end of the war. An Army fighter-pilot like Shepard, he had once received a reprimand for buzzing Griffith Stadium during a Senators doubleheader. The 29-year-old outfielder played six years with Washington before joining the Army, never batting below .291 while scoring 100 or more runs four times and averaging 11 triples a year. After his return he batted .333 over the final 69 games of the 1945 season.

The team also seemed to have cause for celebration with the return of shortstop Cecil Travis in September. During the 1941 season, while Ted Williams was batting .406 and Joe DiMaggio was hitting in 56 straight, it was Travis who led the American League in base hits and who finished second, three points ahead of DiMaggio with a .359 batting average. A .327 lifetime hitter before the war who had only once batted below .302 in his nine-year career, Travis proved of little help on his return as severe frostbite in his feet limited his effectiveness. He retired two years later at the age of 34.

Washington also boasted one of the fastest men in the world in its outfield, five-time American League stolen base king George Case. Occasionally, the Senators would promote special races involving Case including, when both men were in their thirties, a race across the outfield against Jesse Owens. His speed impressed everyone, including Shepard.

"He was *fast*. I talked to a track man in Washington, D.C., and he said that if George Case woulda had training, he could've set records as a track man. He said, 'I don't think anybody could gain on George after he got going.'"

Another of Shepard's fond memories of that time concerns the occasional Griffith Stadium appearances of Washington's biggest baseball legend, Walter Johnson.

"A wonderful man. Gentle as they come. He came out there at the Senators' ballpark and of course everybody's in awe of him. He just threw a few on the sidelines in his street clothes and [Ossie] Bluege, the manager, he said, 'I bet he could still fire them if he had to.'

"Walter Johnson never swore and his catcher, Muddy Ruel, never swore. And Joe Judge, who used to play first base with them, told me they'd be out on the mound in a tight situation and Walter would say,

'Well goodness *gracious*, Muddy, I don't know what to do!' And Muddy'd say, 'Well *dadgummit*, Walter!'

With the major league All-Star game a victim of wartime travel restrictions in 1945, a series of exhibitions were set up across the country to benefit the war relief effort. In cities with two teams (New York, Chicago, Philadelphia, Boston, and St. Louis), contests were arranged between their American and National League representatives. The Senators, without a natural geographical rival, were matched with the Brooklyn Dodgers. The exhibitions were a rousing success, raising nearly a quarter of a million dollars. The largest gathering was in Chicago where more than 47,000 gathered for the contest between the Cubs and White Sox. In Boston, which had been scheduled to hold the aborted 1945 All-Star game, 44 fans donated $1,000 each to sit in box seats.

More than 23,000 fans arrived at Griffith Stadium on the evening of July 10, knowing that Shepard was to be the starting pitcher against the Dodgers. Shepard met with the press and kibitzed with Brooklyn manager Leo Durocher during pre-game festivities and all was well until "The Lip" opened his mouth one too many times.

"Durocher, trying to be gracious, said something that didn't help. Leo and I were standing there talking together, the press taking pictures and interviewing both of us. One reporter asked Leo if they were gonna bunt against me.

"Leo says, 'I'll fine anybody $500 that bunts tonight, 'cause we need the batting practice.'

"But the sportswriters wrote it up as 'Leo Durocher, The Good Hearted Manager Agreed Not to Bunt Against Shepard.' So everybody thought I couldn't field bunts."

After walking Durocher to lead off the game, a fired-up Shepard allowed only one more base runner over the next three innings. Having shut out the Dodgers to that point, Shepard asked Ossie Bluege if he could pitch another inning and the Senator manager consented. He gave up two runs in the fourth on four successive singles, none of which were hit particularly hard, and was awarded the victory when the Senators picked up a run in the bottom of the inning to take the lead for good.

On August 4 the Senators, still in the thick of the pennant race, were in the process of being routed in the second game of a double-header against the Boston Red Sox. Running out of available pitchers, they brought in Shepard to halt what was already a 12-run fourth inning. The bases were loaded as he came to the mound in relief of Joe Cleary (ironically pitching in *his* only major league game, he left the game with a career ERA of 189.00—the highest in history) and Manager Bluege handed the young left-hander the ball. It was the moment Shepard had been waiting for all his life.

"I said, 'Here's my chance.' George Metkovich was the first hitter...and I got the count to three and two and I said, 'Hell, now you got to throw the ball *over*. You don't want to come in here and walk him.'"

He didn't. Shepard reared back and fired strike three past Metkovich and left the mound to a standing ovation. He finished the game, pitching five and one-third innings, allowing only one run and three hits. Elated after the performance, Shepard was sure he would now receive an opportunity to pitch on a regular basis, but he didn't play in another game that season. He never attempted to ask why.

"That's a question you wouldn't ask. We were fighting for the pennant and being very successful and we had some pretty good pitchers. It's hard for the manager to imagine that his best chance of winning today is a guy with his leg off. You just can't imagine that. It didn't bother *me*, but I can see where the other person would have a problem believing that could happen."

Despite his infrequent appearances Shepard was fully accepted as part of the team, as evidenced by his being on the receiving end of his share of pranks pulled by his teammates.

Once, his teammates falsely led him to believe that Cleveland Indians pitcher Jim Bagby wanted to meet him. He went, only to discover that Bagby was afflicted with a harelip that rendered his speech difficult to understand. Shepard's teammates stood around trying not to laugh at their practical joke, while they watched him attempt to decipher the Cleveland pitcher's conversation.

Another time, Joe Kuhel arranged a phony appointment for a non-existent high school newspaper reporter to interview Shepard. Then the rest of the team went to dinner before returning to the hotel to see how long it would take for the pitcher to realize that the "reporter" wasn't going to show.

Shepard gained his revenge against Kuhel that winter. The Senators' first baseman was well known for his sartorial splendor, so Shepard phoned Kuhel's wife and posed as a *Life* magazine reporter writing a story on baseball's best dressed players, which was to include her husband. Then he showed up at Kuhel's doorstep to see his reaction when the ballplayer realized he had been duped.

Although these pranks might seem cruel, they indicated a player's acceptance by his peers. It was something that another player of that era, in a position similar to Shepard's, never learned. He was Pete Gray, the remarkable one-armed outfielder for the St. Louis Browns. Quite naturally, Shepard was often paired with the sullen St. Louis left fielder in photographs and articles.

"Pete could have been such an outstanding celebrity and ball player had he had a different personality. I've heard ball players say, 'Goddam him, he's always asking me to do something and I never heard him say "thank you".'

"I went to room with a player and after about a week he said, 'I've got a confession to make. I never realized how beautiful the word "thank you" was until I met you. A couple of years ago, I roomed with Pete Gray in the minor leagues and it was 'Hand me this…hand me that…carry this…carry that.' And he said, 'Never once did I hear the words, 'Thank you.'

"'When I heard you was coming to room with me, I said, 'There's another damned amputee. Why do I get them all?'"

* * *

Going into the final days of the 1945 season, the Senators were within striking range of Detroit but their season was ending early, with a doubleheader against Philadelphia, while the Tigers and the rest of the American League continued for another week. (One version of the story goes that Washington owner Clark Griffith had not anticipated his team contending for the pennant, so he requested that the Senators be allowed to end their season early so that he could squeeze another week's rent out of Griffith Stadium's other tenant, the Washington Redskins.)

In the Senators' first game of that season-ending doubleheader versus Philadelphia, the teams battled for 11 innings to a 3-3 standoff under overcast skies. The sun finally made an appearance in the bottom of the inning but as Washington outfielder George Binks took his position at the top of the 12th, he neglected to take his sunglasses with him. Sure enough, a fly ball went to Binks and while he, as newspaper accounts described, "gave a fine impression of a man chasing bees as the sun blinded him," the ball fell safely for a double. George Kell then singled into the corner and Philadelphia won the game, dealing a severe blow to Washington's pennant hopes.

At the same time, Detroit was not playing particularly well and the Tigers were stung by criticism that they were "backing into" the pennant. Nevertheless, they went into their final two games against the St. Louis Browns needing but a single victory to capture the flag.

Virgil Trucks, fresh out of the Navy, was chosen by the Tigers to make his first start of the season, but it rained. And it rained. And then it rained some more. Finally, after three days, Detroit and St. Louis were scheduled to meet in a doubleheader to close out the regular season.

Despite Trucks' fine performance, the Tigers were trailing 3-2 in the ninth inning of the first game and facing the specter of having to win the second game or board a train to Washington for a play-off to determine the American League champion.

Detroit loaded the bases in the ninth against St. Louis screwballer Nels Potter and then Hank Greenberg sent a shot into the bleachers, just inside the foul pole for a grand slam and a pennant for Detroit. The teams began the second game, but the rain returned minutes after the game started and washed out that contest. The Senators had come close. Washington would finish fourth in 1946 but after that, never again would a team based in the nation's capital finish in the first division.

* * *

Shepard stayed busy during the off-season, visiting veteran's and children's hospitals and making a training film for leg amputees just back from the war. He barnstormed that winter with the American League All-Stars and later reported to the Senators for spring training in 1946. He pitched in a couple of exhibition games, registering six scoreless innings, but with the stars returning from the war he wasn't given a serious chance of making the team. Instead, he remained with Washington as a coach.

"They'd say, 'What's our future in a guy with his leg off?' I wasn't getting to play and I didn't get on the regular active list, so then I asked to go down to Chattanooga and finish the season."

There Shepard won two and lost two on the mound and surprised everyone by hitting a double and scoring from second on a single to left field.

Once again, he barnstormed during the winter of 1946 with the American League All-Stars, playing through the Pacific Northwest. He pitched occasionally, but actually preferred playing first base because there he could play every day; even before losing his leg in the war, Shepard had always played the outfield or first base in addition to his pitching duties.

He was having a successful tour in 1946 and looked forward to a visit to the Northwest by Bob Feller's All-Stars, probably the top barnstorming team that winter.

"In Calgary, I hit two home runs, and I was really enjoying playing first base. We played Feller's All-Stars in Seattle and I saw that I wasn't in the lineup. I said, *'Hey*, wait a minute. How come I'm not playing tonight?'

"They said, 'Well, Feller's out there and he has to bear down and we're afraid you might get hurt.'

"I said, 'Look, you guys, I've done everything I'm supposed to do up till now and, by God, I'm *playing*.' So I played first base, made a couple pretty good plays and I got one for two off of Feller and I got one for two off of Johnny Sain."

The next season, Shepard was visiting Griffith Stadium, having undergone some planned reconstructive surgery on his leg, and ran into Yogi Berra for the first time since that 1945 exhibition game between Washington and New London Naval Base.

"I'm on crutches, not wearing the prosthesis, and I'm sitting down talking to [Yankee infielder] Bobby Brown, because he was studying to be a doctor. He was real interested in the amputation and so forth.

"Yogi Berra come by and so Brown introduced me to Yogi. I told Yogi that I was very glad to meet him, but I said, 'I pitched against you in 1945. I was the left-handed pitcher that started for the Senators when we played you up in New London.'

"'Oh,' he said, 'No shit. It's too bad that you lost your leg because you looked like a pretty good pitcher.'

"I said, 'Well I had it off then, Yogi.'

"He couldn't believe it. So I thought that was a pretty good compliment: that I'd pitched five innings against him and he didn't know I had an artificial leg."

* * *

In November 1946, Shepard checked into Walter Reed Hospital for additional reconstructive surgery. The doctors in the German hospital had done the preliminary work, leaving the remaining surgery to be completed on his return to the States. The re-amputation should have had a recovery time of six weeks but there were complications that led to four more operations. He was on crutches for two and a half years before receiving medical clearance to play and by that time his shoulder muscles had tightened so much that his arm never fully recovered. Shepard took a job in 1949 as manager of the class "B" team in Waterbury, Connecticut.

He registered a 5-6 record on the mound that year in addition to his managerial duties and also played nearly 50 games at first base, hitting four home runs and driving in 21 in only 131 at bats. Two of his home runs came in one game on July 6 against Bristol. He also *stole* five bases during the year and excited the crowd by beating out a bunt for a base hit. While managing that season, Shepard encountered a young pitcher who might have reminded him of himself as a young man, struggling with control problems in Longview, Texas, back in 1939.

Waterbury needed pitching help, so Shepard phoned Hank Greenberg, who was running the Cleveland Indians' minor league system at the time, and asked if he had any pitchers with a live arm on whom he'd given up. Greenberg sent a pitcher named Bob Muhr, with the disclaimer that, "he always walks the ballpark." Shepard had a plan in mind for taming the wild hurler.

"Muhr came to the club and I started him a couple nights later and he went about an inning, and he'd walk about six or seven and so I took him out. I told him, 'I like what I saw. I'll start you in four days.'

"He said, 'You're starting me *again?*'

"I said, 'Sure, everything looked good to me.'

"So he went about four innings the next time out. I says, 'Okay, prepare yourself to start in another four days. You're improving, you look good.' Then I had a talk with him. I said, 'What are you trying to do here when you pitch?'

"He said, 'In that situation I try to hit the low outside corner.'

"I said, 'What if the other manager gave everybody the take sign?

You would walk *everybody* if you threw the ball where you're trying to throw it. Even if you make perfect pitches. You've got great stuff. Why don't you try throwing to the center of the plate, and if you're six inches off either way, you still have a strike. You don't have to be afraid of throwing the ball over.'

"He went about six or seven innings the next time. And then he won ten straight for me. Oh, he was tough. He went to spring training the next year, and didn't make it because I'm sure the manager says, 'Oh hell, he's wild,' and sent him home."

* * *

Bert Shepard remained in Waterbury for only one season before deciding to retire, passing on the opportunity to continue as a manager because of the tenuous nature of the profession. He attempted a comeback in 1952, playing for four different teams, and later took a job managing a semi-pro team in Willistown, North Dakota. The Willistown ballclub featured a speedy second baseman Shepard thought was a major league prospect. He remembers that the ball player, "could really run, but never got a chance to prove himself." The young infielder was Mike Ilitch and while he never received an opportunity in baseball, he amassed a fortune with his pizza franchise Little Caesar's. Ilitch did eventually reach the major leagues in August 1992—by buying the Detroit Tigers from rival pizza baron Tom Monaghan.

In 1955, Shepard was working out with Los Angeles and Hollywood of the Pacific Coast League, hoping for an opportunity to sign with someone when he was offered a contract by the Modesto Reds of the California League.

Pitching in the first game of a doubleheader against Reno the day after his signing, Shepard surrendered two runs in the first inning before settling down and picking up a complete game victory. No Reno base runner advanced past second base after the first inning. As he was being interviewed between games, the fans crowded around him and urged him to pitch the second game, a plea Shepard good-naturedly brushed aside, saying, "Perhaps later in the season."

Later didn't come as that complete game victory proved his last hurrah. In two more starts, he was blasted for 12 runs in two and one-third innings. Hanging up the spikes for good, Shepard finally headed into private life and jumped into the world outside baseball in

BERT SHEPARD

Born June 28, 1920, Dana, Indiana
Ht. 5'11" Wt. 185   BL TL

MAJOR AND MINOR LEAGUE CAREER

Year	Team, League	W-L	Pct	G	GS	CG	SHO	IP	H	R	ER	BB	SO	ERA
1939	Jeanerette, Evangeline				DID NOT PITCH									
1940	Wisconsin Rapids, WI St	3-2	.600	9	—	2	—	43	44	34	29	48	25	6.06
1941	Anaheim, California	0-1	.000	3	—	—	—	11	—	—	—	—	—	—
	Bisbee, Arizona-Texas	3-5	.375	30	—	—	—	73	102	82	67	51	36	8.25
1942-44					MILITARY SERVICE									
1945	WASHINGTON, American	0-0	—	1	0	0	0	5.1	3	1	1	1	2	1.69
1946	Chattanooga, Southern Assn	2-2	.500	7	5	1	0	29	34	31	24	27	8	7.45
1947-48					DID NOT PITCH									
1949	Waterbury, Colonial (Mgr)	5-6	.455	20	9	4	0	73	97	65	50	44	21	6.16
1950-51					DID NOT PITCH									
1952	St. Augustine, Fl St (Mgr)	2-2	.500	4	—	2	0	22	28	18	11	8	10	4.50
	Paris, Big State	0-0	—	3	—	0	0	5	14	7	7	4	1	12.60
	Corpus Christi, Gulf Coast			LESS THAN 45 INNINGS – NO RECORD										
	Hot Springs, Cotton States	1-3	.250	5	—	2	—	27	—	—	—	—	—	—
1953	Tampa, Florida Inter-national	0-0	—	2	—	—	—	2	—	—	—	—	—	—
1954					DID NOT PITCH									
1955	Modesto, California	1-1	.500	3	3	1	0	9.1	20	14	13	5	2	12.54
	MAJOR LEAGUE TOTALS	0-0	—	1	0	0	0	5.1	3	1	1	1	2	1.69
	MINOR LEAGUE TOTALS	17-22	.436	86	—	—	—	294.1	—	—	—	—	—	—

the same way he had played the game: asking for no special favors and fully confident of success.

"I went to work for IBM, but before I started, the guy said, 'Well, I think you'd make a pretty good typewriter salesman, Bert, but you gotta walk upstairs and carry that typewriter and I don't think you can do it.'

"I said, 'I tell you what. You go get your strongest salesman in New York. We'll put one under each arm and start walking down Fifth Avenue and I'll bet you $100 he puts his down first.' I got the job.

"When I went to work at Hughes Aircraft, the guy says, 'Yeah Bert, I got a good job here for you but it's too bad, you have to walk all over the plant and I know you can't do it.'

"I said, 'Well, I walked eighteen holes of golf Saturday. I pitched nine innings of baseball yesterday. Do you have to be in better shape than that?'

"He said, 'What the hell am I worried about? C'mon and go to work.'

"But you see, who else could challenge the employer that way? Even though I didn't make any money in baseball, the reputation that I developed, and the confidence that I developed bein' able to play, enabled me to get jobs."

Shepard worked as a safety engineer for Hughes Aircraft and several Southern California insurance companies. He also worked in the same capacity for Fluor Construction in both Saudi Arabia and Venezuela before retiring in 1983. He is a two-time National Amputee Golf champion, winning the title in 1968 and 1971, and plays with a four handicap while stalking the course on an artificial ankle he has developed that allows him to walk 36 holes in complete comfort.

Shepard is proud that he was viewed as an inspiration to other amputees and still encounters those who were helped by the stories of his success. He has always made himself available to help others dealing with the loss of a leg. Among those he has aided in the past was Hall of Famer Joe Tinker, at the time going through severe depression after undergoing an amputation in 1947. Clark Griffith wrote Shepard of the hard time Tinker was having and urged him to write the old ball player as encouragement and to offer advice on using an artificial leg, which he did. Tinker wrote back, "Dear Bert, Your fine letter received and I don't know how to thank you. As it is just what I wanted to know about my leg—now I feel I do not have to worry about my loss. I can carry on just the same as you boys that went over."

More recently, Shepard received a phone call from a man who had never met him, but knew of his story.

"He's seventy-eight years old and they had to cut his leg off. I could tell over the phone that he was hurting. Really suffering. And he lived in San Bernardino, about forty miles away, and I thought well I'll go down and see him a week or two later. But I could tell he was suffering. So I said, 'Hell, I'm gonna come down now.'

"So I hopped in the car and went down and took some tools with me and some things to help him.

"Say somebody put a sharp nail in your shoe and you had to walk with it for a month. You'd give anything for somebody to take it out, wouldn't you? And that's just the way that amputee was. I wanted to do whatever I could to help him."

Shepard's outlook on his "misfortune" in losing his leg is that it isn't misfortune at all.

"When Karen, my daughter, was ten, she and I were sitting on the bed and I had the [artificial] leg off. And she said, 'Daddy, I'm sorry that you lost your leg.'

"I said, 'Well, Karen, I'm not. If I hadn't lost my leg, I wouldn't have met your mother and I wouldn't have you. And I wouldn't take anything in the world for you.' And that's the way to look at things.

"I've always enjoyed the situation of competition. I've never been *afraid* to fail. Then, of course, I've had a couple other setbacks, losing a leg and so forth, and I found that wasn't as bad as I thought it'd be. I felt that I could've done a pretty good job [for the Senators] had I had the opportunity. But I'm sure a lotta ballplayers feel the same way.

"When the Germans interrogated me and they asked me to answer some questions and I wouldn't do it, I said, 'When I went into pilot training and came over here to combat, I was willing to accept whatever consequences happened.' You take whatever happens and do the best with it that you can."

RON NECCIAI

Pitcher, 1952 Pittsburgh Pirates

I've seen a lot of baseball in my time. There have only been two young pitchers I was certain were destined for greatness, simply because they had the meanest fastball a batter can face. One of those boys was Dizzy Dean. The other is Ron Necciai. And Necciai is harder to hit.
> —Branch Rickey
> quoted in *Branch Rickey*
> by Murray Polner

He had a curveball that, if Ted Williams was standing right here, I'd say, "Ted, put two strikes on ya with Necciai on the hill...and you're out. Strikeout. Here it comes."
> —former teammate Bill Koski

You always figure you're young. That was the most difficult part for me...after I'd hurt my arm...that one day came the realization that it was never gonna get better. But up until that time, it's always, "Hey, I'm young. You know, I'm twenty years old. This is gonna heal. Young people don't stay hurt forever, they get better." Then one day you realize that, no, maybe you wouldn't.
> —Ron Necciai

Every year, players pop up out of nowhere in baseball, sure as spring, promising to make fans forget Babe Ruth and Walter Johnson and re-write the record books in the process.

Then the season begins.

Most of these "phenoms" are quickly forgotten. Some fatal flaw in their talents is exposed and exploited by opponents until it becomes difficult to recall what was at all impressive about them in the first place.

Yet a few of these players created such a sensation that they are remembered; sometimes in awe of their talent, sometimes in derision regarding their failure. But they *are* remembered. These players are the stuff of baseball legend, the tales of their exploits and "what might have been" echoing between generations. They are also a reminder that life *isn't* always fair.

In the summer of 1955, a sore-armed pitcher sat in the stands watching his minor league teammates play a game in Waco, Texas. Two years before, he had attempted to rush his arm into shape following his discharge from the Army, leaving him with a torn rotator cuff to show for his efforts. After an aborted comeback attempt in 1953 he was forced to sit out the entire 1954 season, unable to throw more than two or three pitches before pain forced him to stop. Now, Ron Necciai felt that he had reached the end of the line.

"I just decided, 'To *hell* with it. I give up.' I wasn't gonna stay there the rest of my life...sit on the bench and work out before the games then change clothes and go watch in the stands. I decided I better go find something else.

"It was pretty tough for awhile. You're kinda lost and wanta go hide, really. You're young. You finally got to the big leagues and you've only been there a month or two and all of a sudden, your arm's *gone* — the thing that got ya there. And you can't figure out *why*. You say, '*Why me?* What the hell did *I* do?' I've never had a sore arm all that time, and I get one sore arm and it lasts a *lifetime*."

Just three years before, Ron Necciai had been on top of the world. Just three years before, he'd picked up his first big league victory and Branch Rickey was comparing him to Dizzy Dean and Christy Mathewson. Just three years before, he had struck out 27 batters in a minor league no-hitter.

At the age of 23, the dream was over.

* * *

Sports was a natural outlet for a young man in western Pennsylvania at the time Ron Necciai was growing up. Sports was practically the only way a young man could escape life in the steel mills of Monongahela and Gallatin, two towns straddling the Monongahela River just upstream from Pittsburgh, where Necciai has lived all his life. The region has been hit hard in recent years by the decline in the steel industry but even at the conclusion of World War II, when the demand for steel brought prosperity to the area and the mills operated in 24 hour shifts, there were not unlimited opportunities for a young man seeking a different kind of life. While Necciai loved living in Monongahela, he definitely wanted a different life than the mills had to offer.

"You just go in every morning at seven o'clock and you do the same thing all day until three-thirty. And you go home and you go back the next day...and that's it. It was heavy industry. You worked and you either bend springs or bend axles or load them or unload them or lubricate them or assemble them...but it's all basically the same thing. I wasn't there very long. But I was there long enough to know that I didn't want to be there forever."

Necciai's opportunity to escape the mills presented itself when he tagged along with a friend to a Pittsburgh Pirate tryout camp. Although he had never before given any consideration to playing baseball professionally, Necciai engaged one of the scouts in conversation and convinced the man to come out and watch *him* play, which eventually resulted in his being offered a contract by Pittsburgh in 1950 as a first baseman.

George Detore, the manager for the Class-D team in Salisbury, North Carolina, where Necciai was assigned by the Pirates, quickly switched the skinny kid from first base to the pitcher's mound after he got a look at the youngster's throws to second base on the first-short-first double play. The teenager's lack of foot speed and his inability to hit curveballs made Detore's decision easy.

The conversion was anything but an immediate success and at one point Necciai left the team and went home.

"I really don't know why I did that at the time. Maybe I was homesick. Maybe I didn't think I could play ball for a living or something. I really don't know. And to this day, I still don't know. It's just one of those things you do when you're young and impulsive."

The steel mills quickly cured the young pitcher's impulsiveness and Necciai returned to Salisbury, only to continue losing. He found himself on the verge of being released. He had attempted without success to master a curveball and made no progress until Detore suggested a technique where the ball is actually released backwards, with the *back* of the hand facing the batter as the ball rolls off of the fingertips. The pitcher snaps his wrist at the release point in the same manner as one does with a yo-yo.

"We tried it and started really at six feet...ten feet...fifteen feet. Twenty feet, thirty feet, forty feet. Till I finally got that thing where I could really turn it over and throw it. We used to call it a 'drop.' Straight up and down. I found that I could throw it backwards easier and it was a whole lot more effective. It looked like a fastball but went straight down."

It was a pitch that not only "dropped," it *exploded* in its downward arc toward the plate. After having lost his first seven decisions for Salisbury, the kid with the funny drop pitch struck out 17 batters in a one-hit shutout for his first professional victory. The legend of Ron Necciai's curveball had begun.

Soon after Necciai had unveiled his new pitch, Pittsburgh's minor league director, Branch Rickey, Jr., visited Salisbury, and the kid with the unusual curveball caught his eye. Rickey, son of the Pirates' legendary general manager, took the 19-year-old aside and impressed upon him that he was too talented to be pitching in a "D" league. If he got his act together, Rickey said he'd show Necciai where he could pitch and "make some real money."

A winning streak earned him a promotion to New Orleans of the Southern Association, the Pirates' Double A affiliate for the remainder of the 1951 season, and although he struggled there, he showed enough to earn an invitation to De Land, Florida, site of Pittsburgh's annual fall camp for their best prospects.

De Land proved to be a big turning point for Necciai, as he impressed the Pittsburgh brass and put himself in a good position to make the team the next spring. Always a self-described "worry-wart," the teenager began to have physical problems while in San Bernardino for 1952 spring training after realizing that he was indeed on the verge of making the major league club. He couldn't eat and was losing weight...weight he couldn't afford to lose. He was spitting up blood.

Diagnosed as suffering from severe ulcers, Necciai was placed on a strict regimen designed to ease his ailing stomach and enable him to regain his strength. Branch Rickey, Sr., offered him the choice of locations where he could round into shape. Knowing that Detore had moved from Salisbury to Bristol of the Class-D Appalachian League, Necciai chose the little Tennessee border town as the venue for his recovery.

"I went there, and they said, 'Fine, you'll only be there for awhile, and then we'll move you as your health progresses and you get yourself back into shape.'"

No one had any inkling that Ron Necciai was about to shake up the baseball world.

* * *

Pitchers in the Pirate organization loved to play for Detore, but for Necciai it was more than that. The ex-minor league catcher and Cleveland Indian infielder was almost like a father to him.

The veteran manager would tell Necciai stories about Ted Williams, who was a teenager himself when he and Detore were teammates on the old San Diego Padres of the Pacific Coast League. He told Necciai that he had the same kind of talent; that he could make it all the way to the major leagues. He always boosted the young man's confidence, helping him to relax and concentrate on his mound duties. He and catcher Harry Dunlop devised a plan where Necciai was to simply pitch and leave the game plan to the manager and his receiver. Just throw to the glove.

Necciai was impressed by his manager's patience, persistence, and competitive nature. He never allowed him to get down on himself. Detore treated all his young charges with the same attention and respect and his players returned the favor. They wanted to win for this man. There was never any question whom Necciai wanted to play for during his recovery; he just felt fortunate the Pirates allowed him to return under Detore's tutelage.

Despite the physical maladies that at first limited his appearances, Necciai's performances for Bristol began attracting attention as he accumulated strikeouts at a record pace. He fanned 20 and 19 in back-to-back games. One evening Detore brought him in from the bullpen against Johnson City in the seventh inning with the bases loaded and nobody out. He struck out the side — and the next eight in a row, his streak of 11 consecutive strikeouts breaking the 42-year-old minor league record of Harry Ables. On May 13, 1952, Necciai grabbed his piece of immortality, striking out 27 batters in a no-hitter against the Welch Miners. (It was the first of *five* no-hitters authored by Bristol pitchers that season: Bill Bell tossed three himself...two of them in consecutive starts, and Frank Ramsey tossed another the day after Bell's third of the year.) It was the equivalent of a golfer knocking in back-to-back-to-back holes in one. Necciai had seemingly taken the art of pitching to an unprecedented level.

Only four Welch batters reached base that night: one on a walk, another by error, a third was hit by a pitch, and the fourth reached base when the ball eluded catcher Harry Dunlop on a swinging third strike with two out in the ninth. Once again, he struck out 11 in a row, tying his own mark of just a few days before, a record that had previously stood for over four decades.

In all, 17 of the 27 strikeouts came on swinging strikes, including the last three in a row. Welch's Bob Kendrick went into the record books as the final unfortunate strikeout victim. Necciai had shattered the previous Appalachian League record for strikeouts in a game, raising the standard by six, and also broke the previous professional record of 25 strikeouts, set by Clarence "Hooks" Iott in 1941.

To this day, Necciai remembers very little about the biggest night of his professional career.

"In those days, I *did* have a lot of health problems and that was one of the reasons for being there. I was there on a kind of a [health] regimen...and to learn to pitch the proper way. George and Harry had a game plan in which I was to throw so many pitches at so many given times. They'd feed me melba toast and cottage cheese and milk between innings, that was the accepted cure in those days for ulcers.

"I wasn't feeling good that night and I was a little bit worried about my stomach. It was burning and I used to take these little black Banthine pills. I was more concerned with not throwing up and having stomach pains than anything else.

"You also have to realize this was not 27 men in a row, which would make you cognizant of everything. You hit one...you walk one...a guy hits a ball. There's *action*. So it's not like Don Larsen in the World Series, everybody up and down.

"There never was a point where I realized how many I struck out. I realized that I had a no-hitter in about the seventh or eighth inning when the guys and the fans started counting. Everybody kept saying, 'We don't want to jinx you, but nobody's got a base hit yet.' They were looking for a no-hitter 'cause we had Bill Bell on the ballclub. I'd never thrown a professional no-hitter.... I wasn't really looking for that. I wasn't really paying that much attention.

"We knew what happened *after* the game, but we didn't think anything about it 'cause after all, this is 1952. You figure *somebody* certainly has done this before.

"The next morning, the phone started ringing. The little gal, Audrey, who ran the ballclub office started calling and saying, 'Hey, this newspaper's on and this radio station's on and this magazine's on and everybody wants to interview you and talk to you about this and that, because its never been done.' Then it caused a commotion."

In *The Sporting News*, a feature article, complete with a photograph of "Rocket Ron" graced the inside pages, along with two other stories about the event and the man in the spotlight. Detore was quoted as saying, 'Of all the pitchers I've seen in the big leagues, Necciai more closely resembles [Dizzy] Dean because of his long arms and speed.' Offers poured in from all over the country for interviews and appearances on television.

"I got real smart real quick to find out which one of them was trying to use you or which one of them was being honest with you. You find that out in a big hurry."

More than 5,000 people, including Branch Rickey, Jr., were shoe-horned into Shaw Stadium for Necciai's next start and after that two-hit, 24-strikeout effort (including a record five strikeouts in *one inning*), it was obvious there was nothing left for The Rocket to accomplish in Bristol. He was promoted to Burlington of the Class-B Carolina League, leaving behind some incredible statistics. Necciai had won all four games he started (he also made two relief appearances), pitching a total of 42⅔ innings. He tossed three shutouts, surrendered only ten base hits and struck out *109* batters. His final ERA was 0.42. Sixty-five percent of the batters that came to the plate against him struck out.

At Burlington Necciai continued to dominate. Despite a record of only 7-9 for the last place team, he led the league with a 1.57 ERA and 172 strikeouts in his 18 appearances. He was the winning pitcher in the Carolina League All-Star Game. He broke "Vinegar Bend" Mizell's league record for consecutive strikeouts. In 169 minor league innings between Bristol and Burlington, Necciai had *averaged* 15 strikeouts per nine innings.

One morning, Burlington Manager Jerry Gardner called Necciai and said, "Pack your bags. You're going up to the Pirates."

"They handed me a piece of paper and away I went. I'd talked to Mr. Rickey. He'd called me a few days before and told me they were getting ready to bring me up. I was tickled to death. I was *ready* to go. I *wanted* to go. And of course, that was home. I lived nearby...twenty miles from the ballpark. I was anxious to go. I wanted to go to the big leagues and see if I could do any good."

* * *

One of the amazing things about Ron Necciai is that for a man whose anxieties resulted in bleeding ulcers, he never seemed to let his distress affect his performance on the mound.

"I had the problem before the game even started," says Necciai today. "I was always a worry-wart anyhow. Not anymore. I think since I left baseball, I haven't worried about anything," he says laughingly. "No, not true. But anyway, I don't worry. I *was* a worry-wart, and still am to a degree, but I think that was it, it was bothering me before the game."

In fact, his stomach had so bothered him the day of his 27-strikeout performance that he almost didn't play. George Detore finally persuaded him to give it a try, explaining to him that if his stomach objected, he could always take him out of the game.

"It's one of those days, if he'd said, 'Go home,' might never have been."

At Burlington, he roomed with Bill Koski, who remarked that on nights before Necciai was scheduled to pitch he would keep Koski up until four in the morning talking about the game, smoking cartons of cigarettes and trying to improve his pick-off move up in their room.

"I kept them all up, all night long. I don't know if I dwelled on the game. Yeah, I guess maybe. Got myself all hyped up or something. But he's right. I probably taught all my roommates how to smoke, 'cause I could get five of them going at a time. I really could. I used to sneak in the dugout in between pitches and innings and everything else. I was really a smoker."

Over time, after his retirement from baseball, the ulcers slowly disappeared.

"I stayed on a diet and maybe [they disappeared because of] new medicines. They always used to say, you get ulcers from what's eating you, not what you're eating. It died down and maybe I *was* tense and tight and…too hot under the collar, whatever. Maybe that *was* it. But over time it went away. I haven't had a problem in years and years and years. In fact I think, they probably went away when I stopped smoking many years ago."

* * *

The 1952 edition of the Pittsburgh Pirates has been widely considered among the worst teams of all time. By August of that year it seemed that bringing in rookies like Ron Necciai and Bill Bell, who had received a lot of publicity for their minor league feats, certainly couldn't hurt the team and might provide a shot in the arm at the box office.

How to best describe the atmosphere in the clubhouse of a team more than 50 games out of first place? Necciai knows about the experience firsthand.

"It's survival, man. You worry about *yourself.* You don't look around …you're not worried about anybody else. You're worried about how well *you* do. It might be a team sport, but they're not gonna pay the pitcher on how many home runs 'Joe Green' hits. You're trying your damnedest to get yourself a spot for next year. That's really what *we* were doing."

Of course, when promising rookies arrive to play for a bad ballclub, they often face unrealistic expectations, especially when they've struck out 27 batters in one game. The fans, starving for a hero on a ballclub that needed a dugout full of them, expected the rookie to continue his strikeout pace in the big leagues.

What made Necciai's potential so tantalizing was that he had his great stuff almost every time out. It was the other ingredient in a pitcher's success that eluded him most often.

"I had control problems and I guess I lost some confidence. Control was the thing. It's the secret to being a pitcher, and there was a difference. I never professed to be a pitcher. I was listed on the lineup as a pitcher, but I was a thrower. And there's a big difference between a thrower and a pitcher. I had a tendency to just go to hell. I could throw ten strikes in a row and eighteen balls in a row."

So nervous he smoked three packs of cigarettes in the clubhouse an hour before the game, Necciai made his major league debut on August 10 against the Chicago Cubs. Later complaining of his inability to get his curveball to spin, the rookie right-hander was tagged for five runs in the first inning, but Manager Billy Meyer left him in the game and he settled down. He was eventually lifted for a pinch hitter in the bottom of the sixth with the Cubs leading 7-3.

In interviews after the game Necciai was clearly disgusted with his performance and volunteered to pitch in relief the next night against Cincinnati. He didn't allow a hit while striking out five of the ten men he faced and later commented that he had never had better stuff on the mound than he did that night against the Reds, even in his famous 27-strikeout game. Pirate catcher Joe Garagiola couldn't stop raving about the kid from Monongahela.

His next start came on August 15 and it was highlighted by one of his most cherished memories: his one big league base hit.

"I remember it real well. It was in St. Louis and the guy pitching was Al Clark. I hit a ball between his legs into center field for a base hit, and I think it surprised me more than him."

Necciai was knocked out of the box soon after but received another thrill when he got the pleasure of meeting Stan Musial following the game. The Cardinal great was from Donora, Pennsylvania, the next town upriver from the rookie's home. Musial offered Necciai some words of encouragement and the young kid from Monongahela came away impressed with the legendary "Stan the Man."

Although he liked throwing to all three Pirate catchers, it was with Garagiola that Necciai felt most comfortable.

"He made you feel easy...didn't make any fast motions or moves or anything. So easy and fluid and just made it a lot easier for you to try to throw the ball to him. He was very supportive and always on my side and praising me. When I got banged around pretty good, he was always the first guy to come and say, 'Don't worry about it. Tomorrow's another day and it'll all even out and you'll get them out tomorrow. Don't let that bother you...you can do it.' He was extremely supportive."

On August 24, Necciai notched his first major league victory.

"My one and only. That was against the *Boston* Braves. That's how long ago that was. And I remember that was in Pittsburgh and Murry Dickson relieved me in the ninth. We beat them 4-3.

"It was a game that I remember. I couldn't throw hard enough that day, that if I'd hit you between the eyes you'd a thought a mosquito bit ya. I don't know how I lasted two innings. I don't understand it. I guess everybody was up there looking for something to come out of a cannon and it was coming out of some little boy's arm and they were trying to hit the ball so damn hard, they off-timed themselves and tapped the ball. That's a day they should have scored twenty. I remember real well, it was very strange."

Murry Dickson, who had saved Necciai's victory over the Braves, was a veteran pitcher younger members of the pitching staff found extremely helpful. "The Little Carpenter from Kansas," a major leaguer since breaking in with the Cardinals in 1939, had won 20 games the previous season—a figure that represented more than 30 percent of the seventh-place Pirates' victory total. In 1952 he began a three-year streak of leading the National League in defeats, an occupational hazard for good pitchers on bad teams, but his 14 victories for the 1952 Pirates accounted for exactly one-third of the team's 42 wins. Dickson remained in the major leagues well into his forties, closing out his career on the Kansas City-New York shuttle, making an appearance in the 1958 World Series for the Yankees.

Necciai, the wild 20-year-old rookie, marveled at the 36-year-old Dickson's control.

"We had a bullpen coach by the name of Sam Narron. Big, big tough guy from North Carolina who'd warm up Dickson. He'd actually sit on a Coca-Cola box, behind the plate out in the bullpen in Greenberg Gardens, and warm up Dickson. He never had to move for the ball. He never threw it too high, never threw it too low. I mean he was *there*. Sam could sit on that crate and warm him up. That's how great a control Dickson had. He could throw you six different curveballs from six different places at six different speeds, and have them all wind up in the same spot. He was just on a bad ballclub."

Control, or lack of it, was Necciai's nemesis and it brought inconsistency. He'd be dominating for seven innings in a 1-0 loss to Cincinnati one start and the next time out surrender eight runs in less than three innings. As the season drew to a close, however, he showed improvement. He struck out eight in seven innings versus the Reds on the last day of the season, but left the game trailing 2-0. (The Pirates tied the game in the top of the ninth, only to lose on a sacrifice fly in the bottom of the inning.) In his start previous to that, Necciai had pitched well in a Pirate loss indicative of the team's 42-112 record. Pittsburgh went into the ninth inning trailing 4-0, but rallied for three runs and had the bases loaded with two out when, inexplicably, pinch runner Brandy Davis broke from third in an attempt to steal home and was tagged out to end the game.

"The best part about it, Ralph Kiner was hitting. I can remember Brandy coming and Billy Meyer's sitting on the end of the dugout and Brandy's staggering home being out by five feet. He ran over and picked up the telephone that was in the dugout and called the press box and said, 'I did that on my own.' We always laugh about that."

As the season reached its conclusion, Necciai had dropped six of seven decisions with a 7.08 ERA for Pittsburgh, but no one could ignore his striking out a total of 312 batters at three different professional levels that season. The Pittsburgh media guide said of him, "Baseball men are virtually a unit in the opinion that it is only a matter of time until he attains a ranking among the greatest pitchers of his day."

"I was real confident. I felt it was just a matter of my getting more experience. I was looking forward to going to play winter ball that year, figuring that's what I really needed. I just needed more work on my control against better competition. I felt that I coulda handled those guys [in the majors] with a little more experience and a little more knowledge and a little more confidence. In fact, I was getting a little cocky at that stage. I could see, as they say, the light at the end of the tunnel."

Two months later Necciai was served with his draft notice and, despite his bleeding ulcers, was inducted into the Army in January 1953. At the time there was a perception that while other young men were fighting and dying in Korea, baseball players were getting out of duty because of their occupation. To this day, he feels that to be the reason the Army took him despite the x-rays and doctor's letters that clearly documented his being unfit for active duty.

The Army has never had the reputation of making allowances for special dietary needs. After his Banthine pills ran out, Necciai was not able to keep any food down, was losing weight, and ended up in an Army hospital. Finally, he was discharged in April 1953. After three months of Army life he was back where he had been 12 months before and needed once again to go on a strict regimen to regain his health.

"I was trying to whip myself into physical playing shape, which didn't work, and I think that's when I hurt my arm. I *know* that's when I hurt my arm. I can remember when I hurt it."

It was a pain that he thought would go away in a couple of weeks.

* * *

Although he is now reconciled to the events that curtailed his career and was awarded a place in the Pennsylvania Sports Hall of Fame in May 1990, at the time of his forced retirement it took a couple of years away from the game for Ron Necciai to gain his bearings. Branch Rickey offered him an opportunity to stay in baseball in another capacity, but he declined because of differences he had with others in the Pittsburgh organization. He certainly had no differences with "The Mahatma," as Necciai still admires him perhaps more than any other figure he encountered in baseball.

"To me, I think he was the smartest man God put on this Earth. From the way he treated me...I've read a lot of things about Rickey, including Happy Chandler's book and everybody else's. And what they have to say and what I have to say is a whole lot different.

"He treated me fantastic. He was kind to me, he was considerate. He encouraged me and he pushed me along. He told me what he was gonna do and why he was gonna do it. And he did it. And he paid me. I can't complain about the pay—or anything else. He was in my corner. I must've wound up being his fair-haired boy or something for some reason, but I just think he was fantastic."

Making use of contacts from his days in baseball, Necciai ventured into the sporting goods business and discovered he possessed a talent for, and an enjoyment of, that line of work. As a sales representative, he was able to travel and stay involved in sports. Today he is a partner in Hays, Necciai and Associates, a firm that deals in hunting and fishing equipment over a 17-state area. He travels extensively for his company, expresses great satisfaction with his life, and disdains dwelling in the past.

"Well, I mean, what's to be gained? There's no sense in me wishing. I've done real well in any stretch of any imagination of the things that I wanted to do and get outta life. I was very very fortunate. I had the chance to play in the big leagues, and there weren't very many people that ever did that, albeit as short as it was. But I can at least say I played the game, and I won one, and I got a base hit in the big leagues, a legitimate one.

RON NECCIAI

Born June 18, 1932, Gallatin, Pennsylvania
Ht. 6'4" Wt. 190   BR TR

MAJOR AND MINOR LEAGUE CAREER

Year	Team, League	W-L	Pct	G	GS	CG	SHO	IP	H	R	ER	BB	SO	ERA
1950	Shelby, Western Carolina	0-0	—	1	—	0	0	0	1	3	3	2	0	Inf.
	Salisbury, Carolina	0-0	—	2	—	0	0	3	4	7	7	6	0	21.00
1951	Salisbury, Carolina	4-9	.308	20	—	5	0	106	91	72	57	87	111	4.84
	New Orleans, Southern Assn	1-5	.167	8	7	1	—	33	44	35	31	42	11	8.45
1952	Bristol, Appalachian	4-0	1.000	6	4	4	3	42.2	10	6	2	20	109	0.42
	Burlington, Carolina	7-9	.437	18	—	13	2	126	73	29	22	60	*172*	*1.57*
	PITTSBURGH, National	1-6	.143	12	9	0	0	55	63	45	43	32	31	7.04
1953	Burlington, Carolina	1-1	.500	6	—	1	—	17	12	11	11	18	23	5.82
1954					INJURED—DID NOT PLAY									
1955	Hollywood, Pacific Coast	0-0	—	3	1	0	0	10.1	5	3	3	13	1	2.61
	Waco, Big State	1-0	1.000	2	—	—	—	—	—	—	—	—	—	—
	MAJOR LEAGUE TOTALS	1-6	.143	12	9	0	0	55	63	45	43	32	31	7.04
	MINOR LEAGUE TOTALS	18-24	.429	66	—	24	5	338	239	166	136	248	427	3.62

Italics in boldface type indicate led league

"So, it isn't anything that I wake up and say, 'Boy, I could have won thirty,' or 'I could have won twenty-five,' and I could have done this and I could have done that and it bothers me. It bothered me only in the sense that, at that time, that was really all I knew how to do. I didn't know anything. I went to high school. I didn't know anything else. What the hell was I gonna do? I played baseball.

"When they take away the only thing you can do, and nobody really took it from me...I just couldn't understand it.

"I just decided, I...I gotta get off of this, man. I'm not gonna die at twenty. I can't play baseball anymore at twenty, but I'm not gonna die. So...I gotta pretty good family and a very close family and they support me.

"Even though I had an arm injury and didn't stay around very long, I got a whole lot more outta that game than I ever put into it, believe me. I just think it's an occupational hazard. Pitchers...a lot of other guys had the same thing I had, but didn't strike out twenty-seven, so they didn't get the publicity. It's just an occupational hazard, that's all.

"When you can get paid for something you really like to do, that's not bad. I can't say it any other way, 'cause I liked baseball and I'da probably done it for nothing. And what I do now, they pay me and I'd probably do *it* for nothing, I like it so well.

"I've done well, I can't complain...they won't have to hold any benefits for me."

DOUG CLAREY

Second Baseman,
1976 St. Louis Cardinals

I think what struck me, the first couple of games I played professionally, is that you think you're hot stuff and you're great and you get all these accolades in high school. Then you see all these other players out there and you say, "My gosh!"

You start questioning your ability after awhile. And that was a really strange realization: that maybe there're other players out there that can play as good or better than you can.

The belief in oneself has to be there, or else you just get sucked up by everything you have to put up with in the minor leagues: the travelling, the conditions, the meal money, the scraping just to get by. If you don't like the game and have that belief that you can make it up to the big league level...
—Doug Clarey

As is our confidence, so is our capacity.
—William Hazlitt

On April 28, 1976, St. Louis Cardinal pinch hitter Doug Clarey hit a game-winning, two-run home run in the 16th inning of a contest against the San Francisco Giants. Coming in one of his four big league at bats, the blast was Clarey's first and only base hit, making him one of 12 players through the end of the 1991 major league season whose only hit was a home run. (Ron Allen, whose brothers Dick and Hank had more substantial major league careers, accomplished the same "feat" in August 1972 against the San Diego Padres; his only hit in nine at bats. As an interesting footnote he too was playing for the St. Louis Cardinals.)

Clarey was optioned to Triple-A not long after his game-winning heroics, recalled briefly in August that year and then returned to the minor leagues. He appeared in a total of nine games with St. Louis, all as a pinch hitter or defensive replacement.

"I never really got any particular opportunity," says Clarey now regarding that period of his career. "I really had thought that I might, you know, get a chance to maybe start the next game or something like that. I was just hoping. You know, as a 'thank you,' or something like that. But I guess that's not the way it works."

* * *

Doug Clarey's earliest childhood recollections always include a bat or a glove or a ball. As he puts it, "It was just kind of a love affair that I started with as long as I can remember." From the age of three he was always doing something with a baseball, not because his parents pushed, he just seemed to have a natural interest. Later it became apparent he had a natural aptitude as well. Clarey was a standout on just about every team for which he played from Little League on. Attending high school in Sunnyvale, California (a suburb located about halfway between San Francisco and San Jose), Clarey quickly gained the attention of professional baseball scouts.

Turning down an athletic scholarship to UCLA to sign with the Minnesota Twins shortly after graduation in 1972, Clarey was drafted as a shortstop and then shifted by the Twins to second base after his first minor league season. Although reluctant at first to make the change (he would have preferred moving to the outfield), it was at Wisconsin Rapids in 1974 that he came under the tutelage of a former second baseman and future Minnesota Twins manager, Johnny Goryl. Clarey had a tendency to get down on himself after making errors and

Goryl helped the young infielder learn the finer points of playing the position, especially in his mental approach to the game. That season Clarey flourished under the veteran coach's tutelage, leading Midwest League second basemen in fielding percentage, assists, and double plays. Although hitting only .232, he made the All-Star team and exhibited some punch in his bat with nine home runs and 57 runs batted in.

His performance attracted the attention of the St. Louis Cardinals and after two and a half years in the Twins organization, Clarey was informed by a friend living in Minnesota that he had been purchased by the Cardinals in the 1974 winter draft. Sure enough, a couple of weeks later a letter from St. Louis arrived welcoming the infielder to the organization and informing him that he was to report in the spring to the Cardinals' Double-A affiliate in Little Rock, Arkansas.

The Texas League provided a new perspective of life on the road. The Arkansas Travellers had no problem living up to their nickname as Texas League road trips were, and are, an endurance test.

"Some of the bus rides *were* memorable," remembers Clarey. "The trip from Little Rock to El Paso was about twenty-two hours. And as soon as we got off the bus, we had to go out to the stadium, check into the hotel, get a bite to eat, and come back to the ballpark."

There are many adjustments that a ball player must make when entering the professional ranks, among them the realization that the fans and press will not be as kind or understanding as when the player was a campus hero. The protective environment surrounding the gifted student-athlete disappears with the signing of that professional contract. No longer are his talents constantly praised. Criticism begins to surface. He is no longer "special"; he is surrounded by people just as talented as himself. It matters little to the critics that this is an 18-year-old boy away from home for the first time, far removed from family and friends.

"I think especially if you've gone into baseball at a young age where you're basically coming outta the cradle into the big world out there, you get so spoiled. Especially if you're a big shot, you get pampered. You don't know what it's like to have hard knocks out there. And for a lot of people that can be devastating."

The obstacles blocking the path of a young man aspiring to a future in the major leagues are innumerable. Some are on-field: minimal instruction, lack of confidence, physical shortcomings, curveballs. These factors have all claimed their share of minor leaguers short of the goal.

Also well documented are those *off* the field. The road claims its share of victims as well. The key in a player's staying out of trouble lies in his ability to remain focused on his ultimate goal, the major leagues.

"For me, it was *very* easy. Some guys, you know, had a problem with that. There's no doubt about it. Some guys are out partying every night. I saw, when I look back on it now, the potential for really becoming an alcoholic in baseball. You get guys that are coming right outta college or right outta high school and, in a lotta these states, the drinking age back then was *eighteen*. Some of these guys came from states where you had to be twenty-one. And they start drinking and they don't know how to handle it. They want to be a part of the group, and the other guys are drinking heavily, so they start doing it too.

"The peer pressure was definitely there. But once you made a stance, once you made it clear that, 'If you guys want to party, that's fine. I'm not gonna be a part of it,' things were fine from there."

Clarey may not have struggled with temptation, but he did struggle at the plate in 1975. In 130 games with Arkansas he hit only .206, with three home runs and 44 RBIs. In his mind, a lot of his problems were—in his mind. He added pressure on himself when placed in the second spot in the batting order. There he felt he was to fill the stereotypical role of hit-and-run specialist: being a contact hitter who moved runners along. Much more a free-swinging type of hitter, in trying to be something he was not Clarey became tentative at the plate and it remained a weakness right up until the very last season of his professional career.

During the final month and a half of the 1975 season, Clarey was paired with a new double-play partner. A 19-year-old prodigy out of Texas, Garry Templeton arrived in the Traveller clubhouse from "A" ball and hacked his way through Texas League pitching, hitting .402 over the final 42 games of the season.

"It was incredible to see him play. You know, I'd heard about this hot-shot guy and how he was gonna be the Cardinal shortstop of the future. And you don't hear hype like that very often. And when I saw this guy play...when I saw what he could do and how effortlessly he did it, I said, 'God, how can a guy have so much ability?'"

* * *

Although he had not hit well during the 1975 season, Clarey was in the Cardinals' minor league camp the next spring, ticketed for promotion to the organization's Triple-A affiliate in Tulsa, Oklahoma—only one step away from the big leagues. Toward the end of spring training he pulled a hamstring which put him out of commission for about a week and a half. Meanwhile the parent club made its final cuts, sending a couple of infielders to Tulsa, and Clarey was placed on the St. Petersburg roster (in an "A" league) until the Cardinals could settle the roster situation, which was fine with him since he couldn't play anyway. He was to report back to Tulsa when his hamstring healed.

As he convalesced in Florida, St. Louis starting second baseman Mike Tyson was kayoed by a runaway base runner while turning a double play and had to be placed on the disabled list. The infielders St. Louis had sent to Tulsa at the end of training camp were out of options and could not be recalled. The Cardinals needed someone to play second base and with Clarey the next logical choice, St. Petersburg Manager Hal Lanier had a surprise in store for the young infielder as he reported to the clubhouse to work with the trainer.

"I came in early to get my leg worked on and Lanier said, 'Doug, come over here. I want to talk to you.' He's real serious and everything.

"He said, 'I just got a phone call. They want you to report to St. Louis tonight.' And he just put a big smile on his face and jumped up and grabbed me and said, 'You're going to the big leagues!'

"I said, 'You gotta be *kidding*.' I was in a state of shock. I couldn't believe it.

"So I had to go back to my apartment and put all my things together. I made a couple of phone calls: one to my parents and one to a couple good buddies, and let them know I was going [to the big leagues]. I just said, 'God, I can't believe this is happening to me.' It was one of the most unbelievable feelings I've ever experienced in my life. It lasted for a good two or three days.

"I was so intimidated the next day. I had arrived [in St. Louis] about ten o'clock that night, so I rented a car at the airport and found someplace to stay and then came [to the stadium] the next morning. I walked into the stadium...I didn't know where to go. So they directed me…and everybody took it just matter of factly, like it was just another day of business. *I'm* sitting there just about jumping outta my pants.

"They told me, 'Hey, you gotta sign this contract and then go down to the locker room and you can put all your stuff down there.'

"I go down there and my uniform's all ready, in front of a locker, with my name on the back of it and everything. I was going, '*Wow*, hey, that looks pretty nice!'

"I think I stayed there a couple of hours just checking things out. The main thing was, I knew I was up there basically just as a fill-in. In the back of my mind I was saying, 'Boy, you know, if I get an opportunity and I really show well, maybe I have a chance to stay.' There's always that hope. In the meantime, I was just thrilled to be there."

The Cardinal clubhouse was an interesting, if not winning combination of future stars, current greats, veteran journeymen, and all-around characters. Clarey found it a very friendly clubhouse. Lou Brock was the biggest name on the team and a season away from breaking Ty Cobb's all-time career stolen base record. He was also one of the first to come up to the 22-year-old rookie and welcome him to the St. Louis Cardinals.

"He was so easygoing. He seemed to have a special aura that just made you want to be around him. On the field, he was one of the most *determined* players I have ever seen. Always hustling, always thinking. Never any mental mistakes and always played with so much confidence. One of my first days there, we had a luncheon to go to and we sat at the dais in alphabetical order. I sat between Lou Brock and Willie Crawford. I remember the whole evening Lou Brock was talking to me and joking. He was talking about his florist business…how it's great to be a rookie and don't let things intimidate you. Just as nice as he could be. And Willie Crawford too. Super nice guys."

The St. Louis locker room was full of contrasting personalities. On one hand was Ted Simmons, the All-Star catcher with the mild-mannered, laid-back attitude that reminded Clarey of a "hippie type of philosophy." Certainly not a person one would picture as a future major league general manager. On the other hand was Reggie Smith, who was anything but laid back and mild mannered and Al Hrabosky, whose image on the field was more intense than even

Smith's, but off the field was a heck of a nice guy. (Hrabosky had become a national celebrity the season before with his Fu Manchu mustache and "Mad Hungarian" act.) Always in the background was utility infielder Lee "Bee Bee" Richard and his omnipresent ghetto blaster.

Keith Hernandez, Garry Templeton, and John Denny were youngsters headed for stardom while Ron Fairly and Don Kessinger, two veterans nearing the end of their playing careers as regulars, were also on the roster. Manager Red Schoendienst was coming to the end of a 12-year run at the helm of the Cardinals. The longest such stint in team history, the former second sacker had taken the team to two World Series appearances and only three losing seasons prior to 1976.

It was Kessinger, the long-time Cub shortstop and future White Sox player-manager who took the young Clarey under his wing, acting as his advisor and mentor. Clarey has nothing but kind words for Kessinger to this day, and the great treatment he received from his teammates during his time in St. Louis remains one of his greatest memories from professional baseball.

Unfortunately, Clarey's hamstring problem returned his very first day with the team as he ran in the outfield during a rain delay. Realizing it would not be prudent to begin a major league career by informing his manager that he would be unavailable to play, Clarey refused to let anyone, even the trainer, know that he had re-injured himself.

"I just gritted my teeth and pretended like I didn't have anything wrong with my hamstring, but it was killing me the whole time I was up there."

* * *

April 20, 1976, was Doug Clarey's 22nd birthday. It was also his first day as a major league baseball player as he sat on the bench watching his new teammates play against the New York Mets. In a game where Cardinal pitcher Lynn McGlothen hit Met hurler Jon Matlack in the ribs with a fastball (after plunking New York outfielder Del Unser earlier because he'd had the audacity to hit a home run), Clarey watched a brawl erupt when Matlack tried to retaliate against McGlothen. Clarey had barely put on his uniform and introduced himself to his teammates and already he was in the middle of a riot.

"I'm just kinda standing around and all of a sudden I feel this *big* arm just give me a bear hug from the back and [it] just lifts me up.

And I turn around and it's Ed Kranepool [the New York Met first baseman].

"He just says, 'This is no place for you. Why don't you get over here and watch?' And he had a big smile on his face. So I went over with him and just started talking to him a little bit. It was really something, but I tell you, I've never felt anything so strong as a bear hug from Ed Kranepool."

After the dust had cleared, Matlack continued on his merry way, carrying a lopsided 7-0 lead into the eighth inning. With the pitcher due up, Red Schoendienst looked down the bench directly at Clarey and said, "Why don't you go up there and see what you can do."

After picking out a bat from the rack he kneeled in the on-deck circle, so nervous the bat felt like "a toothpick" in his hands. He recalls feeling, "Like I could swing the bat two hundred miles an hour." After hearing his name announced, Clarey rose and walked to the plate for his first major league at bat.

"I think I swung at all three pitches...I struck out. I swung at all three pitches and I felt I was right *on* that ball. How could I *not* hit that ball? He threw me two fastballs and a curveball and see you later. It was very frustrating, but I remember I felt very relieved. It was like, 'Oh, I got it under my belt now.' I felt that I was part of the team."

After his first pinch-hitting performance Clarey was used for the most part as a late-inning defensive replacement at second base. This is not an easy role since a player must be ready to enter a close game, after sitting for two hours, where one miscue can end the game on a sour note. It was not a situation he relished. Instead of playing aggressively, he would tell himself, "Don't blow it," and measured his success by his ability to go unnoticed.

A week after the Kranepool hug, the Cardinals were visiting Candlestick Park, playing the final game of a three-game set against the San Francisco Giants. This being the rookie's home turf, several of his friends were in attendance, but he had yet to appear in the series.

The game was a pitcher's duel from the outset, played before slightly more than 4,000 fans during a typical Arctic Wednesday afternoon at Candlestick Park. The crowd was especially disappointing in light of the fact that the Giants just months before had been literally only minutes away from moving to Toronto when Arizona cattleman Bud Herseth rode to the rescue to join Bob Lurie in keeping the team from moving to Canada.

As the winds whirled and whipped off San Francisco Bay, John Denny battled the Giants' John "The Count" Montefusco to a 1-1 standoff through seven innings before being lifted for pinch hitter Ron Fairly in the top of the eighth. Montefusco departed for a pinch hitter himself in the bottom of the inning, having struck out 12 Cardinals without issuing a walk.

At one point, Clarey appeared in the on-deck circle as a prospective pinch hitter, where he could hear his friends even through his nervousness as they yelled, "There he is! Hey, Doug! How you doing?"

Their excitement in the potential of seeing him play after three days of waiting dissipated as Clarey was called back to the dugout. The situation that would have resulted in his being used at that time failed to materialize and he went back to the bench in a vain attempt to stay warm.

The game continued, a 1-1 tie, through the 11th, 12th, and 13th innings. The teams then traded single runs in the 14th and threw goose eggs on the scoreboard again in the 15th. Despite having collected 16 hits (including five by Willie Crawford and four by Lou Brock), the Cardinals had used 19 players and seemed unable to put the Giants away.

With two out in the St. Louis half of the 16th inning and Don Kessinger on base, reliever Mike Proly was due up. Clarey remembers Preston Gomez filling in for Red Schoendienst that day and recalls Gomez saying to him, "Go up there and pinch-hit. Just make contact and put the ball in play."

As he went to the plate, Clarey felt none of the nervousness he had experienced earlier. As he looked toward the mound at Giants southpaw Mike Caldwell, he felt as comfortable as "getting up in the morning and putting on my slippers."

"I took a swing and I think I fouled it down the third base line. Then a couple of pitches later, he threw me a hanging slider and to be honest I don't remember swinging the bat. But my eyes must've just lit up and I made good contact with it and hit a line drive over the left field fence.

"I remember running around the bases. As I headed toward second base, I must've really been running hard because by the time...I hit first base...I saw Gary Matthews, the left fielder, I saw him jump up and he didn't come down with the ball. I looked at the second base umpire...and he was doing that little twirl of his finger. I said, 'Oh, you gotta be kidding.'

"A couple of the guys were at home plate to greet me and everything and everybody was happy and Kessinger picked me up and hugged me. It was just the greatest experience in the world. It happened so *quickly* though."

Danny Frisella then took over on the mound for the bottom of the 16th and, after a one-two-three inning, secured a 4-2 victory for the St. Louis Cardinals. He was the 21st player the Cardinals had used in the game. But it was the 20th player utilized who was receiving all the attention.

"I remember going on the radio after the game and talking about the whole thing. All the sportswriters were in the clubhouse after the game, God, I couldn't believe it. I'd never had that happen to me before, all these microphones being shoved in my face.

"I was the last guy in after doing the interview outside and...at Candlestick, you have a long walkway to go to the clubhouse. Well, my teammates had laid down all these towels leading right to my stall, like they had rolled out the red carpet for me.

"We had to hurry up because that was 'Get-Away Day' for Los Angeles and I guess we had to make the flight real quickly. So, I just showered and hopped on the bus to the airport and I remember that's when [St. Louis catcher Ken] Rudolph presented me with the home run ball. He gave the guy [who had retrieved it] three balls in exchange for that one."

* * *

Despite his game-winning long ball, Doug Clarey never started a game in the majors. When Mike Tyson returned from the disabled list, Clarey was sent to Tulsa, his original spring training destination. He remained there as others were recalled, leaving him perplexed when he did not re-join the Cardinals when the rosters expanded in September.

"I just started wondering if I really *did* have any kind of a future with the Cardinals at that point in time," says Clarey.

His answer to that particular question came at the end of March when he was traded to the New York Mets for outfielder Benny Ayala. Slated to be the starting shortstop for the Mets' Triple-A team in Tidewater, Clarey was allowed a week to reacquaint himself with the position (having not played there on an everyday basis for five years), only to see the Mets send middle infielders Leo Foster and Rick Auerbach to Tidewater and him to the bench. It was extremely frustrating as it marked the first time in his life that Clarey had not had a regular position. For the first time in his life he watched teammates play and tell himself that he was better. For the first time in his life he would gaze out onto the field at the players on his team and, while not rooting for something bad to happen, would certainly hope nothing good happened either.

"You catch yourself doing that, and I *hated* that. Somehow, you just say, 'Hey, they're getting *their* chance right now.' After awhile, you just start saying, 'Hey, it's not really what *they* do or what they don't do, it's what *you* do when you get the chance.'"

Clarey never really got his chance with the Mets. He landed in manager Frank Verdi's doghouse after throwing his batting helmet in reaction to being replaced by a pinch hitter. That summer, the New York Mets traded Tom Seaver to the Cincinnati Reds and acquired several young players in the deal, some of whom were assigned to Tidewater. To make room for the new players, Clarey was sent to the Milwaukee Brewers and he finished the season for their Double-A team in Holyoke, Massachusetts.

The Brewers in turn sent Clarey to the Baltimore Orioles organization at the end of spring training in 1978, assigning him to their Double-A affiliate in Charlotte, North Carolina. He was with his fourth organization within a year, but here he had landed in a good situation.

The previous spring, before being traded by St. Louis to the Mets, Clarey's play had caught the eye of Lance Nichols, the Cardinals' Triple-A manager. He had been experimenting with Clarey at third base before the transaction that sent the infielder to Tidewater. In the intervening year, as Clarey had caromed across country, Nichols had joined the Oriole organization—as their manager at Charlotte.

Nichols told Clarey, "I could never understand why they traded you last year. I told them what *I* thought." While he could not offer Clarey a regular spot in the lineup because he had younger prospects the Orioles were committed to, Clarey knew he would get a fair shake from Nichols.

Soon an injury opened a spot at third and Clarey smashed a dozen home runs in the first month and a half of the season. Then just as suddenly as his break appeared, he went without warning into the worst slump of his professional career.

After two months of adjusting mentally, physically, and any other way he could, he finally figured out what his problem in hitting had been all along. One day someone, Clarey does not now remember who it was, told him, "Just the way you're swinging the bat, it's like you don't see it, Doug, until it's right *on* you. *Then* you react."

Clarey replied, "Yeah, I feel that way. It's like I don't see the ball."

The now anonymous benefactor then told Clarey to ignore completely the pitcher's windup. Instead he was to keep his eyes glued on the pitcher's release point. "Just look at the little spot where the ball comes from."

"And the very day I did that, I hit four line drives right on the nose. I just picked up the ball and everything came right back."

It is difficult to say why after months of advice, one simple suggestion can turn things around, but that's the way it works sometimes.

"A lotta people are anxious to give you their opinions," says Clarey. "They'd say, 'It looks like you're dropping your shoulder a little bit,' 'Why don't you lay the bat on your shoulder?,' and 'Why don't you spread your feet out a little bit more?' All these little tricks like that, and you start thinking about *that* instead of really what the problem was. And the problem was I just wasn't seeing the damn ball.

"[In high school], you're only playing twenty games a year and you don't have *time* to get into a slump. And you don't work on it on a daily basis either. Once you start playing 120 games a year, you get a lotta bad habits that are hard to get out of."

Clarey was again hitting the ball with authority at the end of the 1978 season. Other than a .226 batting average, his final totals included 19 home runs and 69 RBIs and career highs in almost every offensive category, but to his disappointment the Orioles assigned him to Charlotte once again for 1979. He contacted the parent club to inquire of their long-range plans for him and was informed that the organization envisioned him as a player-coach. Clarey basically replied, "Thanks, but no thanks." His only reason to continue playing was the possibility of returning to the major leagues.

Offered the chance to remain with Charlotte as a player in 1979, but without any real hope of returning to the majors, Clarey received permission to contact other teams in an attempt to make a deal for himself. He soon realized that wherever he played he'd only be going through the motions. With the burning desire to play gone, the decision to retire was an easy one. He'd just been married the year before and his wife had not had a pleasant experience in Charlotte. Spending another year in North Carolina as a baseball wife was not something she was looking forward to. Without any realistic chance of getting back to the show, the sacrifices necessary to play in minor leagues did not seem worth it. At the ripe old age of 25, Clarey was too old to be a prospect in the minds of baseball people. It was time to get on with his life.

"Actually I was fairly relieved, because I was not only living my own life...a little bit of my parents' life was being lived through me also — having like a celebrity in the family type thing. I added a lot of pressure to myself because I didn't want to disappoint my high school coach. He'd be real disappointed if I wasn't playing anymore. As it turns out, that wasn't the case at all, but I was thinking that I'm letting a lot of people down if I don't have a good season."

* * *

At the suggestion of a family member Doug Clarey went into the field of commercial real estate after his baseball career came to an end and since 1987 has had his own firm, Clarey Commercial Brokerage. He enjoys the competition of the business world, but does not miss that aspect of baseball.

"One thing I *do* miss is the shape I was in when I was playing. Being active every day and being in good shape. I took real good care of myself when I was playing. And I'm not in as good shape as I was. I miss that. I also miss the camaraderie with the teammates.

"I really have no desire to go out there [and play]. I enjoy the hell out of *watching* the games. I love to be at the games themselves and watch them. But as far as participating and everything, I'm still burned out with it. I think I had my fill. It came to the point where it wasn't fun anymore."

Looking back, Clarey readily offers an honest self-analysis of his seven-year professional baseball career and how his experience follows him in what he does today.

"I think that the *talent* was there. I don't have any doubt about that. Especially on a defensive basis, I felt I was as good as any second

DOUG CLAREY

Born April 20, 1954, Los Angeles, California
Ht. 6'0" Wt. 180   BR TR

MAJOR AND MINOR LEAGUE CAREER

Year	Team, League	G	AB	R	H	2B	3B	HR	RBI	BA	SA	BB	SO	SB
1972	Melbourne, Florida State	49	185	35	41	6	0	1	18	.222	.270	22	32	5
1973	Geneva, NY-Penn	65	232	34	55	7	0	5	24	.237	.332	23	42	1
1974	Wisconsin Rapids, Midwest	120	427	47	99	18	2	9	57	.232	.347	48	88	7
1975	Arkansas, Texas	130	433	51	89	17	2	3	44	.206	.275	38	56	1
1976	St. Petersburg, Florida St	3	8	0	3	0	0	0	1	.375	.375	0	1	0
	ST. LOUIS, National	9	4	2	1	0	0	1	2	.250	1.000	0	1	0
	Tulsa, American Assn	63	167	29	38	8	2	7	31	.228	.425	31	35	1
1977	Tidewater, International	28	80	7	10	0	0	3	9	.125	.238	5	21	2
	Holyoke, Eastern	70	235	37	63	10	5	6	35	.268	.430	16	53	0
1978	Charlotte, Southern	138	473	61	107	23	0	19	69	.226	.395	52	98	5
MAJOR LEAGUE TOTALS		9	4	2	1	0	0	1	2	.250	1.000	0	1	0
MINOR LEAGUE TOTALS		666	2240	301	505	89	11	53	288	.225	.346	235	426	22

1972 – Led Florida East Coast League Shortstops in Assists (159).
1973 – Led New York-Penn League Second Basemen in Assists (176) and Errors (24).
1974 – Led Midwest League Second Basemen in Fielding (.963), Assists (319), and DP (80).
1975 – Led Texas League Second Basemen in Assists (320), Errors (29), and DP (74).

baseman out there. I'd always had problems with *hitting,* but yet I was always very, very positive about it. 'Hey, you know, *something's* gonna happen. I'm gonna break through.'

"I think probably the biggest hang-up was mental. Once you stop believing in yourself and you don't think you can do something, all of a sudden, things start to disintegrate a little bit. When I was really going through bad times, batting slumps or whatever, and I remember how terrible I'd feel when I was playing baseball. I'd wake up in the morning, almost feel depressed, 'Oh God, another day I gotta go out there and go oh for four again?'

"It helps knowing that I went through all that and things in the long run come out okay. And just going out there day after day, even when things weren't going good...to keep trying and keep trying and keep trying...I think that has really helped out, especially in *this* profession. 'Cause I get a lot of 'no's' and 'Get out of my office.'

"You just pick yourself up and say, 'Hey, let's go down to the next door and see if we can help them out down there.'

"The rejection has always been, for me anyway, a real tough thing to handle. You know, you put on a smile, and I'm a very pleasant easygoing guy anyway, and to hear the rejection gets to you after awhile. But eventually, you're going to find that person that says, 'Hey, I'm *glad* you stopped by here. You know, I could *really* use some help. Can you help out?'

"It makes everything worthwhile."

MARSHALL MAULDIN

Third Baseman,
1934 Chicago White Sox

I've had a good life. When I come out of baseball, I went to work for Fulton County. I was Superintendent of Parks and Recreation and that's where I retired. I retired January 1, 1985.

I had a good time. We built about seventy some odd ballfields in the Atlanta area. I go by now and then...one of the gymnasiums we built and you see forty, fifty, sixty kids hanging around ...they're all playing basketball now. Course, in the summer, you go to the fields and you see all those kids out playing Little League ball.

And I enjoy that very much. Just seeing those kids out there.
— Marshall Mauldin

All success consists in this: You are doing something for somebody — benefiting humanity — and the feeling of success comes from the consciousness of this.
— Elbert Hubbard

Marshall Mauldin grew up in a poor section of Atlanta, Georgia, during the 1920s and 1930s. It was a place with no baseball fields. Mauldin and his friends would improvise in a local cow pasture, laying out a rough diamond and dodging balls rife with wicked hops caused by unseen and devious stones. It was a place where the boys could dream, envisioning themselves as Babe Ruth, Lou Gehrig, Tony Lazzeri, and the rest of Murderer's Row.

After the hard-fought contest, Mauldin and his group would wander down to Ponce de Leon Park, home of the Southern Association Atlanta Crackers. Over time they had devised schemes to sneak into the ballpark — most commonly by scurrying through a hole in the fence at the far reaches of the outfield corner. The possibility of seeing Nick Cullop, Ben Paschall, and the rest of their hometown heroes made the risk of getting caught well worth it.

The experience made Mauldin a life-long fan of the Atlanta Crackers and when a unique opportunity arose to give up playing major league baseball and return home to play for the team he idolized in his youth, he never hesitated.

Mauldin also never forgot the neighborhoods in which he was raised, or the children living there today. After his playing career ended, he spearheaded an effort to build playing fields, gymnasiums, and parks for these youngsters so they wouldn't have to play in a cow pasture as he had.

The Atlanta Crackers are but a memory now; they have not existed for almost three decades and most of the children playing at those recreation centers today probably don't know that such a team ever existed. Thanks to one former Cracker, however, they can take advantage of an opportunity that would otherwise have never existed for them.

* * *

Marshall Mauldin's organized baseball career got its start on the Atlanta sandlots where he was a five-foot-eleven, 150-pound shortstop for Wesley Memorial Church in the city Sunday School League. His play earned him a tryout with Chattanooga of the Southern Association in 1933, but he still proved a bit green and was returned home to play semi-professional baseball with a team sponsored by Bonnie Smith Furniture in Barnesville, Georgia, about an hour south of Atlanta.

Mauldin was offered another tryout with a Southern Association team, this time for New Orleans. Again, while the team was interested it was felt he needed more experience and the New Orleans ballclub loaned him on a "gentleman's agreement" to Lafayette of the Evangeline League. At the end of the 1934 season, Lafayette was to return Mauldin to New Orleans.

The young infielder didn't seem to need much more experience, hitting an impressive .318 in a league where, as he recalled in an interview later that year, "Nobody hits over .340. If they did, they'd have to hit laying down. Those pitchers down there had a system. If they got two strikes on you, the next one is at your head."

According to the same interview, when Mauldin wasn't ducking 0-2 pitches, he might be attempting to field strange objects thrown by his own teammates. Not so many years ago, leagues like the Evangeline employed only one umpire to control the action on the field, leading to all sorts of innovative maneuvers on the part of players in an attempt to gain advantage.

"I remember one day when our team was leading 1-0 and the other side had men on second and third with one out. Our catcher called for a pitchout to try to get the man off third. Well, he threw wild into left field and the man on third and the man from second came legging it home. Imagine their embarrassment when our catcher stood right in front of the plate and tagged each one out with the ball. While the boys, out yonder, were chasing an iced potato, whitewashed. He brought it along from home for an emergency.

"The umpire, of course, was standing behind the pitcher with men on the bases and a big beef went up, naturally. Our catcher claimed he just happened to see the potato lying there and was throwing it off the ballfield, but I guess the umpire didn't believe him 'cause he just put the men back on base."

(More than 50 years later, another minor league catcher, Dave Bresnahan, pulled the same trick. A great-nephew of Hall of Fame receiver Roger Bresnahan, the Cleveland Indian farmhand was fined and released soon after the game, although he did achieve far more notoriety for that incident than he had for his .149 batting average.)

Just when the officials in the New Orleans front office were rubbing their hands together in anticipation of Mauldin's return, Lafayette received an offer in August 1934 from the Chicago White Sox. Completely ignoring the gentleman's agreement with the Southern Association club, Lafayette struck a deal and Mauldin, only a few months removed from playing for a semi-pro team sponsored by a furniture store, was headed straight to the major leagues.

* * *

Mauldin had never before been out of the South; in fact he had been out of Georgia only once in his life, but was fortunate in that Chicago's future Hall of Fame shortstop Luke Appling was a friend and his roommate. They had been raised in the same West Atlanta neighborhood where Mauldin, who was five years Appling's junior, often acted as batboy for amateur teams the future White Sox great played for.

Elated at his arrival in the Windy City, Mauldin reacted with a sense of excitement and nervousness when catching his first glimpse of Comiskey Park. Most of the venues in which he had played seated no more than a couple thousand. *This* was the big time. Mauldin wandered through the Chicago clubhouse, seeing players he'd only read about: Luke Sewell, Al Simmons, Ted Lyons, George Earnshaw, Mule Haas, Jimmy Dykes. Now he could experience what he had before only been able to imagine.

For a month he imagined more than he experienced; not playing in a single game during that time. He sat on the Chicago bench, his chances of cracking the lineup not enhanced by the fact that Jimmy Dykes, the team's incumbent third baseman, also happened to be manager of the White Sox. In the meantime, the teenager occupied himself sightseeing as the team embarked on a long road trip through Washington, Philadelphia, Boston, and St. Louis—cities the wide-eyed teenager was seeing for the first time. The experience sparked a life-long interest in travel. He bantered with the writers covering the team. Accepting an offer to display his prowess at the typewriter, he dashed off part of a story one columnist was writing about him. His biggest thrill was arriving in New York, home of Babe Ruth and Yankee Stadium. Checking into the Hotel New Yorker with the rest of the White Sox, Mauldin got directions to Yankee Stadium, rushed to the subway, hopped on board, and arrived two and a half hours before the Chicago-New York game scheduled for that afternoon.

The Chicago dressing room was off the third base line at Yankee Stadium, the same side of the field as the Yankee bench, and to get over to the visitor's side of the field, Mauldin had to come down a walkway that exited into the Yankee dugout and then cross the diamond. As Mauldin came out of the runway toward the playing field, he stopped suddenly, the sight making him catch his breath.

"I looked up and there sat Babe Ruth and Lou Gehrig and Tony Lazzeri and Bill Dickey. Ruth happened to be the closest to me and just like a kid I said, 'Mr. Ruth, I've *always* wanted to meet you.' He was very nice to me. Last thing he said to me was, 'I wish you the best in the world.'

"Ruth had a big body on him from his hips on up, but down his legs...they were spindly. But I tell you one thing, I never seen anybody could hit a baseball as hard as he could. I've seen all the great ones, I guess, since 1934...Williams, DiMaggio, Mantle, Greenberg, Foxx, and all those boys. I've never seen a man could hit it as *hard* as Ruth. I would wager anybody that if he played today, he'd hit eighty to one hundred home runs a season, 'cause the ball's more lively today than it used to be.

"I remember one day we were playing the Yankees. [Ted] Lyons was pitching [for us]. When Ruth came up to bat, Lyons took the ball and put just enough speed on that ball to get it up to the plate. Just about like he was warming up.

"Old Ruth, he swung and he knocked the ball what looked like four hundred feet right straight up in the air. And old Lyons told me, 'That's the only way you pitch to him. If you try to overpower him with something, he'd knock your brains out.'"

On September 10, Mauldin found his name on a major league lineup card for the first time.

"I was as nervous as anything you've ever seen and I was playing third base and almost shaking. They put me in there against Washington [the defending American League champions], and I went along pretty good for the first couple, three innings and finally someone hit me a ball down at third base and luckily I got a good hop on it. After that, I was never nervous again."

Mauldin doubled off Washington starter Jack Russell for his only hit in four trips to the plate. The next day he once again started against the Senators and went one for four, but was deprived of an opportunity to be the hero. With the score tied 2-2 in the 11th inning, Chicago had the bases loaded and one out with Mauldin due up next. Jimmy Dykes, however, chose to pinch hit himself for the rookie and singled in the winning run. It was Dykes' only pinch-hitting appearance that season. Mauldin shrugs off the memory, remarking in a matter-of-fact tone, "I always wanted to get up there, but the manager...he makes out the lineup card."

The 37-year-old Dykes was in the first of 21 major league seasons as a manager (plus several more in the Pacific Coast League), having taken over for Lew Fonseca 15 games into the year. An All-Star in the inaugural contest a year before, he was still a solid player despite his advanced age and would remain so for two more seasons. A product of the Philadelphia sandlots, Dykes had been one of Connie Mack's favorite players, manning several positions during his 15 seasons under "The Grand Old Man." No shrinking violet when it came to turning the air blue with his tirades (quite unlike his mentor), Dykes was nonetheless popular with most of his players and would run the White Sox through 1946. When Mack retired (or was retired), following the 1950 season, Dykes was tabbed as the successor to the venerable patriarch of the Athletics.

Despite the White Sox skipper being his chief impediment to playing, Mauldin is more than gracious in his assessment of the gruff Sox manager with the omnipresent cigar.

"Dykes was great. He was a great manager. He could get along with his ball players. He'd chew you out good one minute, but he's the best friend you ever had ten minutes later. But if you made a dumb play, he'd jump all over you.

"I will never forget, we were playing Cleveland one day in Chicago there. An outfielder named Joe Vosmik...he could hit that ball hard and I backed up a couple, three or four steps and I looked up and he was *bunting*.

"I came in and I got the ball, and I threw to first base about half off balance and I missed the first baseman, Zeke Bonura. I missed him by five feet. I threw it right over his head. I didn't know *what* Dykes was gonna say to me when I went in.

"I got in the dugout and he met me, and he said, 'Son, that's the way to do it. When you throw one away,' he said, 'do a good job.' Of course, that calmed me down a little bit."

At the time Mauldin joined the team, the Chicago White Sox franchise was still trying to recover from the Black Sox scandal of 14 years before. An American League power during the first two decades of this century (with four pennants and ten finishes of third place or better), by 1934 the White Sox were a collection of ex-Philadelphia

Athletics picked up during Mack's big post-season fire sale of 1932, and several one-dimensional ball players employed to fill in around Luke Appling and Ted Lyons. While the crosstown Cubs chased the Gashouse Gang and Bill Terry's Giants for the National League flag, the Chisox finished in the junior circuit cellar with a 53-99 record. It was their eighth straight losing season.

The team did not lack for characters and one of the more colorful members of the Pale Hose was Zeke Bonura, the big, slow-footed slugger Jimmy Dykes directed to stand by the first base bag whenever the White Sox were on defense. Bonura led the league in fielding percentage three times, primarily because his interest in getting near a baseball without a bat in his hands was as limited as his range. He rarely made errors because he rarely used his glove.

"He wasn't what you'd call a good first baseman," recalls Mauldin. "There was one day in Chicago I threw him a ball and he got his feet crossed up. The ball liked to hit him in the head. He didn't even get his glove up. [Laughs.] He wasn't a good fielder, but old Zeke could knock in a few runs and he could *hit*."

Mauldin started several games at third base for the Sox in September and on the 22nd stroked three hits and drove in three runs in a 9-8 loss to the Cleveland Indians. One of his hits that day was his only major league home run, off the Tribe's Oral Hildebrand.

"I hit it, and I knew I hit it fairly well, but I was the most surprised person in the ballpark. I was so shook up, I don't know *what* I was thinking as I rounded the bases. I know I touched them. Hank Aaron hit only about 740 or 750 more."

Shortly after that game, his offense almost totally disappeared. Mauldin accumulated only three singles in his final 14 at bats and suddenly the season was over. In his two months with the White Sox, he collected ten hits in 38 at bats for a .263 average, including one home run and three runs batted in.

"I made a stupid mistake. I was going real well for a few games and I hurt my hand. I couldn't grip the bat properly, and I didn't tell Dykes about it 'cause back in those days, if you're a rookie and you got in the lineup, you better stay in there as long as you could."

* * *

The reviews on Marshall Mauldin's 1934 performance for the White Sox were generally good. The Chicago press remarked, "While he was a trifle jumpy when it came to fielding, he hit well enough and has the physical appointments necessary for a successful career. Even if the White Sox find it to the advantage of the lad to farm him out for a season or two, Marshall Mauldin bears much promise as a future great for the Chicago club."

Future was the key word in that phrase. At his age and with Dykes at third, Mauldin stood little chance of making the extra $100 per month he would receive on top of his prior year's salary should he make the big league roster.

He attended spring training with the Sox in 1935, which was held at Brookside Park in Pasadena, California, across the street from the Rose Bowl. Making his first trip out West, he and a few teammates toured a movie studio and watched comedian Joe E. Brown film some scenes for a motion picture he was starring in. Enjoyable as the camp was, Mauldin didn't stick with the team as Dykes, impressed by the youngster's speed, farmed him out to Longview of the West Dixie League where he was to learn to play the outfield. There, Mauldin hit .337, with a league-leading 179 hits, and was second in runs scored.

In 1936, he moved up to Knoxville of the Southern Association and had the best season of his career, hitting .378, finishing second by six points to Chattanooga's Fred Sington for the batting title. He rapped out 42 doubles, eight triples and seven home runs among his 218 hits. It proved to be a most opportune time for Mauldin to have his best year.

*   *   *

The relationship between major and minor league baseball was changing rapidly in the 1930s, and not for the better as far as Commissioner Kenesaw Mountain Landis was concerned. Branch Rickey had invented the farm system in the 1920s, providing his St. Louis Cardinals an edge when it came to acquiring, and hoarding, talent. Rickey signed players both with an eye toward developing athletes for the Cardinals and keeping talent away from his competitors. The system had transformed the Redbirds from perennial doormat to powerhouse, and it had also transformed the minor leagues from a competitive to a subservient role. This development destroyed the integrity of the minor league pennant races in Landis' eyes. A team in the Sally League for example, might be in a tight battle for the flag and suddenly be forced to give up its best players in the middle of the season because their contracts were owned by someone else. Few minor league franchises had the resources to compete independently, especially after the onset of the Depression, and there became fewer and fewer powerhouse minor league teams, teams that in the past had arguably been better than some of their weaker major league counterparts.

The White Sox, following the example set by Rickey, had begun developing their own talent and by 1936 emerged as a contender for the first time in 15 years, finishing only one-half game behind the pennant-winning Detroit Tigers. Players from the Sox farm system such as ex-Cub Mike Kreevich and fellow outfielder Rip Radcliff combined with pitchers Vern Kennedy, John Whitehead, and Monty Stratton in making a contribution to the team's rise in fortune. The front office made some excellent player acquisitions as well, purchasing veteran catcher Luke Sewell from Washington and obtaining pitcher Thornton Lee from Cleveland in a three-way deal involving next to nothing. Lee won 74 games in his first five seasons with Chicago.

In 1937, they once again chased the Tigers, falling three games short, but found themselves paying a price for the success of their farm system and their efforts to retain the talent they had developed. They became one of many victims of Commissioner Landis' decision to remedy what Rickey had wrought.

Anticipating what was to happen to the minor leagues should he not act, Judge Landis throughout the 1930s routinely canceled contracts of players he felt were being hidden in the minors by major league organizations. One of those emancipated was Mauldin. He was a free agent, 39 years before Andy Messersmith.

Twenty-three years old and sporting a lifetime .348 batting average in 362 minor league games, Mauldin quickly received offers from the Cleveland Indians and Philadelphia Athletics, but his thoughts were turning toward home. Spending the 1936 season in the Southern Association had provided him the opportunity to play in Ponce de Leon Park, against the Crackers he had so loved as a boy. It rekindled Mauldin's desire to play in his own backyard among the treasured memories of his youth. When offered the choice of teams for which he could play, Mauldin signed a contract with the minor league Atlanta Crackers.

Atlanta may have been *in* the minor leagues, but the Crackers were anything but a minor league organization. The team travelled first class, stayed in the best hotels, and the players simply signed for their meals with no restrictions.

It is important to realize that there were minor league teams in the past, in Baltimore, Minneapolis, Newark, San Francisco, Atlanta, and other places, that were minor league in name only. In terms of business operation, facilities, salary, and talent, these were teams every bit the equal of the majors. Many players actually preferred the minors. The major leagues covered only the Northeast and Midwestern portions of the country until the late 1950s, so a great minor league team in the South or West was able to attract a large and loyal following. Many of the players could make two or three times more as a starter in the minors than they could enjoy in the big leagues. In many of the smaller towns, people would slip twenty-dollar bills into the pockets of a player who hit a game-winning home run (not to intimate in any way that the fans had possibly won the money through betting in the stands). The minor leagues were not always thought of as a poor step-child of the majors. Mauldin certainly did not feel that way.

"Atlanta was home. I was born there. I had a wonderful time playing for Atlanta. I enjoyed my years [with the Crackers]. I wouldn't trade them for anything in the world. I was the first Atlanta-born player that ever played for the Atlanta Crackers at the time I come. I was proud of that. Back when I was a kid the Atlanta Crackers to me was just like the New York Yankees. I'd go out there and I wouldn't have the money to get in the ballgame, but I'd slip through the fence or something.

"A lot of days...I played with the Crackers nine years...I'd be out there playing and I'd look over there at the fence where we all used to sneak in."

* * *

Mauldin was slight of build throughout his career, usually carrying about 170 pounds on his five-foot eleven-inch frame. He rarely walked and rarely struck out, exhibiting good bat control with little power; the quintessential line-drive hitter. He always choked up on the bat and pulled most of his hits into left field.

After hitting .290 in his first season with Atlanta, Mauldin had a great all-around year in 1938, playing all over the infield and outfield while reaching double figures in doubles, triples, home runs, and stolen bases. He was second on the team in RBIs while batting in the lead-off position.

The Crackers, managed by Paul Richards, took the Southern Association pennant and went on to win the Dixie World Series from Beaumont of the West Dixie League. The Texas ballclub, an affiliate of the Detroit Tigers that featured in its pitching rotation "Schoolboy" Rowe and "Dizzy" Trout, managed only a single tie in the five-game series against the Georgians.

Mauldin still rates Paul Richards as the finest manager he ever played for or against.

"He knew more 'inside baseball' than anyone I was in contact with. It's the little things in baseball that count. He emphasized that when you hit a ball, no matter where it goes, you're to *run*. And brother, I guarantee you if you *didn't* run, he'd take some of your money.

"Richards also didn't like for you to let anybody make a double play. If you were on first base, he expected you to kinda bump up into that second baseman or shortstop if you could possibly get to him.

"I tried to learn the inside of baseball the best I could. I tried to play an intelligent game. Paul Richards put all that in me to tell you the truth. All the ball players that ever played for him — he did that to all of them."

In a 1970 interview with Charlie Roberts of *The Atlanta Constitution*, Mauldin related his favorite Paul Richards story.

"I remember one time in Birmingham, Paul was catching and went out and told our pitcher to walk the next batter. He told Paul it was hot, he was tired, and he wasn't going to do it.

"Paul told him to put the guy on or he'd fine him $100. The pitcher said, 'I didn't say I wouldn't put him on. I'm tired and I'm not going to throw four pitches and walk him when I can hit him with one.'

"And that's what he did. He conked the guy."

After the Dixie Series, Richards worked with Mauldin on hitting the ball to all fields instead of pulling every pitch that came his way. After a .272 batting mark in 1939, Mauldin would never hit less than .311 again, racking up five straight .300 seasons through 1944.

In 1943, he struck out only 13 times in 504 at bats while hitting .333. The next year, his last with the Crackers, Mauldin hit .324 and had the best day of his professional career on the Fourth of July, 1944.

In a game against the Memphis Chicks, a team featuring the phenomenal Pete Gray, Mauldin set off his own fireworks display, going six for six. It was part of a streak of 11 straight base hits.

He retired at the end of the season with over 1,800 hits in the minor leagues and a tidy lifetime batting average of .316.

Marshall Mauldin never regretted his decision to sign with a "minor league" team.

* * *

Mauldin officially closed out his professional career in the International League in 1946. Drafted by Toronto during the winter after sitting out the 1945 season, he went four for nine in two games before hanging it up for good.

In his 1970 interview, Mauldin claimed he quit "because my eyesight got weaker or the pitchers got better. They put glasses on me and I hung it up."

Looking back at his 1944 statistics, one might see that Mauldin's observation regarding his eyesight could be borne out to a degree (he more than tripled his strikeout total from the previous year in 115 less at bats). It should be pointed out, however, that in a later conversation he explained that although his eyesight did weaken, he was generally not at all thrilled with being drafted and playing up in Canada, far from home.

"I just didn't like the playing conditions up there. We opened the season, it was about 28 degrees and snowing. It was just miserable up there. I come out of the Deep South, I'm not used to all that cold, cold weather."

Mauldin spent a half-dozen years promoting golf exhibitions and tournaments for the Parks Department in Fulton County after returning from Toronto. Despite a shoestring budget, he helped bring in greats such as Ben Hogan, Byron Nelson, and Carey Middlecoff. When the department shifted its emphasis away from such ventures, Mauldin returned briefly to baseball, scouting for the Baltimore Orioles for whom he signed Jerry Adair out of Oklahoma A&M (now Oklahoma State University).

"I didn't enjoy scouting because they played all night ball out there in these amateur and semi-pro leagues and you'd go to a ballgame 'bout seven thirty to ten, ten-thirty at night. Then you get in a motel and you don't have anything to do all day but just sit there and wait for a ballgame."

Mauldin returned to the Parks Department soon thereafter, and in the late 1960s led a movement to dot the Atlanta area with recreation centers and parks so that the children of the city neighborhoods would have an opportunity to enjoy the game he loved so much. He created athletic programs at the Fulton County prison camps feeling it provided the inmates the opportunity to "become goal oriented instead of drifting." Sportsmanship awards were presented by Mauldin to deserving prisoners, who had the merit noted on evaluation sheets that were forwarded to the parole board. Mauldin had justifiable pride in the program, noting the enthusiasm of the participants and their ability to play outside teams without incident. In recognition of his efforts, a baseball field in South Fulton was named in his honor in June 1972. Warden Robert C. Wright remarked to those in attendance at the ceremony that Mauldin was being "honored in the way a true professional should be."

* * *

Looking back at the early portion of his career, Mauldin did feel the White Sox rushed him; that he was in awe of his surroundings in Chicago and would have benefitted playing in the minor leagues for two or three seasons before promotion to the majors.

"Well, it was a *large* place. Of course, where I'd been playing baseball in this little class 'C' league...they had a seating capacity of about 2,000 people. In Chicago I looked at that big stadium and I think they seated about 58,000...something like that. It was a big thrill to go up there. I didn't stay too long, but I enjoyed it.

"Today, people play baseball for the money. Back when I played, I think people enjoyed playing and *wanted* to play. I had a desire to play baseball when I was a kid. I was born and raised in a poor neighborhood in Atlanta...in a large family, and we didn't have the money that a lot of people had. But it taught me one thing. If you set your mind out to do something, I don't care who you are, if you work hard enough you can accomplish it."

The boy who had been out of Georgia only once prior to his 19th birthday later made up for his lack of travel experience thanks in large part to 70-year friend and decade-long companion Lucille Yancey Primm. The two travelled the world, usually in the company of good

MARSHALL MAULDIN

Born November 5, 1914, Atlanta, Georgia   Died September 2, 1990, Union City, Georgia
Ht. 5'11"   Wt. 175   BR   TR

MAJOR AND MINOR LEAGUE CAREER

Year	Team, League	G	AB	R	H	2B	3B	HR	RBI	BA	SA	BB	SO	SB
1934	Lafayette, Evangeline	88	340	53	108	12	4	2	40	.318	.394	—	—	—
	CHICAGO, American	10	38	3	10	2	0	1	3	.263	.395	0	3	0
1935	Longview, West Dixie	133	531	91	*179*	30	9	5	65	.337	.456	34	48	10
1936	Knoxville, Southern Assn	141	576	98	218	42	8	7	64	.378	.516	14	34	10
1937	Atlanta, Southern Assn	138	545	83	158	28	4	3	46	.290	.372	27	33	9
1938	Atlanta, Southern Assn	153	622	92	172	30	10	10	73	.277	.405	20	49	14
1939	Atlanta, Southern Assn	123	471	62	128	22	1	1	43	.272	.329	21	23	22
1940	Atlanta-Knoxville, South Assn	141	545	62	179	29	5	0	42	.328	.400	14	27	16
1941	Knoxville, Southern Assn	155	659	84	205	30	7	2	58	.311	.387	28	28	10
1942	Memphis-Atlanta, South Assn	143	562	93	175	29	3	0	52	.311	.374	41	20	12
1943	Atlanta, Southern Assn	126	504	82	168	27	5	6	65	.333	.442	18	13	3
1944	Atlanta, Southern Assn	95	389	68	126	18	7	1	43	.324	.414	27	43	11
1945					DID NOT PLAY									
1946	Toronto, International	2	9	—	4	—	—	—	—	.444	—	—	—	—
	MAJOR LEAGUE TOTALS	10	38	3	10	2	0	1	3	.263	.395	0	3	0
	MINOR LEAGUE TOTALS	1438	5753	868	1820	297	63	37	591	.316	.409	244	318	117

Italics in boldface type indicate led league

friend and Georgia Governor (then Lieutenant Governor) Zell Miller. The experience kept Mauldin active and opened up to him a whole new set of experiences.

"Since retirement I haven't sat around too much. I've travelled all over the world. We went to Russia, Czechoslovakia, China. Then we went to Australia and New Zealand. Went to Hong Kong. Last year, we went to Amsterdam, Holland, and Athens, Greece. We were on a cruise in Athens for four days. We went to Turkey, too. We have a trip planned through Holland, Switzerland, and Germany, including a cruise on the River Rhine."

Of course, Mauldin's proudest accomplishment in life was his work for Fulton County, Georgia, in building those gymnasiums and ballparks for the neighborhood children. He didn't forget about his once being among them, playing baseball all day and then trying to peek over the fence into Ponce de Leon Park at night. By the time of his retirement, recreation centers were a part of the Fulton County landscape, several of which bore his name, and it was a source of great pleasure for him to drive by and see the fields humming with activity. He stayed active after retirement, through travel and his contract with Fulton County to provide recreation for the prison camp inmates. He was honored by the Atlanta Braves in January 1986 for his service to the community.

However, Marshall Mauldin was unable to make his trip along the Rhine. During the summer of 1990, he was stricken with a recurrence of cancer and passed away the Sunday before Labor Day that same year, just three months before the death of his good friend Luke Appling.

· But if you drive by the parks of Fulton County, Georgia (in South Fulton, Union City, Burdette Park, Cochran Mills, Cedar Grove, Sandtown, and other places), during the summer, you can still see Marshall Mauldin — in the children there playing in a facility provided them by a man none of them knew, but to whom they are all grateful. Perhaps among them will be one who will leave the playing fields of Atlanta and travel the country playing baseball; someone who will return and, like Mauldin, give something back to the community. For an old ball player, it is a most fitting epitaph.

FLOYD GIEBELL
Pitcher, 1939-41 Detroit Tigers

I knew that I had, shall we say...I had very little chance of beating Feller. Not only in Cleveland, but anyplace else. I knew that then. I knew the odds were against me or the ballclub winning because Detroit never did hit Feller very hard. [Hank] Greenberg and [Rudy] York, they were up there swinging, knocking all the air outta the ballpark. Course, a lotta people knocked the air outta the ballpark when he was on the mound. But I knew that if I could hang in there pretty close, that we had a chance.

And as the game went on I thought that, especially after we got two runs, unless something happened or I got a little wild, we had a chance to win. Being a control pitcher, I didn't think I was gonna walk anybody much, which I didn't.

No, I...I didn't walk out there thinking I was...that we didn't have a chance at all. I've never been that way.
　　　　　　　　　　　　　　　— Floyd Giebell

He who seizes the right moment,
Is the right man.
　　　　　　　　　　　　　　　— Goethe

Floyd Giebell pitched in 28 games during his major league career, encompassing a grand total of 67⅔ innings spread over three seasons more than 50 years ago. He won exactly three games, yet still receives nearly 70 fan letters a year thanks to a single pitching performance. On a day in late September 1940 he was the Detroit Tigers' surprise starter for the deciding game of an exciting American League pennant race. His opponent was baseball's most dominating and charismatic pitcher of the time, Bob Feller of the Cleveland Indians. Giebell had little to do with the circumstances that had brought him to that point; he had been in the minor leagues the entire season while the Tigers and Indians were battling for the league lead. With the two teams heading into the final weekend of the season for a match-up to determine the American League's representative to the 1940 World Series, Giebell was selected to face Feller in the opener of the deciding three-game set.

The 21-year-old Feller had won 27 games that season and, despite his youth, "Rapid Robert" had 82 victories in his major league career to that point. Giebell had won two.

He would win one more.

* * *

Born December 10, 1909, and raised in central West Virginia, Giebell entered college four years after his high school graduation, staying home to help the family after his father suffered a work-related disability. Giebell was employed by Weirton Steel in Weirton, West Virginia, during that period and later received a full scholarship to Salem College, situated on a small campus not far from his home, where he received a degree in business administration with a minor in physical education in 1937.

Each summer while in college, he worked for Weirton Steel and patrolled the outfield for their company team in the highly competitive industrial leagues; Weirton Steel regularly played exhibition contests against the Pittsburgh Pirates and the Homestead Grays. Primarily an outfielder before college, Giebell took up pitching for the first time during his freshman year despite his preference for playing every day because he felt in light of his age that he could reach the major leagues more quickly.

With the four-year gap in his education, Giebell was older than most of his Salem College teammates and, like many players over the history of the game, he established for himself a "baseball age." (In commenting on his performance against the Indians in 1940, the newspapers marveled at the pitching of the "25-year-old rookie" — in truth, he was almost 31.)

Despite his preference for hitting fly balls rather than preventing them (he led his amateur league twice in batting average), Giebell was correct: Pitching *did* prove a fast track to the majors. Signed by the Detroit Tigers after Weirton Steel won a major-league-sponsored national semi-pro tournament in Dayton, Ohio, he went to spring training in 1938 with Beaumont of the Texas League only to be shifted to Evansville of the Three I League prior to opening day. Within a year, he reached the major leagues after going 18-6 with a 1.98 ERA for the Tiger farm team. Giebell opened the 1939 season with Detroit and quickly received his rookie welcome to the big leagues.

Among the perks awarded a major league player was the privilege of wearing spikes shined to a spit polish every day by the clubhouse boy. As Giebell stood on the Tigers' dugout steps one day admiring his reflection in his footwear, Rudy York happened by chewing a plug of tobacco. Without a word he sent a stream of tobacco juice splattering onto the young pitcher's shoes. This became a daily ritual of York's.

The rookie took that for a few days and then "I went over and got a water bucket and threw it all over him. He never bothered me after that. We became friends. Good friends. I liked Rudy York. He helped make that ballclub, although he wasn't the greatest fielder in the world. The Tigers could certainly use his bat."

As part of what would become a recurring theme, Giebell made his major league debut against Cleveland and Feller, striking out two in a one-inning relief appearance. He continued to pitch out of the bullpen without a great deal of success; due in part to the combination of his lacking experience in that role and long periods of inactivity between appearances. For the first time in Giebell's short career he was not a starting pitcher and it proved a difficult adjustment. Eventually, he was shuttled back and forth between the Texas League and Detroit in order to get some kind of regular work on the mound.

At the beginning of August he was optioned to Toledo of the American Association where he encountered a last-place team that had basically quit playing. This left the ever-competitive Giebell frustrated, as did his 1-10 record for the Mud Hens despite tossing nine complete games in 12 starts and compiling a more than respectable 3.58 ERA.

It was a forgettable ending to what should have been a memorable year for a man making his major league debut that season. Between trips to the minors Giebell made nine appearances for Detroit, all in relief, splitting two decisions. There was one episode in 1939, however, that did leave a lasting impression on the young hurler. In addition to his varied travels, Giebell was witness to one moment of baseball history that season, a moment indelibly etched in his memory.

May 2, 1939, was a day that saw six players, including Cap Anson, Charles "Hoss" Radbourn, Buck Ewing, and Al Spalding voted into the Hall of Fame by the Old-Timers Committee. On the same day, prior to a seemingly routine ballgame between the Detroit Tigers and the New York Yankees, a man who would join these six via a special election held later that year made news when he missed his first game in 14 years. It was on that day Lou Gehrig brought the lineup card to home plate and for the first time in 2,130 games his name was not on it.

The Yankee great had been plagued throughout the 1938 season with attacks of what were thought to be lumbago, but had been re-diagnosed over the winter as coming from gall-bladder problems. On this day, the fans began to realize the seriousness of his malady. After an announcement was made over the public address system that his streak had ended, Gehrig disappeared into a corner of the dugout after briefly doffing his cap in response to the crowd. Rookie Floyd Giebell was sitting on the opposite side of the field with the rest of his Tiger teammates.

"Most everyone had heard and knew just about how badly the man had been hurting. It was not only an emotional time for both the Yankees and the Detroit Tigers, but I am sure the fans realized at that time that this was the passing of one of the truly great stars of the game.

"I remember how the man looked...sitting on the second step down in the dugout. They were on the first base side and our dugout, of course, was on the third base side. And I can still see it like it was last week...him sitting there...just staring off towards the outfield. That's what the man was doing."

* * *

In September 1940, the Cleveland Indians were trying to main-
tain a slim lead over the Detroit Tigers and the New York Yankees in
an attempt to capture their first American League pennant in 20 years.
The race was one of the most exciting in history; between June 20 and
the end of the season, the league lead changed hands 18 times. The
chase was being compared in the papers to the National League
pennant race of 1908 and before September was out, no less than five
teams climbed to within four games of first place at one time or
another. And the front-running Indians were a team in turmoil.

Cleveland's season began on a high note with Bob Feller's
opening day no-hitter. However, the clubhouse atmosphere quickly
deteriorated into mutiny against their sometimes caustic manager,
Oscar Vitt. An ex-Tiger third baseman in his third year at the helm for
the Indians, Vitt was still very popular in Detroit...certainly more
popular there than among his own employees in part due to his habit
of publicly berating his players for their mistakes. He also favored
using astrology in determining his starting pitcher, placing a baseball
under the cap of the chosen hurler after studying the alignment of the
stars. The team's morale plummeted to the point where a petition
demanding Vitt's immediate dismissal, and signed by the team's
veterans, was presented to Indians team President Alva Bradley. *The
Cleveland Plain Dealer* reported that the petition contained the
players' complaints that Vitt, among other things, had, "ridiculed his
players in conversations with newspaper writers, fans and opposing
players and managers." Additionally, the players felt that Vitt's ranting
and ravings had made them "the laughingstock of the league."

A few days prior to the meeting with Bradley, the players had
become incensed at comments made by Vitt toward his ace pitcher,
Bob Feller. On the day in question, Feller was getting knocked around
thoroughly by the Boston Red Sox when Vitt reportedly started yelling
so everyone, including his pitcher, could hear him proclaim, "Look at
him! He's supposed to be my ace! I'm supposed to win a pennant with
that kind of pitching!"

Bradley refused to fire Vitt outright, waiting instead until after
the end of the season, by which time most of the players weren't
speaking to their manager and were employing their own set of signs
on the field, ignoring any signals Vitt might relay.

After the story broke on June 13, public and print sentiment landed squarely on the side of the beleaguered Tribe manager and the Cleveland players found themselves branded "crybabies" in every town they visited. Fans dangled baby bottles in front of the dugout and sang derisively. Through all of this turmoil, the Indians played solid baseball and went into Labor Day with a three-and-a-half-game lead over Detroit.

Cleveland had a strong ballclub. The pitching staff allowed the fewest runs in the league and threw the most shutouts. The defense committed the fewest errors. Lou Boudreau, Ken Keltner, and Hal Trosky provided a solid punch in the middle of the lineup but the team's strength was pitching, with Feller, Mel Harder, 18-game winner Al Milnar, and 15-game winner Al Smith making up a formidable starting rotation.

On the other hand, the Detroit Tigers were a dangerous offensive ballclub, but thin in experienced and healthy pitching. Schoolboy Rowe was the ace but, at age 30, was battling back from a shoulder injury that had threatened his career and limited him to a grand total of 14 games in 1937 and 1938. He compiled a 16-3 record in 1940, but again suffered shoulder miseries down the stretch.

Also anchoring the staff was the always colorful Norman "Bobo" Newsom. At 33, Newsom had the best season of his career, finishing fourth in the American League MVP balloting behind teammate Hank Greenberg, Bob Feller, and Joe DiMaggio while posting a 21-5 record. It was Newsom's third straight 20-win season (he reached the milestone with disparate ERAs of 2.83 in 1940, 3.58 in 1939, and most remarkable of all, "Old Buck" won 20 games with an ERA of 5.08 in 1938).

Another 33-year-old, curveball specialist Tommy Bridges, rounded out the top three in the rotation. Al Benton added six wins and 17 saves out of the bullpen. The rest of the starting corps was culled from a group including second-year men Fred Hutchinson and Dizzy Trout, and rookies Johnny Gorsica and 19-year-old Hal New-houser.

The Tigers' offense could be lethal. Hank Greenberg and Rudy York combined for 74 home runs and 284 runs batted in during 1940. They amassed 727 total bases; Greenberg had 384, York 343.

Second-year outfielder Barney McCosky batted .340 and led the league in base hits and triples. (McCosky is one of the forgotten batsmen of the war-interrupted years; a lifetime .312 hitter, he batted more than .320 four times for the Tigers and Athletics, but suffered from a lack of home run production in an era of DiMaggios, Williamses, and Greenbergs.)

Thirty-seven-year-old Charlie Gehringer still outplayed most second basemen in the field and had one last splendid season left in his bat, driving in 81 runs on a .313 batting average. The catching tandem of Birdie Tebbetts and Billy Sullivan combined for a .301 batting average and 87 RBIs. Detroit also called on future Hall of Fame member (and ex-Cleveland star) Earl Averill to pinch-hit and play the outfield occasionally.

Just after Labor Day, the Tigers swept a three-game series from Cleveland by scores of 7-2, 11-3, and 10-5 to close the gap between them to one game.

The Yankees, who two and a half weeks before had been ten games behind, were now only two out of first. Only four games separated the first-place Indians from the fourth-place Boston Red Sox. The next day the Tigers moved to within percentage points of first place after a dramatic come from behind 5-4 win over the Browns thanks to a three-run ninth inning.

On September 11, as Cleveland fans rained lemons onto the playing field (the first of many fan outbursts during this pennant race), the Indians split a doubleheader with New York, and the Tigers moved into first by virtue of an 11-7 victory over the Red Sox.

Cleveland and Detroit then swapped opponents and when the dust had cleared, the Indians were back in first by a game, the Yankees were three and a half games out, the Red Sox were out of the race entirely, and the Chicago White Sox had come from nowhere to take their place, winning 15 of 18 games to move within four games of the lead and a half-game behind the third-place Yankees.

Suddenly, the Tigers faced a dilemma: Schoolboy Rowe had to leave a game early because of pain in his shoulder and staring at back-to-back doubleheaders against the last-place Philadelphia Athletics, Detroit was in need of a healthy arm to get them through the crisis. Enter Floyd Giebell.

Giebell had failed to stick with the Tigers out of spring training in 1940 after nearly bleeding to death that winter in Weirton following a tonsillectomy. His long recovery left him behind the other pitchers in conditioning and, still weak upon reporting to Lakeland,

Florida, for training camp, Giebell was sent to Buffalo and finally began pitching well after regaining his strength in May.

Despite his 15-17 record in the International League, Bisons Manager Steve O'Neill recommended Giebell to Detroit Manager Del Baker as a temporary replacement for Rowe. Compared by O'Neill to Yankee pitcher Monte Pearson, the Buffalo skipper was quoted as saying that he was, "the kind of pitcher batters like to hit against... but they won't do a lot to him."

A "sinker-slider" pitcher, Giebell relied on his control and ability to keep the ball down in the strike zone. Although not known for high velocity hurling, he could spot his fastball when he wanted to ("I could throw ninety-one, ninety-two. I wasn't a softball pitcher"). He had pitched much better than his record indicated; the Bisons so lacked any offensive punch the team frequently employed him as a pinch hitter. He lost four games 1-0 and during one stretch lost three consecutive contests by a score of 2-1.

On September 19, Giebell took the mound against Philadelphia in Rowe's place and went the distance in a 13-2 victory. Greenberg and York drove in five runs apiece in the game, Greenberg clouting the 13th of 15 home runs he would hit that month. After Dizzy Trout won the nightcap 10-1, Detroit was in a first-place tie with Cleveland and the Indians were coming to the Motor City for the first of six games remaining between these rivals.

As the Cleveland team arrived at Union Depot in Detroit the night before the first game of the series, about 200 Tiger fans were waiting to greet them with overripe vegetables and a chorus of "Rock-a-Bye-Baby-in-the-Tree-Top." Cleveland trainer "Lefty" Wiseman was struck in the back with a tomato. The crowd followed the Indians to their hotel and were finally dispersed by a barrage of official Cleveland Indian water bombs dropped from the windows above.

After drying off, the Detroit faithful were back in high spirits the next day, rolling a baby carriage in front of the Cleveland dugout before the game and greeting Manager Oscar Vitt with warm ovations whenever he appeared on the field. What followed was a pivotal moment of the pennant race: a controversial game that proved a second-guesser's delight. The Indians' Mel Harder had kept the Briggs Stadium crowd quiet by allowing the Tigers only three hits going into the eighth inning. With a 4-1 advantage, Harder surrendered a lead-off double and, after a fly ball and a walk, Detroit had runners at first and third with one out. Despite the fact that Harder had not yet surrendered a run in the inning, out of the Cleveland dugout popped the beleaguered Vitt to summon Feller into the game. Feller had pitched a complete game victory the day before, but this time he didn't have it as Detroit strafed him for three straight hits before the Indians could rescue him. The Tigers scored five runs in the inning and went on to win 6-5.

The teams split the last two games of the series, Rowe stopping Cleveland on a five-hit shutout and Feller coming back to homer and beat Detroit 10-5 in the series finale before a crowd of 56,771. The Tigers led the Indians by one game, with a three-game rematch set in Cleveland the next weekend.

The Indians split their series during the week while the Tigers swept a doubleheader from the White Sox, with Newsom winning both games, to put Detroit two games up on Cleveland with three to play. The Tigers needed but one victory to clinch a trip to the World Series. The Indians needed a sweep. The Yankees were still alive, but barely, two and a half games behind. If they and Cleveland both swept their series, the result would be an Indian-Yankee play-off.

The Tigers had won 17 of their last 22. Cleveland announced that Feller would pitch the series opener on Friday. There was open speculation that the Tigers would save Rowe and instead sacrifice one of their younger pitchers against Cleveland's ace. On Friday morning, Detroit Manager Del Baker announced that the team's veterans had just voted on the starting pitcher for that afternoon. Their choice was Floyd Giebell.

*   *   *

"I knew the night before that I was gonna work. I don't care what the sportswriters said, because Baker came to my room and told me. I've heard two stories about being named starting pitcher. I couldn't say that's definite [about the team vote]. But they knew I wouldn't be walking myself out of the ballgame."

Giebell also knew he wanted Billy Sullivan behind the plate for the biggest game of his life.

"I wanted Sullivan because I had a run-in with Tebbetts. Tebbetts didn't like it because I shook him off in St. Louis one day when I relieved Newhouser. He went in the dugout, moaning and groaning, and went to Baker. And Baker come over to talk to me about the situation. I told him, that out there [on the mound], I knew what my best stuff was. And also, I wasn't sitting on the bench blind. And Tebbetts and I never saw eye-to-eye after that. So I always asked for Sullivan when I was pitching."

The Cleveland crowd, a Ladies Day gathering of 45,553, was in a raucous mood long before the first pitch, eager to retaliate for the treatment their heroes had suffered at Union Depot the week before. The start of the game was delayed so that debris hurled onto the field during batting and fielding practice could be cleared. Once the game began, the fans down the left field line decided Greenberg was an inviting target and showered him with garbage as he caught a first-inning fly ball. Baker came out to protest and threatened to pull his team off the field if the fans weren't quieted. Home plate umpire Bill Summers warned the crowd that if the outbursts did not subside, the game would be forfeited to Detroit.

In the second inning, the Tigers received a break when Cleveland outfielder Roy Weatherly lost Greenberg's fly ball in the sun and it fell safely for a double. A fly out by York moved Greenberg to third, but after Feller walked Bruce Campbell, he induced Pinky Higgins to ground into a double play.

Later that inning, there was some activity in the Tiger bullpen and the crowd, sensing a new target, dropped a basket filled with tomatoes and empty bottles onto Birdie Tebbetts' head, knocking the Detroit catcher senseless. A ten-minute delay was required as the stricken player was carried from the bullpen to the dugout and revived. This incident finally settled the crowd, and after two innings the game remained scoreless.

Giebell experienced his first taste of trouble in the bottom of the third when Tiger shortstop Dick Bartell made an error on Ray Mack's ground ball and Mack went to third on a single by Rollie Hemsley.

"Bartell made an error behind me, and then I got out of that. I struck out [Ben] Chapman, I think three different times on sliders when he coulda hurt me with a man on second or third with only one out or something like that."

In the top of the fourth the Tigers got on the board. Charlie Gehringer drew a walk, and after Feller retired Greenberg, York hit a home run—a fly ball that barely made it into the stands. It was one of only three hits, including Greenberg's sun-aided double, that Feller surrendered.

After York's four-bagger, Giebell continued changing speeds, mixing in his slider and keeping the hitters off balance. Going to the bottom of the seventh, Detroit led 2-0.

"In the seventh inning...if Charlie Gehringer makes an error behind ya...he *never* makes errors. He let one go through his legs. And I got in trouble again with men on first and second with nobody out."

Feller sacrificed the runners to second and third. Once again, up stepped Chapman, and once again he struck out. Roy Weatherly then grounded to Higgins and the Indians' best-scoring threat of the day was wasted.

Word came that New York had been defeated by Philadelphia, ending the Yankees' hopes of winning a fifth straight American League title. Suddenly, this hard-fought pennant race was winding up and the Indians were down to their final three outs.

"I don't know about the first two outs. I know the last out of the ninth, a pinch hitter came up...Weatherly? Or was it...no, who was the other outfielder...Heath, yes. And he grounded out to York. Course, me being a pitcher, you always break towards first base when the ball's hit to the left of you. And I went over to cover first base and York waved me off. And the next thing I know, I'm being carried off the field. York took me up first, and the next man was Billy Sullivan, and I think Trout...anyway, they carried me off the field."

York took the ball he caught for the final out and hid it in his pocket, later presenting the prize to Tiger owner Walter Briggs. To Giebell he gave the bat with which he hit the pennant-winning homer after having it autographed by the entire team. It is a memento that is still one of his treasured possessions; a great reminder of his accomplishment. With his 134 pitches that day, Giebell not only had deprived Feller and the Cleveland Indians of a chance to go to the World Series, the man who after this game would be known as "The Icicle Kid" had shut them out—in their own ballpark, allowing only six hits, four of those scratch infield singles.

"They carried me into the dugout, and then they took a picture on the edge of the dugout steps. 'Course, there's always about twenty-five to one hundred sportswriters around. We got into the clubhouse and some of the team members couldn't understand why I wasn't throwing benches around and popping corks all around. I was sitting over there, trying to unwind a little bit. They thought I should be up and whooping it up and turning lockers over. I didn't feel that way. Good thing we're not all alike. It'd be a dull world, wouldn't it? I was just a very happy man at that time. Something had been accomplished that I'd...that most boys had dreamed about."

Giebell phoned his fiancée, a schoolteacher in western New York State, and wired her money to come to Detroit and attend the opening World Series games against the National League champion Cincinnati Reds. (This is contrary to newspaper reports that Briggs had paid her way. Stories that Briggs gave Giebell a full series share out of his pocket are also inaccurate as his share and expenses came to about a two-thirds portion.)

Giebell was not eligible to play in the series, having been called up by the Tigers after the September 1 deadline, but opposing Manager Bill McKechnie gave Detroit permission for him to be in uniform and pitch batting practice. (Del Baker later took the pitcher aside and told him that if he could, he would have started him in the third game of the World Series.)

A huge celebration awaited the Tigers upon their return to Detroit and preparations for the World Series, and the fans presented each team member with a sterling silver tray to show their appreciation.

"Probably weighs about seven pounds," says Giebell today. "It's got handles on it and it's engraved all the way around the edges. It's about an inch deep. And on the face of that sterling silver tray is a natural autograph of all the ball players and coaches on the team. They got one up at Cooperstown. I kept mine in a safe until I retired, and I have it now on my mantle."

The 1940 World Series was a seven-game affair, the Reds forcing the deciding contest after sending the sore-armed Rowe to an early shower for the second time in four days. Game Seven featured a confrontation between Cincinnati's Paul Derringer and Detroit's Bobo Newsom. Newsom had already won two games, despite the tragedy of his father's sudden death after Game One, and was attempting to become the first pitcher since Stan Coveleski in 1920 to win three games in a single World Series. Derringer had beaten Dizzy Trout 5-2 in Game Four, while Newsom had bested Derringer in the series opener and shut out Cincinnati on three hits in Game Five. The

Tigers' 21-game winner, however, had only 48 hours' rest for the final game.

The Tigers took the lead in the third inning of the deciding contest, thanks to an infield hit by Gehringer and a throwing error by Reds third baseman Billy Werber. For a while, it seemed that Newsom would make the run hold up.

Then, in the seventh, Cincinnati's Frank McCormick led off with a double. The next batter, Jimmy Ripple, hit a ball off the railing in right center that just missed being a home run but McCormick, thinking the ball might be caught, held up, then headed for third, stopped again, and then broke for home and scored the tying run when Dick Bartell took the relay throw and failed to turn around and look at McCormick. Giebell remembers that moment like it was yesterday.

"Here's Bartell, standing with his back to the infield — has the ball in his hand, McCormick is just rounding third base. And that cost us the ballgame. Never turned around, and the crowd was roaring. I don't know if Gehringer was trying to help him, which they was supposed to do, you know. But you don't take anything for granted in baseball. So that cost everybody a ring."

A sacrifice bunt, walk, and fly ball later, the Reds had the lead for good, and the World Championship.

* * *

Floyd Giebell looked forward to the 1941 season with great expectation given his performance under pressure the previous September. He knew that despite his pennant-clinching victory he still remained behind several of the veteran pitchers on the staff but felt confident that if he waited his turn he would surely get a starting assignment by the beginning of May.

"May first came around...and the 15th of May came around, and I'm still in the bullpen. And I went to Baker, and he couldn't give me any satisfaction, outside of saying there's more experienced people than me there. But we're down in fourth or fifth place at the time.

"I went to Jack Zeller, the general manager, and I asked him to trade me. This is about the first of June. And they wouldn't do it. They wouldn't trade me. You have an idea how I began to feel about the first of July, then.

"About the sixteenth of July, they started me. The first time since the twenty-seventh of September the year before. I don't remember now who it was against. Anyway, I was in shape physically, but I was in no shape mentally because I was angry and I was hurt. I think I was around for about four innings, and then in a few days, why, they sold me to Buffalo.

"I was glad to get out of town to tell you the truth. From a major league club to Triple A. It may be hard to believe for some people, but I was glad to get out of town."

Giebell went 5-1 for the Bisons during the remainder of that season while the Tigers, who had finished fifth in 1939, returned to fifth place once again in 1941. Despite the fact that he would end his career with a 3.10 ERA over nearly 1,500 minor league innings, and would not once record an ERA approaching 4.00, Giebell never again appeared in a major league uniform. After spending all of 1942 with Buffalo, Giebell signed up for a three-year hitch in the Navy and on his return discovered that Gabby Hartnett, Buffalo's manager, had committed to a youth movement. Then 36 years old, he quickly saw the handwriting on the wall. Giebell returned to the Texas League with Dallas for the 1947 and 1948 seasons, sporting ten wins and a 2.67 ERA in his final season at the age of 38. He then called it quits when he took notice of teammates dragging their families around the country while trying to avoid that inevitable day when they would wear their spikes no more. The situation took him back to a scene he had witnessed some ten years earlier.

"One of my most disappointing things, when I was in the Three I League, they had this barnstorming team [The House of David] going around, playing in the Midwest. And one of the great pitchers, Grover Cleveland Alexander, I saw him staggering [drunk] down the side street—and that hurt, because I read a lot about him and what a great pitcher he was.

"I saw ball players taking their families around...taking their children out of school...and bringing them up for the season. And I said that's never gonna happen to me. I didn't think it was right. I didn't want to be just hanging on and taking my family around, especially in the minor leagues. It's bad enough in the majors."

* * *

Retirement from baseball did not prove difficult.

"I even gave up *The Sporting News* when I quit baseball. Because

I'm a family man and I made up my mind that when the time came, that I wasn't gonna split any hairs.

"We had some good times together [on the Tigers]. You know, we travelled by train in those days, and after you leave a city to go on to the next city, you get on the train. You sit in a nice dining car, why, have a relaxing dinner...the countryside going by. You know, that's the only thing I miss coming out of pro ball. Dinner and watching the countryside go by."

After leaving baseball Giebell first took a position in Greenville, South Carolina, as a recreation director. While there he instituted baseball programs for both children and adults as well as a women's basketball program. After six years there, he returned to Weirton Steel to "build up a little retirement." He received the honor of being inducted into both the West Virginia Sports Hall of Fame and the West Virginia Intercollegiate Hall of Fame. In each instance he was inducted for both baseball and basketball; the former honor given to him on the occasion of West Virginia's centennial celebration of statehood. Giebell was especially proud to be cited as "a role model for the young people of West Virginia."

After retiring from Weirton Steel in 1972, he moved to North Carolina for a life of travel and fishing. He enjoys visits from his grandchildren and great-grandchildren, one of whom, Michael, has been christened "Little Lobo" because the youngster lives not far from the University of New Mexico. Despite these happy moments, tragedy has unfortunately shadowed Floyd Giebell in his later years.

After moving from Greenville to West Virginia, Giebell and his son Stephen regularly travelled to Pittsburgh to visit Fred Hutchinson, Giebell's best friend from his days with the Tigers, whenever the Cincinnati manager accompanied his team into Forbes Field to play the Pirates. Those trips came to an end after his friend's death in 1964 following a valiant battle against cancer.

Then, in November 1969, Stephen was killed in Vietnam.

"It's a murderous stupidity. And Sunday was his birthday, this past Sunday. Fourth of February. Twenty-two years old. Shot by a sniper. Sure, he's got a lot of medals...given to him posthumously. As far as I'm concerned, one young man's life over there is not worth all of Southeast Asia. We had two presidents...lied to us from the word go; what they were gonna do, and what they did do.

"That's something you gotta fight. Something that...part of

FLOYD GIEBELL
Born December 10, 1909, Pennsboro, West Virginia
Ht. 6'2" Wt. 172   BR   TR

MAJOR AND MINOR LEAGUE CAREER

Year	Team, League	W-L	Pct	G	GS	CG	SHO	IP	H	R	ER	BB	SO	ERA
1938	Evansville, I.I.I.	18-6	.750	25	25	20	—	214	171	61	47	61	141	*1.98*
1939	DETROIT, American	1-1	.500	9	0	0	0	15.1	19	7	5	12	9	2.93
	Beaumont, Texas	6-6	.500	13	12	10	1	98.2	91	39	26	32	43	2.37
	Toledo, American Assn	1-10	.091	12	11	9	0	93	102	47	37	21	37	3.58
1940	Buffalo, International	15-17	.469	37	32	21	4	239	241	119	99	82	104	3.73
	DETROIT, American	2-0	1.000	2	2	2	1	18	14	2	2	4	11	1.00
1941	DETROIT, American	0-0	—	17	2	0	0	34.1	45	29	23	26	10	6.09
	Buffalo, International	5-1	.833	6	—	—	—	—	—	—	—	—	—	—
1942	Buffalo, International	8-6	.571	22	15	9	2	139	128	67	57	75	42	3.69
1943	Buffalo, International	12-17	.414	33	33	20	0	248	252	116	90	99	94	3.27
1944-45	MILITARY SERVICE													
1946	Buffalo-Syracuse, Intl	4-5	.444	17	10	6	1	79	82	42	32	38	36	3.65
1947	Dallas, Texas	11-8	.579	27	—	11	—	176.2	164	81	64	70	59	3.26
1948	Dallas, Texas	10-11	.476	24	23	12	1	172	164	71	51	53	61	2.67
	MAJOR LEAGUE TOTALS	3-1	.750	28	4	2	1	67.2	78	38	30	42	30	3.99
	MINOR LEAGUE TOTALS	90-87	.508	216	161	118	9	1459.1	1395	642	503	531	617	3.10

Italics in boldface type indicate led league

us...is just not here anymore. We're not as light, shall we say. We still laugh once in awhile, the family and I. Our daughter is here in North Carolina, she's a teacher. We're making out pretty good. But we're not as light or as gay as we used to be.

"We all take so much for granted. Think we're all gonna live forever I guess, and our loved ones are gonna be with us. But it doesn't work out that way."

* * *

Floyd Giebell has never returned to Detroit.

"I never have been back. I was invited back by [former Tiger President Jim] Campbell a number of times, but I never had a chance to make it. I thought probably on the anniversary of fifty years since we beat Cleveland and Feller they might invite those people back. But it was never done. I got a letter from a guy I don't know, he's up in the [Tiger] office, said that it had been called to his attention what had happened fifty years ago. I've been surprised in a way [that there hasn't been a reunion], because I had some friends up there."

One senses some frustration remaining when Giebell reminisces about the 1940 World Series.

"I thought we should have won it. We *would* have won it, because here's Newsom in the seventh game. That's too bad. Not because I was with Detroit, but if I'd been from Timbuktu, why, I thought Detroit shoulda won. With Newsom there on the mound, the game he pitched, and what happened with Bartell."

Giebell has fond memories of the man who took the loss in that seventh game heartbreaker despite his magnificent 89-pitch performance.

"He threw from every angle. Overhand, sidearm, and underneath. And he *was* somewhat of a showboat. *Very* colorful. I know. I roomed with him a few times on the road; I know how colorful old Buck was. I really do. I took care of his luggage sometimes for him when he was late getting in or getting out, or something. So I know Bobo.

"It was tougher [being on the road] in the old days than it is now. Because, in the old days, you played all day ball practically. And you spent probably three to four days in each town and you had a lotta time on your hands in the evening. And if you didn't have a pretty good...oh...grip on yourself, if you didn't know what it was all about, or what you were all about and what you wanted to accomplish, well, you had plenty of time to get into something else.

"Of course, I think there's a lot more things out there to get into than there were when I was playing. A lot more things: There's more money involved, and this Pete Rose deal, and these people going in there in rehab. They get cooled out and cooled off and a few other things. All this talent some of these guys have, it's too bad that they throw it away."

As he points out, a great number of athletes have left their promise unfulfilled or had their careers tragically shortened in pursuit of various vices. And while his own major league career was frustrating in its brevity, Floyd Giebell can certainly look back with pride and note that he did not fall into that category. When he was handed his opportunity in the spotlight, although it lasted but a moment, he definitely didn't throw it away.

BERNIE WILLIAMS

Outfielder,
1970-72 San Francisco Giants;
1974 San Diego Padres

I just wanted a chance to play. I wasn't playing every day and I was very dissatisfied. I wasn't using any of my God-given talent. I felt like I very well could've been playing. I'd seen instances where they allowed certain players to play into maturity, but [with the Giants] I wasn't getting any playing time. Plus Candlestick Park was cold as hell. [Laughs.]

When I was drafted by them, I felt great. All the way through the minor league system I felt good. I was protected. I was given major league contracts. But I believe if I had started with another organization that was going through a transition, then I would've been able to have more playing time. I wish I would've come up now instead of during the Mays and Bonds and Henderson era.

— Bernie Williams

Ability is of little account without opportunity.
—Napoleon Bonaparte

As the 1971 National League season came to an end, the San Francisco Giants won the Western Division title and completed their 14th consecutive winning season, by far the longest existing streak in the major leagues at the time. Since capturing their only pennant in 1962, the team had won at least 88 games in nine of the previous ten seasons while featuring four future occupants of the Hall of Fame: Willie Mays, Willie McCovey, Juan Marichal, and Gaylord Perry. No other team from that era has as many inductees. Although faced with grumbling from fans and the press that they were not as dominant as they should be (an observation apparently not lost on the front office as evidenced by the fact the Giants employed six different managers since their move West in spite of the team's consistent success), there was no controversy about the tremendous talent they put on the field.

Twenty-five years ago, when San Francisco drafted Bernie Williams out of Oakland's St. Elizabeth High School, a player was bound to the team that selected him until he was either traded or released. This could place a young man in a predicament should he join an organization already overstocked with talent at his position. When Williams was attempting to break into the Giants' outfield during the early 1970s, his "only" obstacles were Willie Mays, Bobby Bonds, Ken Henderson, Dave Kingman, Garry Maddox, Gary Matthews, Gary Thomasson, and George Foster. Although San Francisco's run of success ended with their three games to one defeat at the hands of the Pittsburgh Pirates in the 1971 National League play-offs, the Giants' pipeline of talent from the farm system to the outfield remained intact, much to the detriment of the local boy trying to make good.

* * *

Bernie Williams first became fascinated with baseball through collecting baseball cards, even though he now laughingly says, "I hated the gum." He was nine years old when major league baseball came to the San Francisco Bay Area and collecting cards made his heroes more accessible. Like most of his friends, Williams dreamed that one day he too would be playing in the big leagues. He remembers thinking, "I had this childhood fantasy that one day I could play with Willie Mays. And it just carried on from there."

A high school star, batting nearly .400 in his senior year, Williams also played American Legion ball. In all he slugged a total of 32 home runs between high school and legion competition in 1966, several of which travelled more than 400 feet. It was a season crowned by his helping lead his team to the Legion World Series Championship in North Carolina.

Signed shortly after New Year's Day 1967 by Giants scout Eddie Montague, Williams was assigned to Medford in the Northwest League where he was Most Valuable Player on a team that won the pennant. He led the league in bases on balls and was second in both home runs and RBIs. The next year, he was Honorable Mention on the California League All-Star team and in his third professional season was named to the All-Star team in the Double-A Texas League.

By 1970 the 21-year-old Williams was a starting outfielder in the Pacific Coast League, chasing fly balls for the Giants' Triple-A affiliate in Phoenix. There he teamed up with a future major league home run champion, a man as religious and reserved as Williams was outgoing. His name was George Foster and despite their apparently irreconcilable personalities, the two were roommates and became good friends.

They were known as the "Jekyll and Hyde" roommates. Foster was the one always carrying a baseball in one hand and a Bible in the other. Williams was the one who wasn't. The two would eventually part as teammates when the Giants made the determination that one of them would have to go in order to shore up the team's infield depth for the 1971 stretch run. Foster had bad knees at the time; Williams remembers him always having a bottle of liniment with him, and this factor would weigh heavily in the Giants' eventual decision.

As the 1970 Pacific Coast League season continued and Williams and Foster became closer, the two developed a friendly rivalry.

"We had a little ongoing bet about who would hit for the highest average and on the last day of the season we each had four hits. It just so happened we came up for that fifth time...and I got a hit. I beat him out by a point."

Phoenix Manager Hank Sauer bubbled over enthusiastically when talking about his two young outfield prospects, saying, "We knew they both could play, but they've exceeded all expectations."

After hitting .309 for Phoenix (to Foster's .308), Williams was rewarded with a September promotion to the major leagues and found himself in the outfield next to his childhood hero, the legendary "Say-Hey Kid," Willie Mays.

"It was awesome. I was so nervous. I really didn't know what to say to him. I didn't know if I was gonna be bothering him if I asked him certain questions.

"He positioned players [during games], he counseled players, he fed players, he listened to their problems, he loaned them money. If he saw them possibly going astray, he would say, 'Hey kid, come on. Let's go out tonight.' Out tonight wasn't 'out.' It was to his room and you talked baseball. That was going 'out.' He would order room service and you'd have the full-course spread. The whole bit. But you would be talking baseball.

"Within my mind I said, 'What would it be like to replace him?' I think I got a little bit arrogant until he told me one day, 'You know, when you're of no more value to a ballclub, or to people, you'll see what happens. Just like that.'"

In mid-May 1972, the day came when Mays' words of warning to Williams hit home. The Giants were in Montreal and Williams heard that Mays was going to New York. His first reaction was, "Why is he going to New York? We're in Montreal playing the Expos."

Suddenly it sunk in. Mays, the man who *was* the Giants, had been traded. To Williams it didn't seem right. Mays should have retired as a Giant. You don't trade a Willie Mays.

Less than two years later, Williams would himself be dealt, accompanying another Giants legend in a trade to the San Diego Padres.

Just like that.

*   *   *

After a five for 16 September trial with the Giants in 1970, Williams opened the 1971 season with Phoenix once again. In early June he was sporting a .329 batting average and was recalled to San Francisco after Ken Henderson was injured and George Foster was traded to the Reds in one of the more famous (or infamous depending on your rooting interest) one-sided deals in baseball history. Placed in left field while Henderson was on the mend, Williams hoped a long stretch of playing time might land him the position on a regular basis. The opportunity failed to materialize.

"Back in those days, if you got hurt and someone came along and did well, you could lose your job. So Henderson made a miraculous recovery and I sat around."

His playing time reduced to pinch-hitting or appearing as a defensive replacement, Williams' rare starts usually came against a tough or unknown pitcher, for example the day the Houston Astros came to town and unveiled a new hurler with an untamed fastball. His name was James Rodney Richard.

"It was a bright Sunday afternoon at Candlestick. He's throwing *peas*, one hundred miles an hour. Richard did seventeen that day. Seventeen Ks. I faced him again down in winter ball in the Dominican and then I learned to adjust to him. Just leave all that other stuff alone and wait for the breaking ball. Usually his fastball was either high and tight or low and away, and the breaking ball, which was *very* sharp, would usually be over the center of the plate."

After two months of riding the bench, the young outfielder was sent back to Phoenix, the Giants explaining that he needed to play every day. Williams was in total agreement, he knew he could never develop as a player while huddling in the corner of the Giants' dugout all summer attempting to keep from freezing to death. He went back to Phoenix enthusiastically determined to keep a positive frame of mind. He knew he'd be back in San Francisco soon enough.

"I was playing, and I really enjoyed that."

* * *

The San Francisco Giants staggered to the last day of the 1971 campaign, ultimately clinching the title by a single game over the Los Angeles Dodgers after allowing a large season-long lead to evaporate. Williams returned to the major league team in September, but had remained on the bench which made it difficult for him to feel a part of the celebration.

"I basically was just backing up. I didn't feel complete as a ball player. Maybe I became a little withdrawn, because this was my *dream*. I'm from the Bay Area. We're getting ready to go to the play-offs and I'm just *here*. It really wasn't a fulfilling moment for me."

Williams stuck with the big league club out of spring training the next year as a reserve, but when Mays was traded five weeks into the season it was Garry Maddox, not Bernie Williams, who moved in between Ken Henderson and Bobby Bonds in the San Francisco outfield. The season, which had started out with a player strike that wiped out the first week of league play, was forgettable for both Williams and the Giants. Once again he sat on the bench while the team suffered through their first losing season since moving West, drawing fewer fans than they had in their final season in New York. At the end of the campaign, Williams had batted only 68 times all year. Among his 13 hits were three home runs (two coming in pinch-hitting roles) and nine RBIs.

For the most part, he rode the pines and worked with coach Jim Davenport.

"He'd say, 'Come over here and field some ground balls, because you gotta field them in the outfield.' We'd sit and kick it around and stuff. Very nice guy. He actually taught me about the breaking pitch. If it's coming at you, you know it's gonna break over the plate. But if it's already over the plate, you know it's gonna be a ball. If you concentrate, there are little points and little things that you can pick up to know if the pitcher is going to throw a fastball or a breaking pitch. As soon as the ball leaves his hand, actually. A baseball player's mind...it really goes into another dimension. You can actually *see* things before they happen.

"Davenport taught me that if I'm looking at the pitcher and his wrist is flat, facing towards me, no way from that point can he throw any sort of a breaking pitch. If his wrist is horizontal, then there's no way he could change that to throw a fastball. It has to be some sort of breaking pitch. If your concentration is there, you can see *before* he releases the ball what the pitch is gonna be. But sitting on the bench, you don't have that one-on-one contact."

After a frustrating year and a half with the San Francisco Giants, Williams was not at all certain in 1973 of making the team. During that spring training, as he struggled to remain in the big leagues, he was faced with a family emergency. His two-year-old son fell seriously ill to a mysterious ailment.

"He was running about 104, 105 fever. My wife had to take him to the doctor and then eventually to the hospital. They couldn't find out what was wrong with the kid. I went to management and I said, 'Can I go home for a couple of days?'

"They're telling me that, 'Well, you know you're fighting for a job.'

"I'm saying, 'What's a job compared to if my son dies?' They told me, 'No.'

"I said, '*What?*'

"I promptly left the office and went back to the hotel and called the airport and got on a plane and came home to see my son. There were certain reprisals, but I didn't feel that I had done anything wrong because it had been done before. I don't know if it had been done for the black ball player at that particular time, but it *had* been done. So I didn't think it was very fair.

"Eventually, my son did get better, but his tonsils were deteriorating and were infecting his body and the doctors couldn't find the problem. If this one doctor hadn't discovered the cause, my son could have died. We worried that he had brain damage because he couldn't even walk. They even had to keep an i.v. in his heel and they literally had to pin him down, tie him down to the bed. I just made a decision... I want to live with myself and my wife needs me, so I have to go. I just have to suffer the consequences."

The consequences were that despite a year at Phoenix where he finished second in the league in doubles and triples, sixth in batting, stole 24 bases and went four for five in the league All-Star game, he was not brought up from the minors in 1973.

It was just one instance where Williams felt the hue of his skin made a difference in the way he was treated.

"If it was a white athlete, I don't believe that he would've gotten the same flak and all. There were times that when a father died or whatever, people were allowed to leave. I even had them call the hospital and talk to the doctors just to let them know that this wasn't a lie. That this was *actually* happening."

Four days after the 1973 World Series (and Willie Mays' final game), Williams received a phone call from a local newspaper reporter who had followed his career from his days at St. Elizabeth. He informed Williams that he had been traded with Willie McCovey to the San Diego Padres for pitcher Mike Caldwell.

* * *

The San Diego Padres had struggled since their birth in 1969, never getting closer than 11 games of escaping the National League West cellar during that time. The winter of 1973-74 was especially trying as owner C. Arnholt Smith, engaged in financial gymnastics that would eventually land him in prison, agreed to sell the team to a buyer who was to shift the franchise to Washington, D.C. The move was all but finalized and preparations were made to move team offices across country. New uniforms were manufactured. Then just before spring training, a 70-year-old hamburger entrepreneur, whose life-

long ambition had been to own the Chicago Cubs, stepped in and
saved the franchise for the city of San Diego. He was the founder of
McDonald's, Ray Kroc. Despite the short and troubled history of the
Padre organization, Williams was not sorry to leave the Giants. He
saw the trade as an opportunity to play regularly and prove his worth.
As to whether he was in San Francisco or San Diego, it didn't really
make any difference. He just wanted the chance to play to the best of
his ability.

Despite his early optimism, Williams and his new teammates
embarked on a somewhat stormy relationship with the hamburger
mogul turned baseball expert. At the April 9 home opener, the locals
were suffering a 9-2 drubbing at the hands of the Houston Astros
when Kroc, incensed at what he viewed as the lack of effort put forth
by his charges, grabbed the public address microphone in the eighth
inning and angrily proclaimed, "Ladies and gentlemen...I suffer with
you. I've never seen such stupid baseball playing in my life." Fans and
players alike were stunned. Williams had never seen anything like it.

"He got on the P.A. and made apologies to the fans and he just
literally called us a bunch of bums. Knowing his background I guess
he felt that we as a unit weren't giving all that needed to be given. He
didn't understand that when you're putting all these people together,
they basically have come from other organizations. They don't know
each other.

"When I grew up in the Giants organization, I played with Foster
and I played with Frank Johnson and Bonds and those people. We
learned one another. We learned to the point where it was like constant communication without saying anything. And I don't think selling hamburgers compares.

"I don't think Kroc ever realized what he'd done. I really don't,
because we never got an apology for it."

Williams started a few games for the Padres until straining
tendons in his throwing shoulder making a throw to second to prevent
a runner from taking an extra base. He underwent a series of cortisone
injections but after suffering an allergic reaction, was shipped out to
Hawaii, the Padres' Triple-A affiliate in the Pacific Coast League, to
undertake a special program of physical therapy. That treatment
proved unsuccessful as well. Months after the injury he was still unable
to do anything requiring such simple movement as reaching across his
car to unlock the door without experiencing terrific pain.

That August the Padres approached the young outfielder and asked if he would consider an operation. Williams thought about the experience of his good friend Jim Ray Hart. The Giants' third baseman had been hit by a Bob Gibson fastball that broke his collarbone, an injury that was repaired surgically. Williams had not only been frightened by the scar Hart carried with him, he was also frightened by the results of the operation. Hart was never able to regain full use of the shoulder after his recovery and his once-promising career went into eclipse.

"When I talk to Jimmy now or when I see him, he doesn't even shoot pool anymore because the shoulder bothers him."

Williams decided against surgery, feeling that even if his career was over, the shoulder would still heal to the point that he could lead a normal life. The Padres then offered Williams the chance to continue his career in Japan.

"So I talked to my wife. I said, 'Well, what do you think?' She said, 'Well, I don't know.'

"I said, 'Well, either I take a ten percent cut in pay and stay here or I make $8,000 more. If I take the $8,000 and go over there and can't play anymore, at least we're $8,000 ahead.'"

* * *

Williams was purchased by the Hankyu Braves of the Japanese Pacific League, a team based in Osaka that had appeared in five of the last eight Japan Series—and had lost all five to the same team, the Yomiuri Giants. (The Giants had just completed an unprecedented run of nine consecutive Japan Series titles.) Despite his shoulder injury, the Braves wanted the 27-year-old outfielder and were confident in their team physician's ability to bring him around. Within a week, there was dramatic improvement.

"They took a chance and the doctor, he looked at it and the only thing I did for ten days was conditioning and therapy. They feel if your [physical] condition is good, that everything else is okay. And they definitely made sure you were in condition.

"Then, after that ten days, I started throwing easy. I started stretching it out...sometimes it would get a little stiff and the doctor would just use a little hot liniment. Then he would literally like *pop* it, and it would relieve the pressure. After that year, it was just fine."

The manager of the Braves was the fiery taskmaster Toshiharu Ueda. One of the most successful managers in Japan, Ueda was famous for his temper, as typified by a well-circulated photo of his foot zeroing in on the hindquarters of a catcher who had dropped a throw...in *practice*.

Ueda was used to dealing with foreign ball players (he regularly brought in Maury Wills to provide baserunning instruction), and was willing to make concessions to their training habits and style of play. Ueda would give players the opportunity to take a day off if there was a rainout or an open day in the schedule, which was unusual for a Japanese manager. At first Williams took the days off, until noticing that all the Japanese players would stay with the team and work out on their own.

"So I began to stick around and work out with them. If it rained, we worked out in the hotel lobby or hotel ballrooms and did all our running and calisthenics. I think that helped my standing with the team."

Williams was playing every day and couldn't have been happier. The team was a contender, he was contributing, and he enjoyed experiencing the feeling of "family" that the Japanese create in their workplace.

"It was a fantastic team. I don't know how it was brought together so intricately, but it's the kind of dream [situation] I think every ball player would love getting into. They were just maybe one or two players away from winning everything and luckily I was fortunate enough to be one of those players, along with another guy out of Venezuela. We came and we melded right in.

"These guys would come after the game and say, 'Hey, we're going over to this place tonight. We want to show you this. Hey, let's go to eat over here...I told them you were coming, and you can eat and drink and just relax over there. It's safe, it's okay.'

"I mean, jeez, these people were great. Next to my amateur World Series experience, I believe that was about the best experience in baseball that I had."

The Braves won four straight Pacific Coast League pennants, beginning in Williams' first year with the team, and three straight Japan Series; beating first the Hiroshima Carp in 1975 four games to none (with two ties), and then gaining a measure of revenge against the mighty Yomiuri Giants in both 1976 and 1977, defeating them in seven and five games respectively.

"Yomiuri...they're the symbol of Japan. They're a very good organization, they pay their ball players real well. Their *demands* are really high on a ball player, from what I learned while I was there. Nothing they do on the field is wrong. The umpires, they make the mistakes, not the Giants. So when we beat them, then the experts said, 'Their conditioning wasn't good.' That was the first year we beat them.

"But that next year, and [Sadaharu] Oh was still playing you know, the next year we beat them, and people said, 'Oh-oh. They're for real.'

"When Cincinnati beat the A's [in the 1990 World Series], my wife said, 'It was just like when you guys played Yomiuri. You guys played together, you guys looked like you enjoyed it. You didn't even look like you were under any pressure or anything. You just went out and played the game.' And that's exactly what we did."

Probably the best native player on the Braves was their five-foot-seven center fielder, 13-time stolen base champion Yutaka Fukumoto. Named the Pacific League's Most Valuable Player in 1972 after stealing 106 bases in 122 games, Fukumoto went on to swipe 295 bases in a three-year span and well over 1000 for his career. On that side of the Pacific Rim, the view is that Rickey Henderson still had one man to beat after passing Lou Brock in order to become the true stolen base king.

Williams thought Fukumoto was a tremendous lead-off hitter and all-around athlete who would have been a legitimate major league player. Fukumoto's teammates gave him a hard time upon the new import's arrival, telling him that the American had enough speed to beat him out for the stolen base crown. Fukumoto took the threat seriously and there was an unspoken rivalry between the two outfielders at the beginning of Williams' career in Japan.

"That first year I had maybe about twenty stolen bases and he had like ten. I was running on my own and after I got close to thirty, I stopped getting the [steal] sign."

It was a lesson in the Japanese ego and their need to save face, and for Williams it was a lesson well learned. Of the 200-plus ex-major league ball players to come to Japan, only 11 played more games than Williams. While some Americans have complained loudly about their experiences, he found it relatively easy to play in the Far East, provided you had the right attitude.

BERNIE WILLIAMS

Born October 8, 1948, Alameda, California
Ht. 6'1" Wt. 175   BR TR

MAJOR AND MINOR LEAGUE CAREER

Year	Team, League	G	AB	R	H	2B	3B	HR	RBI	BA	SA	BB	SO	SB
1967	Fresno, California	7	14	1	0	0	0	0	0	.000	.000	8	11	1
	Medford, Northwest	82	255	58	69	11	3	14	55	.271	.502	71	83	13
1968	Fresno, California	105	336	63	88	18	2	13	53	.262	.443	66	91	21
1969	Amarillo, Texas	132	469	86	132	30	6	5	67	.281	.403	65	93	13
1970	Amarillo, Texas	2	8	1	3	0	0	0	0	.375	.375	1	2	0
	Phoenix, Pacific Coast	113	346	71	107	15	8	9	47	.309	.477	57	50	9
	SAN FRANCISCO, National	7	16	2	5	2	0	0	1	.313	.438	2	1	1
1971	Phoenix, Pacific Coast	73	227	47	70	9	7	9	41	.308	.529	31	46	7
	SAN FRANCISCO, National	35	73	8	13	1	0	1	5	.178	.233	12	24	1
1972	SAN FRANCISCO, National	46	68	12	13	3	1	3	9	.191	.397	7	22	0
1973	Phoenix, Pacific Coast	132	492	85	154	31	15	6	55	.313	.474	59	69	24
1974	SAN DIEGO, National	14	15	1	2	0	0	0	0	.133	.133	0	6	0
	Hawaii, Pacific Coast	24	60	9	13	3	0	1	5	.217	.317	12	16	4
	Alexandria, Texas	38	122	12	28	9	1	3	19	.230	.393	16	33	1
1975	Hankyu Braves, Japan Pacific	123	420	54	100	13	0	15	47	.238	.376	42	95	32
1976	Hankyu Braves, Japan Pacific	128	446	54	121	15	8	15	51	.271	.442	35	77	7
1977	Hankyu Braves, Japan Pacific	125	439	60	110	21	6	16	50	.251	.435	32	62	8

1978	Hankyu Braves, Japan Pacific	117	403	64	119	16	2	18	66	.295	.479	38	69	11
1979	Hankyu Braves, Japan Pacific	105	291	40	67	7	4	11	30	.230	.395	35	48	11
1980	Hankyu Braves, Japan Pacific	120	345	—	87	—	—	21	50	.252	—	—	—	—
MAJOR LEAGUE TOTALS		102	172	23	33	6	1	4	15	.192	.308	21	53	2
MINOR LEAGUE TOTALS		708	2329	433	664	126	42	60	342	.285	.453	386	494	93
JAPAN LEAGUE TOTALS		718	2344	—	604	—	—	96	294	.258	—	—	—	—

"Just go play the game. I mean, that's what you're there for. You aren't trying to change them politically. You aren't there to try to change them socially. That's not your affair. You're there to play the game. You're the one that has to fit into *their* society.

"I understood why the [American player's] strike zone was larger …because of the strength factor. You could take an outside pitch and you could hit it out of the park. They could not take that outside pitch and hit it. They could drive it, but not hit it out of the park with any consistency. The umpires would widen your strike zone. But they were just trying to compensate a little bit."

After six years with the Hankyu Braves, comprising more than 700 games, and four Japan Series appearances, Williams called an end to his baseball career after the 1980 season. Injuries had taken their toll; he'd cracked both a kneecap and an elbow during his time with the Braves, and it seemed to him he was constantly going to the doctor for cortisone shots. He felt his body was saying, "This is enough."

* * *

One comes away with the feeling that Bernie Williams still struggles with life after baseball.

"For a couple of years afterward when February first came, my body would say, 'Oh, it's spring training time.' I believe with a ball player you need between three and five years really to adjust [to retirement]. Especially if you don't have any outside interests. My wife had to put up with a lot from me. I'd say up until about 1985, I acted like a little boy. I didn't want to grow up."

Williams currently works for the University of California at Berkeley as a lead custodian, and also manages several apartment buildings in the Oakland area owned by his family. He's planning to take courses at the university in hopes of pursuing a career in computer maintenance. He would really like to work with young people, but feels they just don't listen to anyone.

"There's just too many bad influences," he says, shaking his head sadly.

The opportunity to play with great players may have proved on the flipside a detriment to his major league career, as these same men blocked his ability to get playing time. Yet Williams still carries lessons learned from these people that he applies to his life outside the game. Many of the lessons he learned were from positive examples, such as Willie Mays, Willie McCovey, and Gaylord Perry (whom he credits with teaching him the importance of setting goals for himself). Some were lessons learned from negative examples, such as another teammate, Bobby Bonds.

"We really didn't get along that well because of his overall personality. As far as a ball player, what can you say? He was a great ball player. But as far as his overall demeanor—what he thought and more or less how he really looked at life—I believe he more or less instilled that attitude within his son [Barry]. I try to teach my son that humility is very important within a person, and I don't think they understand what that means."

Williams also sees benefits he has received in practicing the work ethic he learned in baseball.

"Whenever I do something when I'm at work, if it's not up to my standard, I have to do it over again until I'm satisfied. If it's up to my particular standards, then I know my boss isn't gonna come back to me and say, 'Hey, wait a minute. What's going on here?'

"It's just like playing. You keep working, working, working, until it benefits you. Like a high fastball. I know that I could not hit that pitch consistently. So I told myself, 'Why swing at it?' I had to keep telling myself over and over and over, 'You can't handle that, why swing at it? You tie yourself up.' I had to keep telling myself over and over and over and over and over to where it became automatic.

"God gives us certain talents, but I think to be an athlete, he gave you a couple of extra ones. You really have to be in tune with your mind and your body and it has to become as one. And then you can deal with life."

JOHN PACIOREK

Outfielder, 1963 Houston Colt .45s

I used to do a lot of stupid things. I wanted to be the best that ever was...I wanted to be like Mickey Mantle. So I was always doing exercises, doing some crazy things. I didn't really understand what I was doing, I was just doing exercises.

I wanted to have a nineteen and a half inch neck. I used to do neck exercises...you know how you do handstands? Instead of using my hands, I used my head. And all my weight would be on my neck. Every once in awhile, I'd slip and I'd be out of action for two weeks. It was stupid, the stuff I used to do.

But the only thing I could think about was being the best there was.

—John Paciorek

Nothing is more terrible than activity without insight.
— Thomas Carlyle

It was the final day of the 1963 National League season and two second-year expansion teams, the New York Mets and the Houston Colt .45s, were continuing a rivalry of ineptitude. There was serious debate going on at the time as to whether or not the other teams in the National League should contribute additional players to the doormats of the circuit so they could at least become competitive. Unfortunately, the debate raged only in Houston and New York and the plan never came close to fruition. So, for the time being, these two franchises had to carry on as best they could and play out the schedule.

Actually, of the two squads, the Colts seemed at least to have a pulse. Eschewing veterans, unlike their expansion counterparts, Houston had assembled an impressive group of young players and the strategy seemed to be paying dividends. Although they finished ninth in the ten-team National League, the Colts won 16 of their last 22 games in 1963.

For the last two games of the year, Houston management decided to show off their youth movement by putting an all-rookie lineup on the field. In the final contest, the Colts' right fielder was an 18-year-old, in Houston only by chance, who had spent the season playing in a class "C" league.

The teenager came to the plate five times that day. He collected three singles and two walks, drove in three runs, and scored four times. At the end of the game, he still didn't know the feeling of making an out in the major leagues. You will find his entry, right there between his brothers Jim and Tom, on page 1,313 of the eighth edition of *The Baseball Encyclopedia*. Three hits in three at bats—a 1.000 career batting average.

It was the only major league game John Paciorek ever played.

* * *

"When I was a kid I used to fantasize about being a baseball player during baseball season and a football player during football season," says John Paciorek today. "In between I thought I'd box."

This budding Bo Jackson was one of the state of Michigan's best all-around athletes. He hit .500 with 13 home runs during his senior season at St. Ladislaus High School in Hamtramck, Michigan, and was also heavily recruited in football and basketball. He came from an athletic family: Four brothers would play professional baseball, two of them in the major leagues. He caught the eye of Paul Richards, who had just joined the expansion Houston Colt .45s as their general manager. Paciorek was a big, strong kid who always hustled and worked extremely hard, but his thoughts were of college and football. Richards took the young man aside and advised him that he would offer enough money that he'd never even *think* about the gridiron. Suitably impressed, Paciorek signed in September 1962 and reported first to Apache Junction, Arizona, with the major league team, and then later to Moultrie, Georgia, site of the Colts' minor league spring training camp in 1963. Richards announced after the signing that the big strong teenager, "could become one of the really great power hitters and all-around players in baseball." John Paciorek thought so too.

"I was big and strong and brash and everything. I was real arrogant. I remember even when I was in high school and everything, I just wanted to be the best I could be. If anyone was better than me, if I played in a basketball game or anything against them and they were better, then I'd go out and practice hours and hours until I played against them again and proved *I* was better. I just kept doing that in everything I did and I was expecting to do the same in baseball.

Richards was always on the lookout for players to stock his talent-starved expansion team, resulting in a mix of prospects and suspects, as well as the occasional diamond in the rough he might steal from another organization. While Paciorek definitely fit in the "prospect" group, Jimmy Wynn, an infielder drafted from the Cincinnati Reds, fit in the latter category. On the surface, there wasn't anything particularly impressive about this five-foot-ten, 165-pound "slugger," who would eventually earn the nickname "The Toy Cannon."

"He was the third baseman and he was just a tiny little thing," remembers Paciorek. "He was five foot six at the most. I was playing center field in an intrasquad game, and when he came up I moved way in. Next pitch, he rifled a shot off the 450-foot sign and I said, 'Wait a minute.' It's ricocheting off the wall and I finally held him to a triple.

"I picked up some grass and threw it up in the air. I wanted to see if there was a wind or something. But there was nothing. I thought, 'That's probably the best hit he ever got in his life.' So the next time he came to the plate I didn't back up. I just stayed in the same place and I'll be darned if he didn't hit another one off the wall 450 feet."

Working through his first spring training, Paciorek was sure he was going to make the major league roster right out of high school.

The 17-year-old was shocked when told he was being sent to the minor leagues. The team tried to explain to the teenager that he had too much promise to sit on the bench in Houston; they wanted him to go where he could play every day and develop his talent. For Paciorek it was nothing more than a demotion. He felt they were keeping players who simply were not as good as he was. He felt he belonged in the big leagues.

"When I went down to the minors, I felt like I had to protect myself so I wouldn't get hurt. I used to hear things when I was a kid about somebody who was a good ballplayer, but got beaned. That was in the back of my head and here I was going down to the minor leagues with a bunch of young, wild rookies.

"So I was kinda like a prima donna at that point. Houston thought highly of me; they wanted me to go out there and really rip it up. I didn't do anything. I just didn't feel motivated. I shoulda really capitalized on the opportunities instead of acting like I did."

* * *

Paciorek was sent by the Colts to Modesto of the Class "C" California League. The franchise there, which was in the second year of a working agreement with Houston, was in trouble and the city was in danger of losing professional baseball. The ballpark had been named after Del Webb, part-owner of the New York Yankees, in the hope that he might provide the financing for improvements in the facility, but outside of an eight-year working agreement with the perennial American League champions, no benefits from the relationship were forthcoming.

In an era when the minor leagues were dying, with the advent of television and its ability to provide access to major league baseball for a vast and previously untapped audience, local heroes playing for minor league teams were quickly becoming a memory as ownership began to rely more and more on major league organizations for their financial well-being. Modesto's most productive hitter *and* most popular player in 1962 had been a veteran minor leaguer named Len Tucker. Unable to join the team until June because of his teaching duties at a junior high school 90 miles south in Fresno, Tucker still drove in 101 runs and hit 30 home runs.

Once again in 1963, Tucker was unavailable until the end of school and Modesto General Manager Lee Landers was having difficulty receiving permission from the parent club to offer Tucker more money. Finally, in late April, Landers was able to announce to the local press that Houston had given him permission to up the ante. He and Tucker were "only about $50 apart now." That chasm was eventually bridged and Tucker put the bitter salary dispute behind him, hitting .326 with 26 home runs. He drove in 113 runs on 115 hits.

Paciorek meanwhile was attracting attention for his gonzo work ethic. He did handstands, headstands, neckstands. He ran *everywhere*. He would race from his outfield position at the end of each inning, even in the 110 degree heat of a Bakersfield summer, attempting to beat the rest of his teammates to the dugout.

"I'd be hustling all over," recalls Paciorek. "If I was in right field and our dugout was on the third base side, I'd sprint in and out and I'd try to beat the third baseman to the dugout. It was impressed upon me early in life to hustle. It probably gave everybody a good impression of me because I was always diving and running through people."

Despite fielding a team that made the California League playoffs, Modesto had major problems with attendance. During the first week in May, the Colts were in the midst of a six-game winning streak when they faced the Reno Silver Sox under threatening skies. Five minutes before game time, public address announcer Gene D'Accardo began the starting lineups by welcoming the players' wives and relatives, since almost no one else had come to the ballpark. The paid attendance that evening totaled exactly 29. (The following season, attendance hovered just above the 200 per game mark and the franchise disbanded for a year. The city returned to professional baseball in 1966 with the Kansas City Athletics thanks to out-of-town ownership.)

Among Paciorek's teammates on the 1963 Modesto Colts were future major leaguers Walt Williams, Sonny Jackson, Carroll Sembera, Danny Coombs, Leon McFadden, and Joe Morgan.

There was little to indicate that Morgan was to become a two-time Most Valuable Player and a member of the Hall of Fame, especially on defense. The man against whom others' play at second base is now measured made 15 errors in 45 games before moving on to Durham of the Carolina League.

"The double play combination was Jackson to Morgan to the

bleachers," remembers Paciorek. "Jackson is the one who threw it into the bleachers, Morgan's throw was always in the dirt. He couldn't even throw the ball from second base to first on the fly, that's how ridiculous it was. I mean, he wasn't a bad *fielder*, but he wasn't *real* good and he couldn't throw the ball. I mean, every time he threw it, it went into the dirt. He just worked and worked and worked. I mean, he just couldn't get enough work and he was so smart about how to figure out things."

"He was probably the gutsiest and smartest guy you'd ever want to meet. Here I was, six-foot-two, two hundred pounds, and I was being a prima donna that year that I was sent out. And here's this little guy. They gave us old hand-me-down uniforms. He was so small that when he was wearing a short-sleeved shirt, it covered his wrists. It was a sight to behold.

"And here's this guy, he'd go up there...and in Moultrie, Georgia, where we had spring training for the minor leagues, it was like a cow pasture. If you were standing out in deep left field, sometimes you couldn't even *see* home plate 'cause you were down in a gully. When you were batting there was no green background, you were up against white. You're facing all these fireballing sidearmers, you know. And here I was, I mean jeez, all I wanted to do is preserve myself... I was bailing out and everything.

"I still remember watching Morgan. He was a little left-hander. It didn't matter to him if it was a left-handed pitcher, he just stayed right in there. He just had determination. He looked like he was five-foot-five or whatever it was, but when he stood up there at the plate he looked ten feet tall. I mean he just dug in. He just stuck right in there."

* * *

Paciorek started strongly in his first professional season, batting .326 with two home runs and a team-leading 12 RBIs in the first 13 games. The Colts were 9-4 and had five players hitting better than .300. Paciorek was continuing his crazy exercise patterns.

"I didn't understand what I was doing, I was just doing exercises. There was no scientific logic in what I was doing, I was just doing all kinds of sit-ups and push-ups and all that. I wore lead weights around my ankles. I'd do all these exercises and then I'd go out and throw."

Paciorek began experiencing problems with his upper back,

aggravated by his throwing, and had to come out of the lineup. As he sat on the bench, resting the injury, he began to notice his *lower* back stiffening. Paciorek responded by launching into a new set of stretching exercises — a major miscalculation.

In and out of the lineup for the remainder of the season, his productivity fell off dramatically. His final batting average was only .219 with nine home runs and 49 RBIs in 274 at bats. Despite his lack of health, Paciorek showed definite signs of power: 28 of his 60 hits went for extra bases.

The major league club, concerned with Paciorek's back problems, summoned him to Houston at the conclusion of the California League play-offs so that he might be examined by specialists. While there, the Colts asked him if he was well enough to play in Houston's final game of the season.

"My back was hurting like anything, but I said, 'Yeah!' God, no matter what, I was gonna play."

The Colt lineup that day included the core of the Houston team through the remainder of the decade: Joe Morgan, Rusty Staub, John Bateman, and Bob Aspromonte. Few details of that day stick in Paciorek's mind; he was cocky, only 18, and had no way of knowing that he was playing in his only major league game.

Batting seventh and playing right field, the rookie made two great running catches in the outfield in addition to his reaching safely in all five of his at bats. He had a direct hand in seven runs as the Colts clubbed the New York Mets 13-4. It was the 26th time in 33 games that Houston had defeated its fellow expansion member since the teams had come into existence.

The writer covering the game that day for the *Houston Press* declared the 18-year-old outfielder, "a cinch to make it as a big leaguer." He was called one of "Houston's faces of the future." Paciorek was named Associated Press Player of the Day.

"I was hurting the whole time but I just didn't let it bother me that game. It was really exciting. I was looking forward to more of it."

* * *

During spring training in 1964, the Colts opened the door for Paciorek to make the major league roster. He remembers Houston playing him nearly every day during spring training, and he also remembers not playing very well. His back problem from the year before was, if anything, worse than it had been the previous September. He did not tell the team of his continuing physical difficulties, fearing that disclosure of his back pain would kill his chance of making the team. Paciorek's chances of avoiding another trip to the minor leagues, however, were growing dimmer each day as his back interfered with his ability to play effectively.

"All of a sudden, outta nowhere, I'd be reaching for a ball without thinking and *jeez*...it'd be like a *knife* going through me. So finally, I just couldn't take it anymore. I either wanted to be completely healed or an invalid.

"I just had to tell the team. I said, 'Jeez, I just can't even *move*.' I mean, they knew *something* was wrong, but unless you tell them specifically, they'll just go by what you tell them. They just thought I was looking lame, that's all."

A further physical examination revealed a congenital spine problem for which the only prescribed cure was surgery. The condition was such that it might never have bothered him unless triggered by something, in this case probably the combination of his upper back problem the year before and his exercise routine. The Colts hoped that Paciorek would be able to avoid an operation; that the injury would somehow heal itself or that he could make adaptations in his playing style that would allow him to stay in the lineup.

Assigned first to the Carolina and then the Western Carolina League, Paciorek hit only .135 in 49 games, striking out in half of his at bats. It quickly became apparent that rest and adaptation were not the answer. In June, Paciorek was forced to undergo a spinal fusion.

Following the surgery, he was in a hospital bed for a month, in a back brace for nearly a year, and missed the equivalent of two entire seasons.

"I was real patient with it 'cause I knew that I just had to let it set and everything and get well. And then I thought it was gonna be as good as ever.

"When I was out of the back brace and I could start exercising and stuff—I was real gung-ho on that—I thought I was gonna come back faster than anybody had ever. And I got myself in good shape. But I didn't realize that with the spine being fused...how much the lower back comes into play when you run.

"I was pulling muscles. I never pulled muscles before, especially in my legs. I was always pulling my hamstrings. Then when I tried to throw as hard as I could, I just really screwed up my shoulder because I couldn't follow through right."

Paciorek began attempting his comeback in 1966, playing winter ball in Sarasota, Florida, but his return to the Colts was short-lived. He seemed to make progress that spring but after moving up to the New York-Pennsylvania League, hit only .158 in 46 games. He was released the next season after his shoulder problems rendered him unable even to toss the ball back to the pitcher from first base. He diligently rehabilitated his arm during the off-season and signed with the Cleveland Indians, who sent him to Reno in the California League for the 1968 season after he slugged three homers in 13 games for their Rock Hill franchise of the Western Carolina League.

With the Reno Silver Sox, Paciorek had the best season of his career, hitting .275 with 17 home runs and 65 RBIs in only 82 games. Half of his hits went for extra bases as he amassed an impressive .553 slugging average. He was still plagued by injuries, however, pulled muscles and the like, that limited his playing time to about 60 percent of the schedule.

Paciorek's performance in 1968 nonetheless offered some hope that his potential might still be realized. The Indians promoted the 23-year-old to their Double A affiliate in Waterbury, Connecticut, the next year. Once again, he was plagued by injuries and played in only 29 games with a .213 batting average before the Indians decided that Paciorek's comeback attempt was at an end.

"When they released me, I was almost relieved because I used to have to go out there hours before everybody else to get all stretched out and everything. I opened up the ballpark. It was too much of a pain.

"Being released wasn't real bad because I realized at that point that I didn't really want to go through that anymore. It was just too grueling. I always thought I could adapt and I tried to make adaptations along the way, but I *had* to play at full speed. If I couldn't, I didn't want to play at all."

* * *

John Paciorek's philosophy of life has changed since his playing days. He thinks back to that day when Jimmy Wynn smashed two line drives over his head and how that began to change his perceptions.

"Even as a kid my life was so *matter* based. The bigger you are,

JOHN PACIOREK

Born February 11, 1945, Detroit, Michigan
Ht. 6'2" Wt. 195 BR TR

MAJOR AND MINOR LEAGUE CAREER

Year	Team, League	G	AB	R	H	2B	3B	HR	RBI	BA	SA	BB	SO	SB
1963	Modesto, California	78	274	45	60	15	4	9	49	.219	.401	52	94	5
	HOUSTON, National	1	3	4	3	0	0	0	3	1.000	1.000	2	0	0
1964	Durham, Carolina	39	116	11	18	4	0	4	12	.155	.293	24	52	1
	Statesville, Western Carolina	10	32	2	2	1	0	0	1	.063	.094	6	21	1
1965 1966	INJURED—OUT ALL SEASON													
	Salisbury, Western Carolina	31	85	11	21	3	0	3	20	.247	.388	20	31	0
	Batavia, NY-Penn	46	133	23	21	5	0	3	21	.158	.263	24	61	1
1967	Asheville, Carolina	25	47	6	6	1	0	1	2	.128	.213	8	23	1
	Cocoa, Florida State	7	20	0	1	0	0	0	0	.050	.050	3	10	0
1968	Rock Hill, Western Carolina	13	40	10	9	1	0	3	8	.225	.475	10	11	0
	Reno, California	82	262	46	72	16	3	17	65	.275	.553	25	69	7
1969	Waterbury, Eastern	29	89	11	19	3	0	4	13	.213	.382	19	22	0
MAJOR LEAGUE TOTALS		1	3	4	3	0	0	0	3	1.000	1.000	2	0	0
MINOR LEAGUE TOTALS		360	1098	165	229	49	7	44	191	.209	.386	191	394	16

the farther you can hit the ball. At that point it was such a contradiction. Wynn was so *small*. He was wiry, streamlined, but he wasn't bulky. You know, I thought big rippling muscles and big bulky muscles was what it took to be strong. Quickly I realized, after watching him that it was *speed* that was converted into power. He was kind of an awareness for me."

"Today I'm more family oriented and spiritually based. When I used to think about bulk, I thought about things in a material way. It's the metaphysical that really runs your life, rather than what seems obvious. My life is probably more peaceful now; it's kinda fun."

Paciorek and his wife have seven children, six of whom attend the school where he teaches, a small private school in Los Angeles for pre-school through eighth grade. His eldest son plays baseball at the University of Southern California.

Working with children as he does now reminds Paciorek of his experience with his first manager in professional baseball, Dave Philley. One of baseball's great pinch hitters, Philley had just completed an 18-year major league career, taking his first managerial position when he arrived in Modesto.

"I'm sure he wasn't clairvoyant, but he could, through his experience I guess, know what most of the young guys were thinking or when we were trying to get out of things. We'd come up with all these excuses and we'd think that he had no way of really proving it. But he would just be so determined not to give us the benefit of the doubt because he knew what we were actually thinking. And I can still remember being real adamant about things, actually for something I *was* guilty of, but I couldn't figure out how *he* knew. He'd have to read your mind.

"Then of course, I get the same sense working with kids. But they feel like, 'How the hell do you know…you can't prove it.' They'll deny it. You can't ever prove it, but you know darn well. But if you had to take it to court, you'd lose. [Laughs.]

"I coach all the sports here at the school. Flag football and soccer, basketball, track, and baseball. I guess the competitive fire is still there because when I coach, sometimes I can be real calm before [the game]. Then I get into it when I see my kids and everything. It makes me feel like *I'm* in there.

"I miss competition from that standpoint, but I don't miss some of the aspects of it. I coach four basketball teams and I had to referee these practice games, and I hate it when people act unsportsmanlike instead of just concentrating on the skill of the game. It's just irritating. I just liked the idea of playing and keeping my mouth shut. I tell my kids to do the best they can and not worry about the extra stuff—all the badmouthing and stuff that you see on TV. I always hated yelling at umpires and all that other stuff. I thought it just took away from the game. Managers kick dirt on umpires…people consider it a show. It disgusts me. I just can't tolerate it, anybody yelling at the umpires. They're just trying to make excuses for themselves.

"I also miss so many [of my teammates] in the minor leagues. They were the hits of the team. They're the ones that can sing and play guitar on the bus and all that stuff. They were real characters and jokers and comical guys. Their baseball skills were not that great. They usually got released and everybody was always so disappointed. There's been a lot of them like that. They could never make the grade athletically, but they were the most popular.

"I kinda like what I'm doing, but I always relished the idea of playing. I don't know what I would've done had my back been better. I'd like to think I would've been a star. I wouldn't have settled for anything else but [being] the best."

For one day in September 1963, he was.

FRANK LEJA

First Baseman,
1954-55 New York Yankees;
1962 Los Angeles Angels

The Yankees lied. You never knew who wanted you because they always said, "Nobody wants you." How the hell do you know who wants you? If they put you on waivers and somebody claims you that they don't like, then they can take you back off waivers.

So they ran the whole show. I mean baseball, not just the Yankees, but baseball. It was the same with any organization. That's what you lived with. You became their pawn and you lived your life the way they told you to live it. So if somebody had a hard-nose for you, they could bury you, and you wouldn't know which end was up.

And then they call you a bonus bust. That disgusts the hell out of me. Because, quote-unquote, it didn't happen, sure doesn't mean you're a bonus bust. But it's created somewhere. And who the hell creates it, I feel, but the parent club? Be it Paul Pettit or be it Billy Joe Davidson or be it Billy Consolo. They're trying to say they made a big mistake and then lay it off on the individual.

Then the newspapers pick it up and they'll say, "Oh yeah, good-hit, no-field. You can drive a car through his legs."

In 1962, I'm looking at it right here, I got a Silver Glove from the National Association [as best fielding first baseman in the minor leagues]. You look back and you say, "Jesus, something went wrong."

— Frank Leja

There is no ghost so difficult to lay as the ghost of an injury.
— Alexander Smith

The competition among major league teams to acquire promising amateur talent intensified during the late 1940s, typified by the signing of Johnny Antonelli to a $65,000 bonus by the Boston Braves in 1948. The spending surge had begun in 1941 when the Detroit Tigers signed outfielder Dick Wakefield to a reported $52,000 contract, the largest recorded up to that time. Over the years, team owners initiated a number of measures designed to curb the spending spree, but achieved only mixed results. For example, prior to the 1947 season, a rule was adopted requiring teams to keep on their major league roster for two years anyone signing a bonus greater than $4,000. The spending continued to spiral. Only with the establishment of the amateur draft in 1965, and the resulting loss of leverage for players in negotiations, did the bidding wars abate and the bonuses reach a plateau from which they didn't move significantly for more than a decade.

In January 1950, the magic $100,000 barrier was reached when the Pittsburgh Pirates inked a left-handed high school pitcher by the name of Paul Pettit. A year later, the Cleveland Indians signed pitcher Billy Joe Davidson to a $125,000 bonus. The track record of these "bonus babies" (a term coined to denote both their youth and the fact that many had to be "babied" along in their development), was decidedly mixed; some fell short when they were rushed too quickly, or due to injury, or simply because of the inexact science of scouting talent. Some were in an organization where they didn't really fit, or were victims of heightened expectations. Others, like Al Kaline, Harmon Killebrew, and Sandy Koufax went on to Hall of Fame careers.

During the summer of 1953, Frank Leja was one of the most sought after high school baseball players in the country. Ten years later, he would leave professional baseball embittered and disillusioned with the system, victimized by what he felt was an unseen hand stretching across a decade and four different organizations that, despite his solid glove work and consistently impressive power numbers in the minor leagues, limited his major league career to only 23 at bats.

*   *   *

In June 1953, 18-year-old Frank Leja hit a home run to lead his Holyoke, Massachusetts, high school team to a 1-0 victory in the Western Massachusetts section championship game. Already pursued by the New York Knickerbockers of the National Basketball Association, Leja had his heart and mind set on baseball. His mentor was the coach at Holyoke High, Ed Moriarty, a former infielder who had cups of coffee in 1935 and 1936 with the Boston Braves. Moriarty worked constantly with Leja, hitting him fungoes day after day and convincing the teenager to abandon switch-hitting and concentrate on the tremendous power he generated from the left side of the plate. The ex-major leaguer kept encouraging the young first baseman, assuring him that he indeed had the talent to be a professional.

Leja had been followed by big league scouts from the age of 15 and Moriarty, a former teammate of Al Lopez when both played for the Braves, arranged a tryout with the Indians. At the same time, Leja had been accepted to Dartmouth and was seriously considering the idea of holding off on his professional career.

"Red Rolfe was the baseball coach at Dartmouth," recalls Leja, "and he told me that if I get the money, that I should take the chance and turn pro because you may never get that opportunity again."

During that summer, the teenager was playing in several leagues, including American Legion, and was also working out at the behest of several major league teams, travelling to Comiskey Park, County Stadium in Milwaukee, Municipal Stadium in Cleveland, and the Polo Grounds. The Indians took Leja on a road trip and he roomed with Early Wynn. Interest snowballed and was peaking as he was selected to go to New York and play in the Hearst Game, an all-star exhibition featuring the best American Legion ballplayers in the United States.

"An article came out in the Boston paper with a picture of [Cleveland first baseman] Luke Easter and myself. The headline said I was to be Luke Easter's successor. Somebody got hold of major league baseball and said that I was ineligible to work out with the big league ballciubs and the clubs were tampering.

"When I was at the Hearst Game, a representative from the Commissioner's Office came down to get me. Like I was a criminal. He said, 'The Commissioner wants to see you in his office.' So I went...

and I got grilled...'Did you accept any gratuities? Did they do this for you, did they do that for you?' Well yeah, they gave me meal money, and I remember I told them Billy Glynn, who was then a first baseman for Cleveland, gave me a glove because I only had a high school glove. I wasn't from a wealthy family. And they said, 'That's it!'

"All of a sudden, these clubs got fined and it became front page news. I couldn't understand what the hell was happening because I knew of other players who worked out with big league clubs. That's how they signed in those days.

"I never heard from the Yankees directly until after I was eligible to sign. To this day, I still feel that somebody there had something to do with it [alerting the Commissioner's Office]. For a moment there some clubs seemed to shy away. You got that feeling of 'coolness.'

"Paul Krichell [the Yankees' chief scout] came up to see me and then they really started to get into it. At the time I loved the Yankees. I went to Yankee Stadium and worked out and of the first ten balls, I hit nine in the seats. Now Stengel gets involved. 'We gotta sign this guy' and 'This stadium was built for you.' Then it came down to a matter of money.

"I remember [negotiating with] Cleveland. I was in the room with, I believe the man's name was Shapiro, and I guess he owned a bank and then owned a piece of the Indians. I was sitting there with Al Lopez and Tris Speaker and Hank Greenberg [the Indians' general manager].

"Al Lopez said, if I've got the wording correctly, 'Tell them what you want.' So I told them and this Shapiro almost fell off the chair. And then Tris Speaker said, 'Give it to him, man. Give it to him.' Greenberg turns around and he says, 'Well, no, we'd like to work you out one more time.' I said, 'No, no. I've worked out with you 15 times.' He wanted to take me over to New Jersey and have some guy pitch batting practice to me again.

"They went into a room, a suite there at the Biltmore in New York, and they were in there for like an hour. They never came back out. So my father and I walked outta the room. We're going down the hall and we bump into Paul Krichell and he says, 'C'mon, did you sign with them?' And I said, 'No.' He says, 'C'mon.'

"So we went upstairs to the Yankees' offices and they came in. There's a little squabbling over the bonus, but they gave me a great contract and I said, 'You got it.'"

After the signing, Krichell gazed approvingly at the Yankees' new left-handed slugging first baseman and compared his physique to that of another great Yankee first baseman of the past—Lou Gehrig.

* * *

After signing the contract, which according to Leja included a $25,000 bonus, he reported to Puerto Rico to play in the winter league there but for the most part sat and grew frustrated. He took a lot of razzing and was the butt of several practical jokes: typical rookie hazing, especially for a freshman of Leja's high profile. That was not frustrating, he'd expected it to a certain degree.

What he had not anticipated was his lack of playing opportunity. By his recollection he played in no more than two or three games in a month's time, not realizing until later that the Puerto Rican winter league was taken quite seriously by the teams involved. It was not a proving ground for rookies.

Not understanding this, Leja became sullen and confused, wondering why the Yankees had sent him to the Caribbean to sit. In the back of his mind he wondered if there had been more to the hazing than he had at first thought. Leja was finally told to head home and get ready to report to spring training and his first major league season in 1954.

The next spring, the Yankees assigned Leja to work on his hitting with coach Bill Dickey.

"So naturally, as an 18-year-old, I have to listen to him, right? It's Bill Dickey. He said to me, 'You can't hit like that, son.' He says, 'We gotta work on changing your hands a little bit and getting that bottom wrist straight out.'

"To make a long story short, I never found myself again. It was like I lost the stroke. I was hitting 'thousand-hoppers' to second base. Nobody said anything. Bill Dickey was king. He said, 'You're young, you got plenty of time. It'll come around.'

"From that first spring training, it became a battle. It was an absolute battle for me. There was really no one I could talk to about it. One thing I *knew* I could do, I knew I could field, thanks to my high school coach. That was like my confidence builder. I could pick the ball out of the dirt, I could make the double play, 3-6-3. If I had a bad day at the plate, I didn't feel too bad because I felt it was a matter of time. I felt I could hit, I was a totally confident guy."

Then came an incident that Leja feels doomed his career.

"When I signed my contract, and I think this is the key to the *whole* thing, during the winter of 1953-54, the minimum salary was raised in the big leagues. So I said to myself, 'Jeez, I just picked up a few more bucks. So I got my paycheck and it was at the rate of the 1953 salary. Now this had nothing to do with my bonus; bonuses were under special covenants and they weren't a part of salary. So I said, 'Jeez, there's something wrong here.'

"I went to Allie Reynolds because Reynolds was the player rep. He went upstairs and mentioned it, and the next day I had a note in my locker to come upstairs. So I went upstairs, and I think it was [Bill] De Witt, he said, 'Allie told me about this paycheck and Commissioner [Frick] wants to see you in his office tomorrow morning.' I says, 'What has the Commissioner got to do with this? I'm just asking a question.'

"So the Commissioner wants to see me at ten o'clock in the morning. So naturally, I take the wrong I.R.T. [Inter-Borough Rapid Transit] at 125th Street and I get there about twenty after ten. I walk in the office and Frick's secretary says, 'Where have you been?' I says, 'Jeez, I took the wrong I.R.T., I'm sorry.'

"I go into Frick's office...he's sitting there, and he doesn't even have my contract in front of him. He said, 'What the hell is this about your contract?'

"I said, 'I should've signed a new contract with an update on the '54 minimum salary.' He says to me, 'What the hell are you talking about? They have paid you enough money. Now you get the hell outta here and go back to the stadium.'

"Now I'm *mad*, because this is illegal. I went to a couple of friends of mine and they said, 'Frank, your career...don't bring this up. There's no lawyers that are gonna handle this.' So I don't ever bring it up again.

"Now, nobody [in the Yankee front office] talked to me. I was shunned. The only guy that'd talk to me was Paul Krichell. And I had the feeling, from that point on, 'I'm in deep trouble here.'

*   *   *

After the ruckus over his paycheck, the rookie began to see his position on the team slip, as evidenced by several roster moves made by the ballclub. Leja had signed with the Yankees in part because Joe

Collins was about the only legitimate first baseman in the organization following Johnny Mize's retirement during the off-season.

In addition to Collins, the Yankees picked up veteran left-handed slugger Eddie Robinson from the A's in an 11-player deal the day after the first baseman's 33rd birthday. Then the team also moved a young third baseman in their minor league system over to the first base bag. His name was Bill Skowron, but he would become better known by his nickname "Moose."

Suddenly Leja had dropped to fourth on the Yankee depth chart.

"It became sarcasm from Stengel. Nothing I could do was good enough. He started playing jokes, like one day he was looking for a pinch hitter and he came down the bench and he said, 'Leedge!' And I said, 'Yeah!' He says, 'Sit right there, don't get excited.'"

It soon became obvious Leja was to become an expert at the long-suffering art of riding the pines. A month into the season, he finally made his major league debut—against his one-time roommate with the well-earned reputation of being the meanest pitcher in baseball.

"My first at bat was against Early Wynn. He brushed me the first pitch. On the second or third pitch, I hit a pea into center field and Larry Doby made a shoestring catch. Wynn came over after the game and I came out of the clubhouse and he said, 'You're okay.' That was very nice.

"I figured, here I am, you know, eighteen, and I go up against Wynn and I hit a rocket off him after he brushes me back, and I figured, 'Well maybe this is okay.'"

The teenage left-handed slugger didn't play again for a month.

"I got my first big league hit in Philadelphia—off a left-hander. We were down 3-0 in the eighth inning and I'm sitting with Joe Collins on the bench. Stengel's looking for a pinch hitter and he comes down and he calls me. So okay, I grab a bat. I'm loosening up and I walk up to the plate and he calls me back. And he says, 'What are you gonna look for?'

"I looked at him and I says, 'The ball.'

'He kinda looked at me for a second and he said, 'Good thinking.'

"So, I go up to the plate. First pitch, I hit a rope into right field. Now I'm on first base and he comes down to the end of the dugout and he starts gyrating, saying, 'You see! You see! If you listened to me you'd be the greatest hitter in the world!' And everybody in the dugout's laughing.

"He put me in a game defensively in Detroit and he kept yelling at me. 'Move to the left. Back up. Come in.' I'm doing all this stuff and I feel like an asshole. Everybody on the bench is laughing. Now what the hell is he on me for?

"I remember...[laughs]...I remember, we were in Fenway Park at the end of my first year. I was ready to take infield and Ted Williams was warming up on the side. He looked at me and he says, 'Hey, Leedge! They're really screwing you, ain't they?'"

* * *

When Frank Leja joined New York, the Yankees were not only dominating the American League, but all of baseball, having won in 1953 an unprecedented fifth straight World Series.

"It wasn't a wild clubhouse, it was subdued. There weren't, that I can remember, pranks or any kind of wildness going on. It was kind of a business-like atmosphere. One of the fun guys was Bob Kuzava.

"We had the old clubhouse at Miller Huggins Field [at spring training] and every time cut-down day came, Kuzava would get an axe from one of the workmen and stick it in the wooden floor and say, 'Ooh, what's happening today?'

"For two years I roomed with Yogi [Berra] on the road. He'd wake me up at three in the morning. He'd shake me and he'd go, 'Leedge, are you awake?'

"He was an excellent catcher. He had a good arm, he had a good release. I tell you, he was a helluva ball player. He really was. He was faster than a lot of people thought. And he had the most uncanny wrists I've ever seen on a hitter. He could turn those wrists over. You'd think the ball was by him and he hit a pea somewhere."

For all the tremendous personalities who were a part of the most glamorous franchise in sports, the star of the Yankees was their center fielder. Leja marvelled at his talent.

"For all intents and purposes, I never saw Mickey Mantle, unless it was a ball in the gap, make a running catch. He was uncanny in that when the ball was hit, he just, boom, explodes off the ball and he's standing there tapping the glove. Mickey could fly. If he didn't have problems with his knees, both his knees looked like they had railroad tracks, you wouldn't have heard about Willie Mays."

Leja spent the entire 1954 season on the Yankee bench, appearing in 12 games and batting only five times, including the one base hit in Philadelphia. His prospects of playing appeared no brighter in 1955 since the Yankees seemed to have no intention of using him, and they were required under the rules governing bonus babies to keep him on the roster. In fact, he played even less in 1955, appearing in five games and batting only twice all year. He wasn't even allowed to take batting practice during the 1955 World Series.

Despite his inactivity, Leja was still enjoying the camaraderie involved in being part of a team. As he tells his story, he worries that people will think his anger is aimed at his teammates, and nothing is further from the truth.

"This may sound bitter....It is *bitter*, but the pleasant memories were playing with the guys. It's what happened to you as an *individual*. It's the business side of it."

At the end of that season, the Yankees travelled to Japan on a goodwill tour and Leja had a good time, reuniting with several friends from high school who were stationed there in the Navy. He played in two games on the trip, hitting a home run in one contest, and began to look forward to a minor league assignment in 1956, where he would at last be able to play every day.

"I remember [Yankee part-owner] Del Webb saying to me [on the trip], 'You're gonna sweat next year, son.' I kinda looked at him and I said to myself, 'What the hell's this guy talking about? Why did he say that to me?' Well, I knew I was gonna be sent out, so I figured he's saying that because I'm gonna play every day. But the way he said it, the tone of his voice, kinda hit me wrong."

* * *

Assigned to Richmond, New York's Triple A farm team, at the beginning of the 1956 season, Leja was promised the starting job and then quickly benched. After 36 at bats, he was sent to Double A Binghamton in the Eastern League. Despite decent power numbers there (he was among the league leaders in home runs and had 32 RBIs in 43 games), he drifted down to the B-level Carolina League by year's end. Needless to say, the 20-year-old's attitude was not the best by the time the final pitch was thrown that season.

The next three years proved no less frustrating for the first baseman. He recalls hearing few encouraging words from anyone in the organization, despite back-to-back 100 RBI seasons in 1957 and 1958. The first of those two seasons, he had to fight to play in the Eastern League, threatening to quit baseball if the Yankees sent him as intended to Quincy, Illinois, which was in the lower-classified I.I.I. League. Leja proved he was ready for the stronger competition, leading the Eastern League in RBIs and slugging 22 home runs. In the talent-rich New York organization, however, the performance barely moved him up one rung on the ladder.

In 1959, Leja finally made it back to Richmond, where he had made his minor league debut three seasons previous. Although his batting average dipped a bit, his power numbers were still solid and he was one of the International League's better fielding first basemen. He and Deron Johnson teamed up most of that year to form one of the league's best one-two power combinations.

"Deron Johnson would hit third and I'd hit fourth," says Leja. "I was on a tear there, towards the end of the season and I was moved in the batting order from fourth to seventh. I don't think they [the Yankees] wanted me to lead the team in RBIs."

While Leja was in Richmond that August, Yankee first baseman Bill Skowron broke his wrist. New York was virtually certain to end the season short of the World Series for the first time in five years, and Leja thought perhaps an opportunity had arrived for him to get a real shot at the big leagues.

"All the New York papers had, 'Yankees to Call Up Leja.' So that night after our game in Montreal, they called up Clete Boyer. I remember Clete came to my room and he said, 'Jesus Christ, I feel bad for you.'"

The Yankees platooned Elston Howard and "Marvelous" Marv Throneberry at first for the remainder of the 1959 season while the Yankee bonus baby sat in Richmond. Leja was beginning to feel trapped in the organization: that someone or something was conspiring to keep him from making it to the major leagues. And he didn't know how to improve his situation. After all, he'd already been called on the carpet twice by the Commissioner himself. He felt his only recourse was to get out of the organization; to demand a trade. That just put Leja in more hot water. The Yankees told him that he should keep quiet because he hadn't done enough as a player to make any demands.

"I know for a fact in '59 that Bill Veeck wanted me in Chicago, and the Yankees would not trade me. He called me personally and told me that he offered the Yankees my bonus, all my salary, and three Triple A players. And they wouldn't trade me."

* * *

As 1960 rolled around, Frank Leja was in his seventh season in the Yankee organization. When originally sent to the minor leagues, Paul Krichell had assured him that he'd be back in the majors within two years. It was now going on five and Krichell had died in 1957. Even though he'd had three solid seasons in the high minors, Leja was no longer a prospect, he was a suspect. At 24, when he should have been at the beginning of a long career, he seemed to be nearing the end.

Covering the Yankees for *Newsday* from their spring training camp in St. Petersburg, Stan Isaacs wrote, "He is a six-four, 220-pounder who hits the ball to the fences down here.... If it weren't that his name is Leja, people would get excited.... Not many take Leja seriously; he has the stamp 'reject' all over him.... And now he is an old man of 24."

To a young man whose confidence was shaken, these words, written during the optimism of spring training, were not the antidote to his doubts.

During an exhibition game that spring, Bill Skowron was injured again and Leja was called on to take his place. In a piece of incredible timing, almost immediately he tore his hamstring.

"Now *I'm* hurt bad. I figure, well, that's it. I'm going back to Richmond. Roy Hamey...he tells me, 'You're going north with us. Get your family ready.' I said, 'I'm going *north*?' He said, 'Yeah, you are.'

"I get the car driven home, I fly my family home, and we get to New York. We're ready to come up to Boston to open up the season and the Yankees tell me I'm gonna go to Amarillo [in the Texas League]. *Amarillo*? Your initial reaction would be, 'I didn't hear that.'

"I said, 'What the hell's wrong with Richmond? They've got all the medical equipment and the whole thing. I'll go down there and take therapy [for my hamstring]. I can't play.'

"They say, 'No, no. We got another guy at Richmond now.' So I went home for two weeks. After some battles with Hamey over the phone, I gave in and went to Amarillo."

Leja's stay in Texas lasted 19 games. Hurting, both physically and emotionally, a disillusioned Frank Leja threatened once again to go home. In response, the Yankees lent him to Nashville, the Cincinnati Reds' Double A affiliate in the Southern Association, where he played, but was still hobbled by his injured hamstring.

"They wouldn't send me to Richmond or Denver. Nothing against the trainers [in Nashville], but how much good is a rub gonna do? Or a whirlpool? But in Richmond they had the ultrasound, they had it all.

"I got terribly upset in Nashville, so then Jim Turner [the ex-Yankee pitcher and Nashville's general manager] calls me in and he says, 'We're gonna send you to Charleston.'"

In the space of four months, Leja had gone from making a major league roster to playing first base in the Class A Sally League.

When he received his 1961 contract, it called for him to report to Amarillo. Leja immediately went to New York to speak with Johnny Johnson, who was an assistant under Lee MacPhail, the Yankees' minor league director, and he persuaded Johnson to let him go instead to spring training with Richmond. Leja made the team and then, once again, sat on the bench.

"My wife was at Richmond with me. After a couple of weeks, I said, 'That's it Annie. I've had it here.' So I go in the clubhouse to see Jack White, the general manager. And he says, 'Hey Frank! You're just the guy I want to see.' And I said, 'Yeah? You're the guy I want to see.'

"He said, 'We sold you to Syracuse. Maybe you can play there.'

"I said, 'Do you mean, I am no longer owned by the Yankees?'

"He gave me a slip and it said, 'sold unconditionally' to Syracuse. Syracuse was Minnesota's top farm club."

Given a new lease on his baseball life, Leja jumped into the lineup and vaulted among the league leaders in home runs and RBIs despite sitting on the bench the first month of the season. His final totals for 1961 included 30 home runs and 98 RBIs, the latter figure topping the International League.

"The Twins want to call me up [to Minnesota]. Then I'm notified that the Yankees still own me. I believe it was George Brophy who came to Syracuse and told me. So the Twins took up Joe Altobelli."

* * *

During the winter of 1961, Frank Leja finally escaped the Yankees.

He was sent to the St. Louis Cardinals in a minor league trade, and this time it was for real. The next spring, Leja seemed to have played his way onto the major league roster.

Told he would platoon at first base with Bill White, playing against right-handed pitchers while White moved to the outfield, Leja was satisfied at last. He had a job and he was away from the Yankees.

As Leja sat in a coffee shop one morning near the end of spring training; Cardinal General Manager Bing Devine happened by and asked if he could join him for a cup of coffee.

"He said, 'I've got some news for you.' I'll never forget this statement, he said, 'You've done more for the Cardinal organization than we can ever do for you. We've let you go on waivers and the Angels have picked you up. They don't have a first baseman and you can go over there and play every day. Thank you for what you've done. Frank, don't feel bad, you're still in the big leagues.' And I *didn't* feel bad.

"So I hopped a plane and went to Palm Springs. I get there and [Angels Manager] Bill Rigney says, 'Hey big guy! We've been waiting for you! Are you ready to play?' I said, 'Yeah, I'm ready to play.' So I went right in the lineup and I think I hit three home runs. I was pumped. I was really pumped.

"The strange situation was this: When I got to my locker, my bat order was there that I ordered with the Cardinals two weeks before. I said to the travelling secretary, 'What the hell are these bats doing here?' And he said, 'Hey, Frank...we do good work here.'"

Leja was scheduled to be the opening day first baseman for the Angels when just before the game, Rigney notified him that Eddie Yost was to start instead. Despite Rigney's assurances that he would be in the lineup the next day, Leja was quite upset by the decision. He remembers, "I went absolutely bonkers."

Leja did play the next day, but only sporadically thereafter. Following seven games and 16 hitless at bats, he was traded to the Milwaukee Braves and was in turn assigned to their Triple A affiliate in Louisville where he hit 20 homers and drove in 60 runs with a career high .269 batting average in 122 games. Thinking he would get a chance at replacing Joe Adcock at first base for the Braves (Adcock had been traded to the Cleveland Indians over the winter), the job was instead given to Tommie Aaron. Leja wasn't even invited to the major league camp the next spring.

FRANK LEJA

Born February 7, 1936, Holyoke, Massachusetts   Died May 3, 1991, Boston, Massachusetts
Ht. 6'4" Wt. 210   BL TL

MAJOR AND MINOR LEAGUE CAREER

Year	Team, League	G	AB	R	H	2B	3B	HR	RBI	BA	SA	BB	SO	SB
1954	NEW YORK, American	12	5	2	1	0	0	0	0	.200	.200	0	1	0
1955	NEW YORK, American	7	2	1	0	0	0	0	0	.000	.000	0	1	0
1956	Richmond, International	16	36	2	8	0	0	0	1	.222	.222	6	2	0
	Binghamton, Eastern	43	153	29	37	8	1	6	32	.242	.425	23	27	1
	Winston-Salem, Carolina	65	222	32	48	16	0	6	30	.216	.369	26	53	0
1957	Binghamton, Eastern	135	480	81	117	25	2	22	117	.244	.442	82	83	4
1958	New Orleans, Southern Assn	152	532	98	140	23	3	29	103	.263	.481	109	89	2
1959	Richmond, International	149	499	61	124	17	3	23	81	.248	.433	68	106	1
1960	Amarillo, Texas	19	64	12	13	0	1	1	8	.203	.281	15	17	1
	Nashville, Southern Assn	54	158	17	38	8	0	6	20	.241	.405	26	69	1
	Charleston, South Atlantic	36	123	17	26	4	1	4	13	.211	.358	28	51	1
1961	Richmond-Syracuse, International	142	470	68	122	22	2	30	98	.260	.506	80	129	0
1962	LOS ANGELES, American	7	16	0	0	0	0	0	0	.000	.000	1	6	0
	Louisville, American Assn	122	405	54	109	21	1	20	60	.269	.474	72	100	0
1963	Toronto, International	97	250	32	60	8	0	17	42	.240	.476	41	71	0
MAJOR LEAGUE TOTALS		26	23	3	1	0	0	0	0	.043	.043	1	8	0
MINOR LEAGUE TOTALS		1030	3392	503	842	152	14	164	605	.248	.446	576	797	11

1957 — Led Eastern League First Basemen in PO (1126), Assists (99) and DP (141).
1958 — Led Southern Association First Basemen in PO (1312), Assists (133) and DP (216).
1959 — Led International League First Basemen in PO (1376), Assists (110) and DP (125).
1961 — Led International League First Basemen in PO (1306), Assists (103) and DP (139).
1962 — Led American Association First Basemen in Fielding (.995).

Italics in boldface type indicate led league

He platooned at first base in the International League for the 1963 season, hitting 17 home runs in 250 at bats. He was then released by Milwaukee just before the opening of the spring training camp in 1964.

Despite his two-plus years of major league service, Frank Leja's baseball career was at an end after a grand total of 23 at bats, his only hit coming when Casey Stengel sent him to the plate one day against Philadelphia to face a left-handed pitcher.

* * *

Two of Leja's sons later played professional baseball and, although one served as a batting practice pitcher at Fenway Park for several years, neither made the major leagues as a player. Leja worried that his battles with management may have contributed to their falling short of the big leagues.

After baseball, Leja worked 18 years in the insurance industry, specializing in business insurance, pension plans, and deferred compensation packages. He lived in Nahant, Massachusetts, a town situated on a crooked finger-like peninsula jutting out from the Massachusetts coast into the Atlantic Ocean. There, following his insurance career, he worked full-time out of his home with his middle son running lobster traps.

Leja thought he had been blackballed, probably as a result of his salary dispute in 1954, and although his experiences after baseball had been happy and successful, an important part of his life was still unresolved. It never would be. Leja suffered a sudden, and fatal, heart attack in May 1991. He was 55 years old.

What to make of a promising career unfulfilled? It is an eternal question; there have literally been hundreds of Frank Lejas over the years, athletes who are not made for the system in which they are forced to operate. Bitterness is a normal and understandable reaction. How one reacts to that disappointment is one of the central themes of this book. By all accounts, Leja did not let his bitterness consume his life. But it was there.

It is obvious that Leja and the Yankees were not a match. He played at a time when managers did not give their players what he perhaps needed most: encouragement and a pat on the back. With a Sparky Anderson or a Tommy Lasorda, Leja might have thrived. We will never know.

There are a number of things certain in baseball: Every team is a contender in spring training, 20 years from now Rickey Henderson and Jose Canseco will appear together on a talk show and complain that, "Today's ball players just don't play with the same ability and dedication we did," and there will be talented athletes who will wonder what might have happened had circumstances been different. The last is a question all of us ask ourselves about our lives at one time or another. It is a question to which all of us wish we had an answer.

BIBLIOGRAPHY

Books

Coleman, Ken, and Valenti, Dan. *The Impossible Dream Remembered.* Lexington, MA: Stephen Greene, 1987.

Falls, Joe. *The Detroit Tigers.* New York: Walker, 1989.

Feller, Bob, and Gilbert, Bill. *Now Pitching—Bob Feller.* Secaucus, NJ: Carol, 1990.

Goldstein, Richard. *Spartan Seasons.* New York: Macmillan, 1980.

_____. *Superstars and Screwballs: 100 Years of Brooklyn Baseball.* New York: Dutton, 1991.

Golenbock, Peter. *Bums: An Oral History of the Brooklyn Dodgers.* New York: G.P. Putnam's Sons, 1984.

_____. *Fenway.* New York: G.P. Putnam's Sons, 1992.

James, Bill. *The Bill James Historical Baseball Abstract.* New York: Villard, 1986.

Kuklick, Bruce. *To Everything a Season—Shibe Park and Urban Philadelphia 1909-1976.* Princeton, NJ: Princeton University Press, 1991.

Lieb, Fred. *Baseball as I Have Known It.* New York: Coward McCann & Geoghegan, 1977.

Marazzi, Rich, and Fiorito, Len. *Aaron to Zuverink.* Briarcliff Manor, NY: Stein & Day, 1982.

Mead, William. *Even the Browns.* Chicago, IL: Contemporary Books, 1978.

Okrent, Daniel, and Lewine, Harris, eds. *The Ultimate Baseball Book.* Boston, MA: Houghton Mifflin, 1984.

O'Neal, Bill. *The Pacific Coast League 1903-1988.* Austin, TX: Eakin, 1990.

Polner, Murray. *Branch Rickey.* New York: Atheneum, 1982.

Reichler, Joseph L. *The Baseball Trade Register.* New York: Collier, 1984.

Shatzkin, Mike, ed. *The Ballplayers.* New York: Arbor House, 1990.

Stadler, Ken. *The Pacific Coast League—One Man's Memories 1938-1957.* Marbek, 1984.

Thorn, John, and Palmer, Pete, eds. *Total Baseball.* New York: Warner, 1989.

Whiting, Robert. *The Chrysanthemum and the Bat*. New York: Dodd, Mead, 1977.

_____. *You Gotta Have Wa*. New York: Macmillan, 1989.

Williams, Dick, and Plaschke, Bill. *No More Mr. Nice Guy*. Orlando, Fl: Harcourt Brace Jovanovich, 1990.

Wolff, Rick, ed. *The Baseball Encyclopedia—Eighth Edition*. New York: Macmillan, 1990.

Articles

Biederman, Les. "'A Future Dean' Detore's Tag on Strikeout King." *The Sporting News*, May 21, 1952.

Boardman, Sid. "John Paciorek's 1.000 Average Is a Line for Trivia Buffs." *Kansas City Star*, September 15, 1986.

Goldstein, Richard. "A Day in the Lives of Big Leaguers Was a Career." *New York Times*, June 14, 1982.

Grosshandler, Stan. "Floyd Giebell Recalls His Greatest Day in Baseball." *Baseball Digest*, April 1991.

Herskowitz, Mickey. "Full Speed Ahead for Colt Youth Plan." *The Sporting News*, October 12, 1963.

Holway, John. "Amputee Lived a Major League Dream." *Washington Post*, 1986.

Jordan, Pat. "Kid K." *Sports Illustrated*, June 1987.

Roberts, Charlie. "Mauldin: Mr. Popular." *Atlanta Journal and Constitution*, July 4, 1970.

Salisinger, H. G. "Giebell, Who Pitched Tiger Flag Clincher, 'Icicle Kid' with Cooling System for Batters." *The Sporting News*, March 13, 1941.

Weirich, Frank. "Necciai Whiffs 27 in Bristol No-Hitter." *The Sporting News*, May 21, 1952.

Newspapers

The Arizona Republic	*Newsday*
Atlanta Journal and Constitution	*Oakland Tribune*
(Atlanta) *Sunday American Sports*	*Oneonta Star*
Chicago Daily News	*Pittsburgh Post-Gazette*
Cleveland Plain Dealer	*San Francisco Chronicle*
Fulton County Insight	*San Francisco Examiner*
Houston Post	*The Sporting News*
Kansas City Star	*Syracuse Herald-American*
The Modesto Bee	*Washington Post*
New York Times	*Waterbury Republican-American*

Organization Guides and Handbooks

1971 Detroit Tigers Organization Handbook
1952 Pittsburgh Pirates Yearbook
1953 Pittsburgh Pirates Organization Handbook
1974 San Diego Padres Organization Handbook
1976 San Francisco Giants Scorecard

INDEX

Aaron, Tommie 241
Ables, Harry 140
Abrams, Cal 28
Adair, Jerry 178
Adams, Henry 6
Adcock, Joe 241
Alexander, Grover Cleveland 27, 29, 196
Allen, Ron 152
Altman, George 45-46
Altobelli, Joe 240
American League: 1940 Pennant Race 187-193; 1945 Pennant Race 127-128; 1959 Pennant Race 37
Ames, Red 54
Andrews, Mike 53, 58
Angelini, Norm 81
Anson, Cap 186
Antonelli, Johnny 230
Appling, Luke 170, 173
Arizona-Mexico League 14-15
Ashburn, Richie 27, 28, 29
Aspromonte, Bob 223
Atlanta Crackers 175-176
Auerbach, Rick 161
Aurelius, Marcus 115
Autry, Al 75-88
Autry, Paula 76, 80, 87-88
Averill, Earl 189
Ayala, Benny 160

Bagby, Jim 126
Baker, Del 191-192, 194-195
Bamberger, George 90
Banks, Ernie 107
Barr, George 25

Bartell, Dick 192, 195, 199
Basie, Count 65
Bass, Randy 46
Bateman, John 223
Bell, Bill 11, 140, 141, 143
Bell, Gary 67
Bell, Gus 7, 97
Bench, Johnny 85, 107
Bennett, Tony 65
Benton, Al 188
Berra, Yogi 122, 129, 236
Betto, Kaoru 42
Bilko, Steve 55
Binks, George 127-128
Bluege, Ossie 121, 125, 126
Bonaparte, Napoleon 201
Bonds, Barry 215
Bonds, Bobby 202, 205, 208, 215
Bonura, Zeke 172-173
Boudreau, Lou 106, 188
Bowman, Roger 90
Boyer, Clete 238
Bradley, Alva 187
Bragan, Bobby 63
Brazle, Al 26
Bresnahan, Dave 169
Brett, George 46, 80-81, 85
Bridges, Tommy 188
Briggs, Walter 193-194
Bristol, Dave 77, 83-85
Brock, Lou 156, 159
Brophy, George 240
Brovia, Joe 89-102
Brovia, Kathy 98-99
Brown, Bobby 129
Brown, Joe E. 174
Brown, Joe L. 15
Brown, Lindsay 109-110

Brown, Mace 56, 73
Brucker, Earle 106
Bryant, William Cullen 35
Brye, Steve 46
Bunning, Jim 98
Burlington, N.C. (Carolina League) 11-13

Caldwell, Mike 159, 207
California State University, Stanislaus 17
Camilli, Dolf 22, 105
Camp, Rick 83
Campanella, Roy 40, 102
Campaneris, Bert 66, 76
Campbell, Bruce 192
Campbell, Jim 199
Cardenal, Jose 68
Carlyle, Thomas 217
Carpenter, Robert 24
Carter, Jimmy 84
Case, George 124
Cedeno, Cesar 77
Chambers, Cliff 11
Chandler, Eddie 90
Chandler, Happy 147
Chapman, Ben 192-193
Chapman, Fred 116
Chapman, Sam 106
Chicago White Sox 172-173, 175
Clarey, Doug 151-165
Clark, Al 144
Clarke, Horace 61
Cleary, Joe 126
Cleveland Indians 187-188
Cobb, Ty 1, 46, 156
Cochrane, Mickey 104
Cohen, Sid 110
Coleman, Jerry 29
Collins, Joe 235
Conigliaro, Tony 59, 62, 71, 73
Consolo, Billy 229
Coombs, Danny 221
Coveleski, Stan 194
Craig, Roger 6
Crawford, Willie 156, 159
Cronin, Joe 61, 116
Crosby, Bing 7

Crosetti, Frank 105
Cruz, Jose 77
Cuccinello, Tony 22-23
Cullop, Nick 168

D'Accardo, Gene 221
Dal Canton, Bruce 81
Daniels, Mom 10
Dark, Alvin 9, 68
Davenport, Jim 206
Davidson, Billy Joe 229-230
Davis, Brandy 146
Dean, Dizzy 135-136, 141
Demeter, Don 67
Denny, John 157, 159
Derringer, Paul 194
Detore, George 137-142
Detroit Tigers 188-189
Devine, Bing 241
DeWitt, Bill 234
Dickey, Bill 171, 233
Dickinson, Emily 54
Dickson, Murry 7, 144
DiMaggio, Dom 93
DiMaggio, Joe 29, 46, 93, 102, 105, 107, 124, 171, 188
Doby, Larry 34, 235
Doerr, Bobby 105
Drummond, Cal 63
Duhem, Joe 13
Duke of Wellington 90
Dunlop, Harry 139-140
Durocher, Leo 125
Dykes, Jimmy 170-174

Earnshaw, George 170
Easter, Luke 231
Eckert, William 61
Eckhardt, Oscar 104
"Ed Sullivan Show" 53, 64-65
Ennis, Del 26, 29-30
Errey, Don 119
Essegian, Chuck 42
Eto, Shinichi 46
Evangeline League 169
Evans, Al 121
Ewing, Buck 186

Fagan, Paul 94-95
Fain, Ferris 94, 96
Fairly, Ron 157, 159
Feller, Bob 106, 129, 183-185, 187-188, 191-193, 199
Ferraro, Mike 59
Ferrell, Rick 123
Fitzsimmons, Freddie 22
Fonseca, Lew 172
Ford, Whitey 29, 61-62, 65
Foster, George 202-204
Foster, Leo 161
Foxx, Jimmie 116, 171
Foy, Joe 58, 61-62, 71
Foytack, Paul 98
Frick, Ford 61, 234
Frisella, Danny 160
Fukumoto, Yutaka 211

"Gaijin's Complaint" 45-46
Galan, Augie 105
Garagiola, Joe 11, 144
Gardner, Jerry 142
Gehrig, Lou 171, 186, 233
Gehringer, Charlie 189, 192-193, 195
Gibson, Bob 67, 209
Gibson, Russ 53-54, 62-63, 66
Giebell, Floyd 183-200
Giebell, Stephen 197, 199
Gilligan, Jack 1
Glynn, Bill 25, 232
Goethe, Johann Wolfgang von 183
Goliat, Ed 26
Gomez, Preston 159
Gorsica, Johnny 188
Goryl, Johnny 152-153
Gray, Pete 116, 127, 178
Green, Dick 66
Greenberg, Hank 25, 39-40, 124, 128, 130, 171, 183, 188, 190, 192-193, 232
Gregory, L. H. 111, 113
Griffith, Clark 120-122, 127, 133
Gripsholm 120
Groat, Dick 15

Haas, Mule 170
Haefner, Mickey 123
Haight, Walter 121
Hall, Dick 11-12
Hamey, Roy 239
Hamilton, Jack 71
Hamner, Granny 26, 30
Hankyu Braves 209-211
Harder, Mel 188, 190-191
Hargan, Steve 68
Harrell, Billy 59
Harris, Luman 107
Hart, Jim Ray 209
Hartnett, Gabby 196
Hayes, Frankie 106
Hazlitt, William 151
Heath, Jeff 193
Heintzelman, Ken 30
Held, Woodie 38
Hemsley, Rollie 192
Henderson, Ken 202, 204-205
Henderson, Rickey 211
Herman, Billy 59
Hernandez, Keith 157
Herseth, Bud 158
Higgins, Pinky 59-60, 192-193
Hildebrand, Oral 173
Hogan, Ben 178
Holloman, Bobo 54, 64
Horner, Bob 46
Horton, Tony 66-67
Hostetler, Chuck 116
Houston Colt .45s 218
Howard, Elston 54, 61-64, 65, 71, 238
Hrabosky, Al 156-157
Hriniak, Walt 6
Hubbard, Elbert 167
Huckleberry, Earl 76
Hunter, Bob 96
Hutchinson, Fred 188, 197

Ilitch, Mike 131
Inao, Kazuhisa 41
Iott, Hooks 140
Irvin, Monte 9
Isaacs, Stan 239

Jablonski, Ray 97
Jackson, Reggie 73, 107
Jackson, Sonny 221-222
Jakucki, Sig 94
Jansen, Larry 94
Janssen, David 12
Japan Series 40-41, 45, 47, 210-211
Javitz, Jacob 61
Johnson, Bob 105-107
Johnson, Deron 238
Johnson, Frank 208
Johnson, Johnny 240
Johnson, Walter 124-125
Jolley, Smead 104
Jones, Bumpus 54
Jones, Puddin' Head 29-30
Jones, Sheldon 26
Judge, Joe 124

Kaiser, Henry J. 115
Kaline, Al 230
Kell, George 128
Keltner, Ken 188
Kendrick, Bob 140
Kennedy, Jacqueline 61, 63
Kennedy, John-John 61, 63
Kennedy, Vern 175
Kessinger, Don 157, 159-160
Killebrew, Harmon 230
Kiner, Ralph 7-8, 10-11, 17, 146
Kingman, Dave 202
Kline, Ron 11
Kluszewski, Ted 97
Konstanty, Jim 25, 29-30
Koppett, Leonard 64
Koski, Bill 5-18, 135, 142
Koski, Nancy (née Frazier) 13, 15, 18
Koufax, Sandy 55, 230
Kranepool, Ed 158
Kreevich, Mike 175
Krichell, Paul 232-234, 239
Kroc, Ray 208
Kuhel, Joe 123, 126-127
Kurtz, Hal 69
Kuzava, Bob 236

Lajoie, Napoleon 46
Landers, Lee 221

Landis, Kenesaw Mountain 174-175
Lanier, Hal 155
La Rochefoucauld, François de 103
Larsen, Don 140
Latman, Barry 37
Lau, Charlie 7
Lavagetto, Cookie 22
Law, Vern 10-11
Lazzeri, Tony 171
Le Roux, Buddy 61
Lee, Leron 46
Lee, Thornton 175
Leja, Frank 229-245
Leonard, Dutch 123
Leovich, John 103-113
Lewis, Buddy 123-124
Lindsay, John 61
Liska, Ad 108-109
Lombardi, Ernie 105
Lonborg, Jim 53, 60-61, 71
Lopez, Al 38-40, 231-232
Luby, Hugh 94
Lucas, Bill 83-85
Lurie, Bob 158
Lyons, Ted 170-171, 173

McCormick, Frank 195
McCosky, Barney 188
McCovey, Willie 207, 215
McDowell, Sam 68
MacFadden, Leon 221
McGlothen, Lynn 157
McGregor, Scott 82
Mack, Connie 91, 106, 172
Mack, Roy 192
McKechnie, Bill 194
McKeon, Jack 78, 82
McLain, Denny 79
McLish, Cal 90
McMillan, Roy 97
MacPhail, Larry 22-23, 121-122
MacPhail, Lee 240
McRae, Hal 46, 80
Maddox, Garry 202, 205
Maglie, Sal 66-67, 73
Malzone, Frank 59
Mantle, Mickey 61-62, 171, 236
Marchildon, Phil 107
Marmo, Ben 23

Martin, Pepper 116
Marty, Joe 93
Matlack, Jon 157-158
Matthews, Gary 159, 202
Mauch, Gene 90
Mauldin, Marshall 167-181
Mayfield Clothiers (Kitty League) 7-8
Mayo, Jackie 28
Mays, Willie 102, 202-205, 207, 215
Melton, Cliff 94
Messersmith, Andy 82, 84, 175
Metkovich, George "Catfish" 10, 126
Meyer, Billy 9, 144, 146
Middlecoff, Carey 178
Miller, Zell 181
Milnar, Al 188
Milner, Martin 12
Mize, Johnny 235
Mizell, Vinegar Bend 141
Modesto Colts (California League) 220-221
Monaghan, Tom 131
Monbouquette, Bill 59-60
Montague, Eddie 203
Montanez, Willie 77
Montefusco, John 83, 159
Morgan, Joe 102, 221-223
Moriarty, Ed 231
Moses, Wally 106
Motton, Curt 69
Muhr, Bob 130-131
Munger, Red 98
Mungo, Van Lingle 22
Murphy, Dale 85
Musial, Stan 26, 102, 144

Nagashima, Shigeo 46-48
Nankai Hawks 40-42, 52
Narron, Sam 145
National League: 1949 Pennant Race 25-27; 1950 Pennant Race 28-29
The Natural 31
Necciai, Ron 11, 13, 135-149
Nekola, Bots 56
Nelson, Byron 178
New York Giants 9
New York Yankees 37
Newhouser, Hal 188, 191

Newsom, Bobo 188, 191, 194-195, 199
Nichols, Lance 161
Nicholson, Bill 25
Niekro, Phil 84
Niggeling, Johnny 123
Nomura, Dan 41
Nomura, Katsuya 40-41, 45
Norbert, Ted 108
Nuxhall, Joe 116

O'Connell, Danny 31
O'Dea, Ken 116
O'Doul, Lefty 89, 92-95
Oh, Sadaharu 46-48
Olsen, Barney 110
O'Neill, Steve 190
Orrell, Joe 109
Osenbaugh, Roger 52
Owens, Jesse 124

Pacific Coast League 94-95, 99-100, 104-105
Paciorek, Jim 218
Paciorek, John 217-228
Paciorek, Tom 218
Paepke, Jack 13-14
Paige, Satchel 107-108
Paley, William 61
Paschall, Ben 168
Patterson, Robert 115-116, 120-122
Paul, Gabe 96
Pearson, Monte 190
Peckinpaugh, Roger 104
Pepitone, Joe 61-62
Perry, Gaylord 215
Pesky, Johnny (Paveskovich) 14, 57, 59, 104-105, 111, 113
Petrocelli, Rico 64, 66, 71
Pettit, Paul 229-230
Philadelphia Phillies 27, 29-30
Philley, Dave 227
Piniella, Lou 80
Pittsburgh Pirates 7-8, 10-11, 55
Pollet, Howie 11, 26
Portland Beavers (PCL) 104, 108-109
Posedel, Bill 5, 10

Post, Wally 97
Potter, Nels 128
Primm, Lucille Yancey 179-180
Proly, Mike 159

Radatz, Dick 56, 59
Radbourn, Hoss 186
Ramsey, Frank 140
Rapcliff, Rip 175
Raschi, Vic 29
Reardon, Joe 24
Red Cross 120
Reiser, Pete 11, 17
Reynolds, Allie 29, 234
Richard, Bee Bee 157
Richard, James Rodney 205
Richards, Paul 177, 219
Richmond, Va. (Intl. League) 82
Rickey, Branch, Jr. 138, 141
Rickey, Branch, Sr. 7, 10, 12, 22-23,
    135-136, 139, 142, 147, 174-175
Rigney, Bill 241
Ripple, Jimmy 195
Rixey, Eppa 27
Roberts, Charlie 177
Roberts, Robin 5, 23, 28-30
Robinson, Bill 61
Robinson, Eddie 235
Roettger, Harold 12-13
Rohr, Bill 53-73
Rolfe, Red 231
Rowe, Schoolboy 177, 188-191, 194
Rudolph, Ken 160
Ruel, Muddy 124-125
Runnels, Pete 59
Russell, Jack 171
Ruth, Babe 22, 73, 170-171

Sadecki, Ray 81
Sain, Johnny 6, 82, 129
St. Louis Cardinals 156-157
San Diego Padres (NL) 207-208
San Francisco Giants 202
San Francisco Seals (PCL) 94-95
Sanford, Jack 68, 69
Sanicki, Ed 19-34

Santo, Ron 48
Sauer, Hank 203
Sawyer, Ed 19, 24-26, 31
Schoendienst, Red 157-158
Schuster, Billy 109-110
Scott, George 71
Seaver, Tom 161
Sembera, Carroll 221
Seminick, Andy 30
Seneca 75
Sewell, Luke 170, 175
Sewell, Rip 25
Shellenback, Frank 104-105
Shepard, Bert 115-134
Shotton, Burt 26
Siebert, Sonny 68
Silvestri, Ken 25
Simmons, Al 170
Simmons, Curt 27, 30
Simmons, Ted 156
Sington, Fred 174
Sipek, Dick 116
Sisler, Dick 28, 30
Sisler, George 9
Skowron, Bill 235, 238-239
Smith, Al 188
Smith, Alexander 230
Smith, C. Arnholt 207
Smith, Charlie 63
Smith, Reggie 58-59, 61, 63, 156
Spahn, Warren 96
Spalding, Al 186
Speaker, Tris 232
Spence, Stan 123
Spencer, Daryl 45
Staley, Gerry 38
Stanka, Joe 35-52
Stanka, Joey 45, 48-49
Statz, Jigger 104
Staub, Rusty 223
Steinhagen, Ruth Ann 30
Stengel, Casey 232, 235-236, 244
Stepovich, Michael 111
Stock, Milt 9, 28
Stottlemyre, Mel 65
Stratton, Monty 123, 175
Stuart, Dick 56-57, 59-60, 66
Stutz, Eddie 110-111
Sugiura, Tadashi 40-41, 44, 47
Suhr, Gus 105

Sullivan, Billy 189, 191-193
Sullivan, Ed 65
Summers, Bill 192
Sweeney, Bill 89

Tebbetts, Birdie 189, 191-192
Templeton, Garry 154, 157
Terry, Bill 92
Thomas, George 61
Thomasson, Gary 202
Thompson, Jocko 26
Thorpe, Jim 104
Throneberry, Marv 238
Tiant, Luis 68-69
Tinker, Joe 133-134
"Total Baseball" 40
Travis, Cecil 124
Tresh, Tom 62
Trosky, Hal 188
Trout, Dizzy 177, 188, 190, 193-194
Trucks, Virgil 128
Tsuruoka, Kazuto 43-45, 47
Tucker, Len 220-221
Turley, Bob 56-57
Turner, Jim 240
Tyson, Mike 155, 160

Uecker, Bob 107
Ueda, Toshiharu 210
Unser, Del 157

Veeck, Bill 238-239
Verdi, Frank 161
Vitt, Oscar 187-188, 190
Vosmik, Joe 172

Wagner, Charlie 56
Wagner, Hal 106
Wagner, Honus 9
Waitkus, Eddie 29-30
Wakefield, Dick 230

Walker, Harry 6
Ward, Chuck 23-24
Washington Redskins 127
Washington Senators 123-125
Waterbury, Conn. (Eastern League) 130-131
Weatherly, Roy 192, 193
Webb, Del 220, 237
Wellsville, NY (NY-Penn League) 57
Werber, Billy 195
Werle, Bill 9
Westlake, Wally 11
White, Bill 241
White, Jack 240
Whitehead, John 175
Whittier, John Greenleaf 19
Wilks, Ted 11
Williams, Bernie 201-215
Williams, Dick 58-67, 70-71
Williams, Ken 104
Williams, Stan 68-69
Williams, Ted 46, 59, 93, 105, 107, 124, 135, 139, 171, 236
Williams, Walt 221
Wills, Maury 210
Wilmington, Del. (Interstate League) 24
Wilson, Earl 56, 59
Windemuth, Dick 7, 17
Wiseman, Lefty 190
Wolff, Roger 123
Woodling, Gene 31
World Series: 1940 194-195; 1950 29; 1967 67
Wright, Robert C. 179
Wynn, Early 231, 235
Wynn, Jimmy 219, 225, 227

Yastrzemski, Carl 59-62, 71
Yawkey, Tom 56, 59
Yomiuri Giants 41, 47-48
York, Rudy 183, 185, 188, 190, 192-193
Yost, Eddie 241

Zeller, Jack 195